MARK EVELEIGH was raised in West Africa, dreaming of a life of travel and adventure. He has spent most of the last decade travelling through remote regions of South and Central America, South-East Asia and Africa. At first he financed these trips as a pipe-layer, delivery driver, bouncer, security guard and perfume/oil painting salesman. He screen-printed T-shirts in Ecuador and sold time-shares in the French West Indies before deciding, at the age of 26, to channel his 'travelling career' into the dog-eat-dog world of travel writing.

Maverick in Madagascar

Mark Eveleigh

LONELY PLANET PUBLICATIONS
Melbourne • Oakland • London • Paris

Maverick in Madagascar

Published by Lonely Planet Publications
    Head Office: 90 Maribyrnong St, Footscray, Vic 3011, Australia
                      Locked Bag 1, Footscray, Vic 3011, Australia
    Branches: 150 Linden Street, Oakland, CA 94607, USA
                      10a Spring Place, London NW5 3BH, UK
                      1 rue Dahomey, 75011, Paris, France

Published 2001
Printed by The Bookmaker International Ltd
Printed in China

Maps by Natasha Velleley
Designed by Margaret Jung

National Library of Australia Cataloguing in Publication Data

Maverick in Madagascar

Bibliography
ISBN 1 86450 329 7 (pbk.).

1. Eveleigh, Mark – Journeys – Madagascar. 2. Folklore –
Madagascar. 3. Madagascar – Description and travel.
4. Madagascar – Social life and customs. 5. Mythology,
Malagasy. 6. Vazimbas. I. Title. (Series : Lonely
Planet journeys).

916.910453

Text © Mark Eveleigh 2001
Maps © Lonely Planet 2001

LONELY PLANET and the Lonely Planet logo are trade marks of Lonely
Planet Publications Pty. Ltd.
All rights reserved. No part of this publication may be reproduced, stored in
a retrieval system or transmitted in any form by any means, electronic,
mechanical, photocopying, recording or otherwise, except brief extracts for
the purpose of review, without the written permission of the publisher.

CONTENTS

For Mum and Dad
('whilst' not to be blamed
for my errant and irresponsible disposition)

Also for Claire, Gary and baby Harley
(whose happy arrival coincided
with the finishing stages of this book)

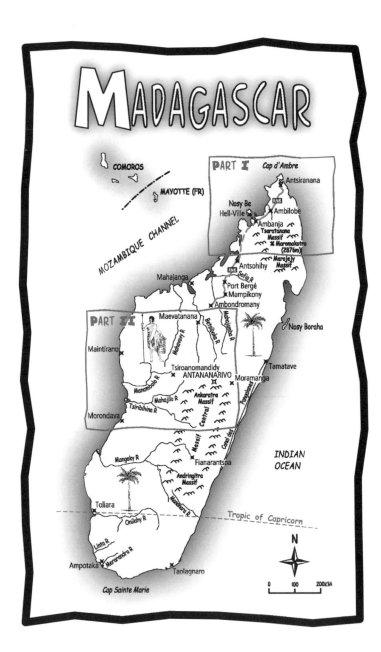

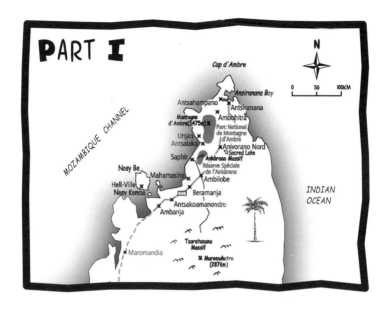

The author would like express his gratitude to Polartec, Lowe Alpine and Air Madagascar for their generous support.

PART I

CHAPTER 1

THE SACRED LAKE, A MALAGASY LEGEND

'This is not my own lie.
This is a lie that the ancestors told me.'
– traditional Malagasy storyteller's 'disclaimer'

A puff of red dust rose with each of his weary steps and the old man tugged the edge of his tattered red lamba up so that it muffled his lower face. He'd passed this way a long, long time ago – in what could have been another lifetime – but he'd never seen it so dry before. The grass that had then been swaying over head height now lay burnt and shrivelled beside the trail.

He shifted the smooth pebble in his cheek – it was a trick that the Sahel camel drivers had taught him, but he was now so dry that there was no saliva left to stimulate. In his thirst and exhaustion he allowed his mind to wander away from the blistering savannah of Madagascar to other lands he had known, in other times. The plains of the Somali peoples, the sands of Rub' al-Khali (where the prophet later became king), the Western Ghats of India, the dripping forests of Ceylon made sacred to the Hindus by Hanuman the monkey prince. He had travelled through so many lifetimes since leaving his home in far-off Sumatra.

A snake, curled on the sun-baked track in ribbons of rich brown and cream, brought him back to the present. As he made a wide detour the old man saluted it politely. In itself the snake was not dangerous, but many in this land believed that snakes were the ancestral spirits and in the old man's profession it was wise to respect the beliefs of all people.

Careful as he was he knew that, along the trails of his many lifetimes, he had left in his wake – beside those who venerated him – a minority who feared his return more than death itself. He had left the Isle of the Moon's most northern point and the bay of Antsiranana, as it gaped open-mouthed towards the expanse of the Indian Ocean, three weeks ago. Strewn behind him was a chain of villages in which the people could talk only of the passing of this strange old man.

Meetings were held under the sacred tamarind trees and people spoke up to say that the mysterious *vazaha* – outsider – was surely from the Antandroy tribe of the far south because of his desert-dweller's habits. Others said: 'He's a Merina noble, exiled from the Highlands. You can tell from his light skin and his red lamba'. Nobody from the village had ever seen a Merina but many believed that it was the colour red that had given them their power of dominion over the island. It was even rumoured that the Merina kings had made it illegal for their subjects ever to wear red.

'Around his neck he wears a *mohara* charm made from a bull's horn. He might be a sorcerer from the Bara cattle-country,' was one wild guess. Yet although he had once been strong and had moved with an athlete's grace, the old man had none of the Negroid features of the Bara.

'He's a Betsileo, one of the Numberless Invincibles: I watched him cook and eat ... he knows how to handle rice and wood with equal skill,' quipped a brave young soul. 'Don't laugh!' cried his father, fumbling with the talisman of wooden beads around his neck. 'He was a Sakalava warrior priest from the long valleys. He's old now, but he was once tall and straight and he knows the ways of charms and curses.'

In a village on the lower slopes of the Amber Mountain a *mpanandro* (shaman), fearing the threat of the stranger's power, ordered the slaughter of six white oxen. It was hoped that such a costly sacrifice would erase any curses that might befall the village with the passing of the old man.

'He was a *Vazimba* spirit!' the mpanandro shouted, his face contorted. 'An envoy from the tomb. He came to us from the other side and if he comes again he may try to take some of us back with him.'

But nobody really knew who the old man was and his trade, which had condemned him to a life of perpetual roaming, had also prohibited him from divulging to any living soul his true origin. He was a sorcerer and it was the loneliest of all professions.

His skill had blessed the nets of the Malabar fishermen during the hunger of the monsoon months. It had brought life-giving rain to the Bantu cattle herders just as it had brought locusts upon a Persian tyrant and scuttled the slave ships at Mogadishu. Yet, though he could dream now only of a cool, bubbling spring, it was forbidden that he should use his powers to soothe his own thirst-swollen tongue. As the sorcerer brooded on this injustice, he realised that the dusty track was leading steadily, though almost imperceptibly, downhill and that a few ragged grass roofs rose above the scrub in the bottom of the basin.

The sun was beginning to spread its crimson skirts over the western hills as the old man staggered gratefully into the centre of the village. The packed red earth between the collapsing ochre-dusted huts had been so hardened by generations of feet that it was almost polished. He caught glimpses of fleeting movements: a small child whisked in through a closing door; the flicker of a dusty lamba as its wearer disappeared around a corner. Stopping, he looked around, but apart from a couple of hens, a scrawny hunting dog and an old black sow, which snuffled busily among the litter, nothing moved.

The pig did nothing to improve the newcomer's first impressions of the village. As a sorcerer all things connected with pigs were *fady*, or taboo, for him. Just the smell of burning bristles was enough to drain his power. He kept one wary eye on the sow's movements as he called to the villagers:

'Here is a visitor – a vazaha and an outsider to your ways and customs. If it be not taboo, I petition you only for a drink of water and I shall be on my way.'

Only the hushed scolding of a sobbing child answered him.

He became angry: 'I bring you no harm! Why do you hide like hedgehogs in your burrows rather than stand forward like proud Antàkarana warriors?'

Still no answer.

Overcome by weariness the old man slumped heavily on the packed earth. From the cracks in the rough woven walls of the huts many dark eyes watched him with bitterness and fear. Angry voices snapped at each other in their distrust and hatred of the wanderer. Only one young woman, blossoming in early mother-hood and flowering with goodwill towards all creatures, felt pity for the old man. Risking the wrath of her neighbours – for they would reason that she had invited a bad destiny onto them and expensive sacrifices would have to be made to cleanse the village – she reached for the earthenware jug that she had carried from the distant stream that very morning. She stepped out into the sunlight and, ignoring the abuse that was flung at her from behind the barred doors, bravely flaunted a smile of welcome for the old man.

'Drink vazaha,' she said kindly, as she held his shaven head. 'I welcome you here, even if my people won't.'

Slowly, sip by sip, the old man's thirst was slaked and it was replaced by a thirst for justice. These people must be taught a les-son that future generations will remember, he thought.

'I thank you,' he said to the young woman. 'You must listen to me carefully and not repeat a word of what I tell you to the oth-ers here. I must go but tonight you must take your family and your cattle and climb as fast as you can to high ground … Soon, there will be more water in this village than anyone has need for.'

The young woman was shocked by the sorcerer's words but she did as he said. As she hurried away from the village that evening she caught the unaccustomed smell of rain in the air and noticed that the stars had been covered by thick clouds. Lightning flashed, thunder roared and, when the family and their cattle reached the top of the hill, they heard a deep, rumbling groan from the direction of the village.

A torrent of water, crashing down from the Amber Mountain and along the trail that had brought the stranger, tore down the village and filled the little valley. But the miserly villagers were not killed: the sorcerer had a more fitting destiny for them. Every one was transformed into a crocodile so that they and their offspring were condemned to live forever surrounded by the water that they had once guarded so jealously.

The young woman and her family founded the hilltop town of Anivorano Nord. They promised that they and their descendants would never refuse hospitality to a traveller and would regularly sacrifice cattle to the accursed inhabitants of the lake. Under their care the crocodiles multiplied and grew to massive proportions.

Many, many years later the 'monsters' of Anivorano Nord's sacred lake became known to sightseers from the cruise and cargo ships that visited the big port in Antsiranana Bay. Villagers began to sell their hardy, humpbacked zebu cattle to crowds of these new vazaha, who were prepared to pay well for the spectacle of seeing them torn apart by the crocodiles. Thus Anivorano Nord became known as one of the few places where people were accustomed to selling their prized zebu, and it was here that I bought a bull called Jobilahy.

CHAPTER 2

DIEGO DOLDRUMS

THE MONSOON WAS driving down in a solid wall as I filed off the Air Mad 737 in Antsiranana, Madagascar's northern capital. The rains were dying hard; they had arrived six weeks late and the locals estimated that they were likely to continue for at least another month. An old Dylan song, 'Hard Rain', was wailing angrily in my head as I waited in the door of the plane for a porter to run from the terminal building with a bouquet of umbrellas, like bony drowned birds.

Ten minutes later I slid into my backpack, hoisted the kitbag and nodded to one of the hustling taxi drivers.

'*Vous allez où, vazaha? ... Vous êtes Américain?*'

'English ... Hôtel La Sirène.'

'Aah, Inglisman! ... Gentleman or hooligan?' It was the only English he knew but I was too tired to dwell on the awful implications of this and sat back to stare at the empty streets through streaming windows. The battle-worn Citroen 2CV lurched onto the wide Boulevard Dupleix, shot past the high concrete walls of the Stade Municipal and skittered onto Avenue Lally Tollendal. Within a few minutes we were rattling between the board-walked bars of Rue Colbert on the wide headland upon which the old part of town lies.

I can now state categorically that there is no Hôtel La Sirène in that most northern outpost of the 'Great Red Island', despite the fact that an Italian traveller I met the night before swore that he had stayed there a week ago!

I had met Elvis (Fake name? Fake hotel?) during the latter, and hazier, half of a 'Gache-tafari' reggae session (as in 'Malgache

Rastafari') in the capital's infamous Hôtel Glacier Bar. He had liked La Sirène so much that he'd made me promise not to even *think* about staying anywhere else.

We cruised around for the best part of an hour as the rain leaked through the tape that held the CV's canvas roof together. It's not that Antsiranana is a big town but, in common with many Malagasy towns, it defies reason in that it doesn't have a centre. The original Malagasy settlement was given a new breath of life by colonial town planners who were devoted to the logical (if not always attractive) grid system. A largely featureless landscape meant that Antsiranana continued to sprawl out from the port long after a French town would have been neatly clipped off by hills or rivers.

Eventually on the edge of a muddy park, strewn with the fallen leaves of storm-wrecked palms, we found a Hôtel Ravinala, named after the national tree of Madagascar, the traveller's palm. There must be a Hôtel Ravinala in almost every town on the island. I was to have extensive experience of Malagasy hotels over the next three months but Antsiranana's Ravinala still stands out from the crowd.

It was barricaded with a two-and-a-half metre wall, which was iced across the top with broken bottles. At first inspection the hotel appeared to be deserted. I found an abandoned reception desk in a hut around the back of the hotel and leaned my backpack against a rusting fridge to go in search of a room.

I didn't need to go far. Roused by the clank of my metal water bottle against the fridge, a tousled head and two bleary eyes appeared from behind the desk. I wondered why the reception desk wasn't at the front of the hotel, until I realised that the few square feet of floor behind that desk were the only dry place in the entire establishment.

Pausing only to pick up a rusty key, fifteen centimetres long, and a wooden broom, the receptionist wordlessly sleepwalked me to a vacant room. There I dropped my bags onto a damp mattress and followed them, as soon as the puddles had been swept out through the doorway.

It seemed to me that I'd been on a collision course with

Madagascar for many years now but so far it was not at all as I'd imagined. The first thing that had struck me on arrival in Antananarivo, the capital, was how Asian everything seemed. During the journey from the airport the bus had trundled through an immense patchwork of paddy fields and swerved, horn blaring, around a hundred rickshaws and painted carts drawn by humpbacked oxen. I'd expected to see Africa and struggled to shake off the idea that I was back in Indonesia. Even the fine-featured, coffee-coloured faces around me were essentially Asian: a living testimony to one of history's most remarkable human migrations.

Since Madagascar first sailed away from the African continent over eighty million years ago, the fierce currents of the 500-kilometre-wide Mozambique Channel have done more to insulate the island than the entirety of the Indian Ocean.

Marco Polo first reported to Europe the existence of 'a great red island' that was rumoured to lie off the coast of Africa. The Arabs had long known it as '*Gezirat Al-Komr*', the Isle of the Moon. In his later (slightly senile) years the great explorer named the island 'Madagascar'; he was thinking of Mogadishu, but of course there was nobody to correct him. The island was 'discovered' – if, as is usual practice, you disregard the fact that the Malagasy tribes had been aware of its existence for a considerable time – on 10 August 1500 by an off-course Portuguese sea captain called Diego Dias.

Most experts agree that the first people on Madagascar were settlers from Indonesia, who arrived on the uninhabited isle between 1,500 and 2,000 years ago. Whether they made the trip in one single voyage of over six thousand kilometres, or over the course of several generations and many coastal settlements, is still a matter for debate.

Human remains from before this period have never been found on the island. On this evidence alone experts deny local claims that the first Malagasy were not Indonesian seafarers, but a mysterious tribe of 'white pygmies' called the Vazimba. Malagasy folklore has it that the Vazimba still exist in remote mountain hide-outs and in some places they are still actively worshipped as the most ancient of the ancestors. In a country where daily life is governed by supernatural powers it should come as no great surprise to hear that the Vazimba of today are invisible and telepathic, and that they have the power to put spells on wanderers who come too close to their hide-outs.

I had recently spent three months in Kalimantan, Central Borneo, looking for the last bands of totally independent nomads of the Punan tribe, about whom similar things had been said. But I couldn't picture the Vazimba as Stone Age hunter-gatherers, living in seclusion in some forgotten valley. Even amongst the authorities who agreed that the Vazimba had existed, opinions were radically divided over even the most fundamental points of their appearance. These enigmatic 'white pygmies' had also been described as 'tall, strong and dark-skinned' and, as I researched, I came to realise that the Vazimba mystery had become something of an anthropological 'Chinese whisper'.

UNESCO's *Africa from the 12th to the 16th* Century said vaguely that there were no Vazimba people and that the traditions mentioning them are probably evidence of the prior existence of certain populations, 'which are difficult to identify'. Yet to quote another UNESCO publication, *Ancient Civilisations of Africa*:

> the ancient Vazimba led a rather primitive life economically … gathering berries, hunting and collecting honey were probably enough for their needs … They may have led a very similar life to the Iban of Borneo.

Arthur Stratton wrote, in *The Great Red Island*, that: 'mankind had found this once desert island, first the mysterious Vazimba, who were, perhaps black, possibly Pygmies, and, probably from Africa'. In *Madagascar Rediscovered* Mervyn Brown, one of the most respected writers on Madagascar, voiced a different opinion: 'It is now generally accepted that the Vazimba were (and are) descendants of the earliest Proto-Malagasy immigrants who were pushed into the interior by later arrivals'. It occurred to me that to a later wave of immigrants, the statuesque Bantu cattle-herders from Africa, the short, wiry Indonesians could well have looked like 'white pygmies'.

Madagascar has sometimes been called the Island of Ghosts, after its most famous inhabitants, the lemurs (named after Roman ghosts that were believed to wander at night). This could just as effectively have been a reflection of the ancestor worship and the spirit-world that is such an essential part of the culture of the island's eighteen tribes. I hoped to travel through the territory of some of these tribes and to see how their versions of the Vazimba story fitted into the island's most ancient mystery. I was aware that a band of invisible pygmies, surely a paradox in itself, were not likely to be easily spotted. But, being neither an anthropologist nor a historian, I wasn't deterred by the almost overwhelming chances of failure. It was the quest itself that had brought me to Madagascar and the basis of my plan was to buy a packhorse and set out on a 2,200-kilometre, three-month trek down the western edge of the world's fourth largest island.

When I woke, several hours later, the gentle tapping on Hôtel Ravinala's iron roof told me that it had almost stopped raining. I lay on my back and looked at the pictures that countless rainy-seasons had painted on the mildewed ceiling and that old Dylan song groaned through my head again.

Looking at my watch I realised that it would be dark within a couple of hours. Lying where I was, just over a thousand kilometres south of the equator, one couldn't expect more than five minutes of dusk at any time of the year – and it would never fall more than fifteen minutes either side of six o'clock.

I smelt the freshly washed, steaming vegetation of the tropics and thought about getting up. A gecko chirruped on the ceiling behind my head and I twisted to look at it. It was no more than eight centimetres long, and was so transparent that I could make out the vertebrae in its tail and its little heart beating beside a front leg, which was tipped with bulbous toes. It was subtly pink all over except for the two grey bumps on its head – the dispropor-tionate eyes that made it such a voracious nocturnal hunter and would help it to do its utmost to diminish the room's mosquito population.

In South-East Asia, geckos are considered good luck – blessed is the house that has a gecko in every room. But the feeling of well-being that this little reptile brought to me as I lay on my mouldering mattress, impregnated with the smell of mosquito coils, was without any such convenient definition. The smell of the steaming mud street, the tap-tap of rain onto the iron roof, the line of ants marching up the rotting timber of the doorframe and the happy chirp – '*chin-chock*' – of a hunting gecko: there is something about the tropics that can make you feel so good – and often for all the wrong reasons. I was chuckling to myself as I laced up my boots and headed out to see what Antsiranana had to offer.

There isn't much to chuckle about in Antsiranana these days and it wasn't long before I found myself a terrace table and a bottle of Three Horses Beer *(grand modèle)* at Bar La Vahinée. Three bored Malagasy girls at a table gave me the eye and I pulled out a book to hide behind: every bar that I'd so far been in had its bevy of resident 'sporting ladies'.

'You don' like Diego girls, mister?' asked a small voice at my shoulder.

Antsiranana means 'where there is salt' but the town is universally known as Diego Suarez after the sailor (described by contemporaries as 'a thief and a murderer who transported Malagasy slaves to India') who secured a tentative foothold here for the King of Portugal in 1543.

'You speak English?' I asked in surprise.

Ant was thirteen years old and he informed me that, in addition to Malagasy and French, he had learnt passable English, German and Portuguese from the steady stream of sailors that passed through Diego. I ordered my second bottle of THB and asked Ant in Spanish if he'd like a coke. He replied in Portuguese and I was flattered that he'd understood.

Ant talked incessantly – in several idioms – as we strolled up the steaming tarmac of Rue Colbert to the end of the headland and turned onto a waterfront avenue where crumbling colonial mansions were fronted by sagging balconies. He kicked an empty tin can all the way from Rue Richelieu to a scrap of rubbish-strewn waterfront waste-ground. A wrought iron bandstand testified to the fact that this little park had once drawn more impressive crowds than the three goats that shied away from the clattering can as Ant booted it off the cliff.

Diego Bay is the finest natural harbour in the Indian Ocean and the town has a reputation (gained I can only imagine from some incurable romantic who had never been there) of being 'the Rio de Janeiro of Madagascar'. It's true that, *if* the wind is offshore at the fish factory and *if* you can ignore the dead dogs and windblown garbage, a small Sugar Loaf Mountain is visible from the lookout above the grandly named Anse de la Dordogne. Then, *if* the sun is shining, it is possible to imagine what a beautiful sight this vast bay must have been to the pirates who, under a swashbuckling visionary now known only as Captain Misson, founded the communist republic of Libertalia here.

The story of Captain Misson is a fantastic one, worthy – as sceptics claim – of invention only in the mind of Daniel Defoe, who first recorded it in 1726. If reports are correct (and this character wears a cloak of mystery that amply complements his air of romance) Misson, a gentleman buccaneer from Provence, sailed into the deserted Diego Bay sometime around 1660 in his frigate, *La Victoire*.

He had joined the French navy at sixteen and had quickly risen through the ranks. The navy of those days was driven by a brutally enforced hierarchy and the suppression of individual freedom was considered vital to the discipline of a man-of-war. But Misson was an educated man and a thinker, and the violent and often cruel naval life did nothing to dampen his fervent idealism. While on shore leave in Genoa he met a young priest named Caraccioli. Misson was still only a junior officer but his ideals and philosophies were already powerful enough to convince Caraccioli to leave the clerical life and follow him to the sea and adventure. Otherwise Misson kept his cards close to his chest and bided his time.

Sure enough, several years later off Martinique, destiny in the form of an English battleship played *La Victoire* straight into Misson's hands. The French ship was hopelessly outgunned and English grapeshot splintered the decks and shredded the rigging. All seemed to be lost until a French gunner scored a direct hit on the English powder hold – she exploded and sank.

By the time the French crew had seen to their casualties it was clear that only one of their officers had survived the battle. This was the opportunity that Misson had waited for. Standing on the poop deck stained with gunpowder and bloody from the battle he began his audacious experiment in democracy. It may not have sounded that way, as he convinced his shipmates to help him steal *La Victoire* and take up a life of piracy, but when he called for a vote every single man chose to follow him. The new Captain Misson gave the order to hoist the Jolly Roger and there was no turning back.

Misson may have been an idealist, but he was no dreamer: the men would only follow him as long as he led them convincingly. He was a skilled commander and was quick to enter battle; by the time they rounded the Cape of Good Hope, *La Victoire* was a rich and happy ship.

It was undoubtedly Misson's intelligence as much as his sense of honour that led him to restrain his men from unnecessary bloodshed. Described as 'a Robin Hood of the waves', he always freed slaves and often went so far as to return them to their homes. The crews of plundered ships were allowed to sail away unharmed and *La Victoire* soon gained such a reputation for magnanimity that it was not unknown for her to win a prize without firing a shot.

Misson must have cut a dashing figure as he led his growing band of followers into the increasingly familiar coves and reefs of the Indian Ocean. The beautiful Arab princess he married in the Comoros, after routing her family's enemies, didn't do anything to hurt his image either!

As I stood on the lookout by the dilapidated bandstand, in Diego's surprisingly chill drizzle, it was impossible not to imagine that the sun was shining on the day when Misson and his buccaneers arrived in the deserted bay. There may have been just enough of a breeze to ripple his white chemise and to tug at the princess's blue-black hair, but Misson is one of those characters in history upon whom you feel sure it can never have drizzled.

Perhaps there were a couple of hunters from the Tsimihety or Antàkarana tribes to witness the arrival and to watch Misson raise the flag of the 'International Republic of Libertalia'. It was not the Jolly Roger but a standard that read *'A Deo a Libertate'* – For God, for Liberty. Probably they crept back from time to time to see what these strange vazaha were doing: laying out vegetable gardens, tending poultry and felling trees to build houses and barricades along the shoreline. It must have seemed mystifying behaviour to hunters and gatherers who lived in wooden huts on the rainforested slopes above the town. But the 'Liberi' appeared to be friendly and slowly the more curious tribesmen – and women – began to come closer to the town. The Tsimihety of today still claim partial descent from the Liberi pirates.

Misson built a school and a church and did all he could to construct a firm moral foundation for his fledgling state. Libertalia was governed by a General Assembly in which any man could have his say, but Misson (who naturally had a slightly greater say than the average Jolly Jack Tar) used his influence to 'protect' the sailors' morals and to encourage marriage with the local girls. This seems as hard to imagine in a town full of hard-bitten, battle-scarred pirates as is Misson's total ban on blasphemy and swearing of any sort!

Misson worked tirelessly to promote Libertalia. He even started an international language and set up a printing press to send out literature advertising the new republic, and he invited the crews of plundered ships to join him in a new life, free from oppression. For a middle-aged Cockney sailor – with two decades on the high seas behind him and a future of poverty and hunger in the taverns of Gravesend ahead – Libertalia would have been an irresistible retirement home. In 1697 when Captain William Kidd limped into Diego in the crippled *Adventure Galley* many of his crew were at just that stage of their lives. More than half of them deserted him before he sailed out again in a captured Armenian trader called the *Quedagh Merchant*.

By the time Kidd – deserted by his 'sponsors' and found guilty of murder and piracy – was swinging from the London gallows, the loyal Caraccioli and the Arab princess too were dead – and Libertalia had been destroyed. While the majority of the pirates were away on one of the campaigns that were still occasionally necessary to support Misson's quest for 'liberty and freedom of choice', their town was attacked by a native war party. It seemed to be an unprovoked attack but it is possible that some of the local menfolk were not overly impressed by the moral constraints that Misson had put on his men.

After almost forty years devoted to his Libertalia-Utopia, Captain Misson – a broken-hearted old man – did the only thing that, it seems now over the distance of three hundred years, he could do.

He buried the Liberi dead and sailed away into the sunset. In a fittingly romantic end to this saga neither he nor *La Victoire*, nor the treasure she was carrying, were ever heard of again.

The only people who pretend to see anything romantic in Diego these days are the new French 'libertines' who congregate at La Vahinée in the evenings – and the young Malagasy prostitutes who live off them. Ant told me that many of them were construction engineers, working for Malagasy contractors, and some were anglers who apparently returned as much for these dark-eyed lovelies as for the sea-fishing. The girls were from all over Madagascar but the majority were from nearby villages and some were perhaps descendants of the Tsimihety girls who had married Misson's pirates.

'A short time back,' wrote Arthur Stratton in 1965, 'it was said that 80% of the wild tribal people carried congenital syphilis, left behind by the seventeenth century pirates of the Spanish Main'. More recently it was reported that one-tenth of consultations at Diego's Centre Hospitalier Régional are for gonorrhoea.

Madagascar has very little in the way of tourist infrastructure and the regional offices of Air Madagascar operate as surrogate tourist information bureaux. So, when I'd said goodbye to Ant (and given him a spare English paperback for his 'homework'), it was here that I made my first 'up-country' enquiries.

'Excusez moi mademoiselle, could you tell me where I might buy a horse?'

The girl pushed herself back from her desk as if to focus more clearly on me ... or to open an escape route. Apart from her coffee-coloured shoulders and straight black hair, everything about her seemed to be pink: pink flowery dress, pink blusher, pink lipstick, dangling pink earrings.

She seemed to get slightly pinker, then sighed deliberately with an assumed air of patience: 'No horses here'.

'No, I know. I mean, I want to buy a horse to travel with and ...' I stammered on, 'well, I wondered if you'd know where they have horses'.

'No horses here. All dead – *la fièvre* ... Malaria.'

At first I didn't believe it and, in growing desperation, I continued my inquiries elsewhere; but the tone with which the townspeople advised me only betrayed the Malagasy's resignation to the whims of nature and the tropical climate. Finally I was forced to accept that, within the last few months, every horse in Northern Madagascar had died in some sort of equine epidemic!

As I stared at my maps in a leaking, cockroach-ridden room a distinct air of gloom descended over my expedition. Only twelve per cent of Madagascar's roads are blue metal and most of the dirt tracks that crisscross the country are impassable during the rainy season. I knew of people who had set out to travel from one end of the island to the other in Landrovers and had very quickly found it impossible. Nevertheless, I had three months to devote to the trek and I hoped that with some sort of pack animal I would somehow get through to Cap Sainte Marie, the sacred beach at Madagascar's southern tip. I had deliberately planned my arrival for what should have been the end of the rains to take advantage of good grazing conditions for at least the first part of the trek. Now I found myself becalmed in the Diego doldrums before my journey had even began.

My timing could not have been worse and the epidemic seemed almost inconceivable, until I remembered the story of two Welsh pioneer-missionaries who arrived on Madagascar's eastern coast in 1818, with their wives and newborn daughters. By the end of six weeks only one, David Jones, was still alive. Cerebral malaria, known in these parts simply as Malagasy Fever, had killed all his companions!

Jones took all this as a test of faith and set off alone on the long journey to the highlands where another great trial awaited him: that of writing the first Malagasy dictionary.

I decided that I could only try to copy Jones's *fahatokiana* (courage) and head for the *havoana salasalany* (hills) myself in search of alternative transport.

CHAPTER 3

AMBER MOUNTAIN

'A journey is a fragment of Hell'
– Mohammed

Route Nationale 6 is the only 'reliable' strip of blue metal in Northern Madagascar and, for the first 250 kilometres, it's as good as it gets. It sweeps southwards from Diego, steadily climbing through cattle scrubland before it skirts around the cloud-shrouded volcano of Montagne d'Ambre (Amber Mountain) and drops down to where the village of Anivorano Nord guards its sacred lake.

Perforated only occasionally with potholes, it ripples onwards past a savage forest of limestone needles on the Ankàrana Massif and across a shimmering plain of traveller's palms as it links the wilderness outpost of Mahamasina to the dusty highway town of Ambilobe. Here the sun-softened tarmac spans the red current of the Mahavavy River and sweeps westwards towards the coast, where it meets a balmy sea breeze wafting out of the mangrove swamps, near the village of Beramanja. It runs straighter now through a chain of villages. Almost hurrying, as if sensing the sea, it passes rows of bamboo stalls offering bananas, mangoes, oranges and coconut wine and it spares barely a glance for the sacred mango tree of Antsakoamanodro.

The tarmac comes to an abrupt end some kilometres south of the regional capital of Ambanja. Now Route Nationale 6 joins the eighty-eight per cent of Madagascar's roads that are unpaved and, even in such formidable company, the next 460-kilometre strip is often considered the roughest road trip in Madagascar.

I was already walking past the last of the mud and thatch shanties of Diego when the equatorial sun blasted over the horizon, drying the road of the night's downpour. I passed a police roadblock where a dog's carcass lay swelling and stinking in the sun and wondered why nobody thought to drag it away.

A truck squealed to a halt and the driver tugged his T-shirt over his face to cut out the stench of rotting flesh. The *gendarme* – who didn't seem to notice – looked up from scribbling the truck's details in an exercise book to ask if I wanted a ride. I thanked him and hurried past, sweating under the weight of my backpack and kitbag, iron-willed in my determination to continue on foot …

… An hour later I was enjoying the cool breeze at the tailgate of a rattling bush-taxi as it climbed steeply through a thickening tangle of vegetation and stands of bamboo onto the rainforested slopes of Montagne d'Ambre. The pick-up truck was piled with sacks of rice, baskets of fish and boxes of 'Lucky Cow' condensed milk. Although the two rows of seats along the sides were full to capacity my fellow passengers greeted me, and my bags, with smiles and a cheerful chorus of: '*Salut vazaha!*' The Malagasy are notoriously easy to talk to and, in a mixture of doubtful pidgin French (mine) and a sign language that was seriously hampered by lack of elbow room, I learnt much of what there was to know about Joffreville even before I arrived.

Joffreville – now known officially (though infrequently) as Ambohitra – was once a hill-station for the local *colon* civil servants to escape the lowland heat. Although it had a large school, a French Legion barracks, a reputation for fine vegetables and roses and a celebrated calendar of social events, it is hard to imagine now that Joffreville was ever anything more than a backwoods boondocks village.

Today Joffreville, with its Catholic church and the abandoned Hôtel Joffre, has a sleepy, decaying charm and its greatest claim to fame is that it is the gateway to Parc National de Montagne d'Ambre. It was this charm that had attracted an unlikely French 'adventurer' away from *la vie Parisienne* to a life in the Chez Henriette guesthouse. Guy had succumbed so completely to the ambience of sleepy Joffreville that in two years he had never once set foot on the forest-clad slopes of the volcano. He spent his days in the hotel bar drinking rum, smoking Gauloises and working through an endless supply of word-search puzzles.

'Business goes slowly,' he grumbled. 'It's been a while since anyone stayed here on their way to the park ... One cannot say why.'

The horses that had once been for hire here had apparently succumbed even more forcefully to the rigours of the climate than had Guy. They had been among the first victims of the mysterious equine fever.

From two days after my arrival in the country, I had been dogged by some vague and fleeting fevers and a throat infection myself. But salvation was on hand in the form of a thick zebu steak, 'French fries' (cooked by Guy's Malagasy wife) and a rum toddy, followed by a cool highland night wrapped in thick blankets. The fever broke powerfully, drenching the bed in sweat, and it wasn't until I awoke late the next morning that I even realised how weak I'd been.

By the time I had finished breakfast, Henriette – as cheerful and as noisily energetic as her husband was lethargic – had already found me a 'trainee guide' who worked occasionally leading tourists around the park. She helped to further prepare me by generously supplying a bag of *beignets* (banana fritters) – energy for the trail.

Ton was just seventeen and arrived on the hotel veranda with a dangerous-looking carving knife in his belt and a plastic shopping bag containing everything else needed for a full-blown jungle expedition. He was dark-skinned with unusually wild bushy hair and his features betrayed an unusually large share of East African blood. Ton spoke only very basic French but he was cheerful and strong and, for a supplementary fee, was happy to shoulder one of the bags.

For years I had prided myself on Travelling Light – on fitting everything I needed for three months in the tropics in a 35-litre backpack (recommended in catalogues for 'dawn-till-dusk treks').

Soon I began to go further 'Off the Beaten Track' and, after a brief 'mercenary period' when I only wrote-to-travel and struggled to sell magazine articles to fund my trips, it dawned on me that I was beginning to travel-to-write. I exchanged my point-and-shoot camera for a fully manual SLR that could go through most things I could with the minimum of mollycoddling, and the accompanying paraphernalia of lenses, flash, tripod, and a hefty bag of slide films (difficult to find in most countries). Then I began to court sponsors for my trips and these sponsors – Polartec, Lowe Alpine, Air Madagascar and even Heineken Export – all wanted reassurance that I was fully prepared and would be using the equipment designed for such expeditions. I had to find space for an extensive medical kit, a specialist tent, a hand-held GPS unit that allowed me to navigate via satellite and charts, survival packs, spare water bottles, etc. etc. etc. The kitbag that I was now heaving onto Ton's back contained the equipment that had spilled out of the top of a 75-litre pack!

We hadn't been on the trail long when we overtook our first Malagasy wayfarer: a panther chameleon in full rainy-season breeding colours, the most eye-catching of all of the world's chameleons (half of which can only be found in Madagascar). He looked like he had been finger-painted in some kindergarten art class. A pale-blue lightning streak flashed horizontally along his flanks, which were scrawled with blue and green tiger-stripes. His swivelling eyes were splotched with deep scarlet and a downward-turned, unhappy clown's mouth was daubed bright yellow as if the infant artist had lost interest at this stage and rushed to finish the job.

Many chameleons are able to surprise predators with a frightening shriek or a sudden flash of gory colours. Having clamped onto some part of their attacker's anatomy they will fight tenaciously to keep their grip and are quite capable of drawing blood. As I stretched my hand towards him, he turned and yawned shocking yellow jaws at me – deterrent enough. Like many of his family this panther chameleon's survival tactics depended upon his unshakeable willingness to turn defence into attack. It's for this ferocity that chameleons are named from the Greek: 'Dwarf Lion'.

Madagascar's isolation made it one of nature's greatest laboratories, a 'naturalist's promised-land' where plants and animals have evolved in unique ways. In 1771, the French naturalist Joseph Philibert Commerson reported that:

> ... here nature seems to have withdrawn into a private sanctuary in order to work on designs which are different from those created elsewhere. At every step you are met by the most bizarre and wonderful forms.

In 1630, Richard Boothby waxed lyrical to say simply that Madagascar was 'the chiefest paradise this day on earth'. Long before that (sometime around 1298) Marco Polo was rather liberal with his quill when he wrote: 'more elephants are bred here than in any other province ... they have leopards and lynxes and lion also in great number'. He went on to describe a bird so huge that it could pounce on an elephant and carry it off to its nest. It seems that Madagascar was never the great man's strong point.

Since only twenty per cent of Madagascar's flora and ten per cent of its fauna are found anywhere else on earth it is not really surprising that leopards, lynxes, lions and elephants are on that extensive 'missing list.' Unfortunately Marco Polo's monstrous 'gryphon bird' (more often known as the Roc in the stories of Sinbad) is a relatively new addition to a missing list that is in danger of getting ever longer. Within a short time of human arrival in this Garden of Eden, two dozen species of large animals were extinct. These included the three-metre tall 'elephant bird' (the *Aepyornis*, capable of laying eight-litre eggs, but not of flying off with even a pygmy hippo – now also extinct), the giant tortoise, the Malagasy Jumping Aardvark (I'm not joking), and fifteen species of lemurs, some as big as gorillas.

The dripping rainforest through which Ton and I were now trekking was one of the last bastions of many unique creatures. Among them were nine species of lemur, the ring-tailed mongoose and the fosa, the largest of the island's eight carnivores: like a skinny, dog-faced puma measuring up to 1.5 metres long. Malagasy belief has endowed it with numerous cunning devices for securing dinner: including the strategy of soaking its bushy tail in river water to extinguish a campfire so that it can steal the roasting meat! Although there have been no reliable reports of fosa attacks on humans, Ton upheld the traditional Malagasy claim that a hungry fosa will often actively hunt zebu calves and children.

Within an hour we were already drenched by the afternoon downpour and had left the dense, misty jungle for the grasslands on the lower eastern slopes. The clouds cleared momentarily and Ton and I stopped to enjoy the view northwards across the sloping countryside and over Diego Bay. The sky above Diego was blue and the town appeared to be basking in the sun. While Diego gets 900 mm of rain a year, the mountain where we were standing receives up to four times that. As I felt the muddy water squelching in my boots, I allowed myself a moment of fondness for 'the Rio de Janeiro of Madagascar'.

Ton was cheerful but shy and, as he led me through a seemingly endless chain of muddy ravines, I stopped trying to draw him into conversation and saved my breath for the march. Twice he made a wrong turn and we had to retrace our steps through several kilometres of oily swamp.

Back in the forest we forded a rushing creek, stumbling thigh-deep against the current. It would have been pointless by this stage to take off our boots and as we splashed onto the opposite bank a cloud of cobalt butterflies erupted around us. There was a flash of shimmering blue and a Malagasy kingfisher landed on a branch barely two metres away. He was a living jewel, glittering blue on his back and shimmering copper-gold on his belly – the black dagger beak, almost as long as the bird himself, looked lethal and vicious in comparison with his beauty. I stood frozen until, with a flash and a swoop, he took off downstream.

We sat under the dripping canopy for a while and ate beignets, allowing the butterflies to drink the sweat from our shirts. I was uncomfortably aware that, amongst its more attractive invertebrate inhabitants, this steamy forest is home to twenty different types of mosquito including some particularly voracious *Anopheles* – one of which was to leave me with a recurring souvenir of Montagne d'Ambre.

In the late afternoon, tired and soaking, we stumbled through a storm-wracked plantation of sugarcane, bananas and jackfruit, and into the communal area between the four ramshackle timber huts that comprised the village of Unjan. These square, stilted huts (there are no typically African *rondavels* in Madagascar) reminded me of others in which I had stayed in Indonesia, the main difference being that these were constructed primarily of timber and woven saplings rather than bamboo. With their sloping palm frond roofs and immensely wide eaves they were a natural reaction to the climate of Montagne d'Ambre and, like the wildlife, could just as easily have evolved in situ.

Ton led me to the largest of the huts and shyly introduced me to his brother and sister-in-law who seemed almost to have been expecting us. I shrugged off my pack, unlaced my boots and gratefully stepped into the shelter of the hut.

There, looking like a modern art exhibit, was a magnificent wrought iron bed, pulled away from the walls to escape the creatures that inevitably trooped around the corners of the room. I was fascinated by the mystery of its arrival high on the side of a volcano.

'No mystery,' explained Ton. 'From Diego on a bush-taxi roof. Then carried eight kilometres, one piece at a time, from the road.'

The ornate bed, with its ragged mattress stuffed with kapok, looked distinctly out of place. But later, as the young couple said goodnight and pulled a moth-eaten piece of cotton over themselves, I had to admit that it showed a certain amount of style.

Ton's sister-in-law cooked some rice and tinned ravioli (that I'd carried from Joffreville), on a sandbox fireplace in the back doorway. I was grateful for some sweet coffee to wash it down. As I sat back against the wall listening to my hosts' mysterious Malagasy chatter it seemed amazing that only two days ago I had been lost and lonely in a dreary Diego hotel room.

I had a small, freestanding tent which could be used indoors as a sort of mozzy-net, but I didn't want to protect myself from the environment that my hosts were forced to sleep in every night. So, lying on a woven palm sleeping-mat in the doorway, I pulled the cotton sheet up to my chin and lay awake listening to the croak of tree frogs and the grunts of nocturnal lemurs. Three fearful, almost human, shrieks split the night like lightening and I wondered if I had heard the last cry of a fosa's dinner.

The household awoke at cockcrow – which in Unjan happens to be at 3.45 am. I was glad to see that it wasn't raining and we breakfasted quickly on reheated rice and ravioli. We filled my water bottle with coffee that I was sure would go a long way towards fuelling another day's footwork. I left rice, a packet of coffee and a tin of 'Lucky Cow' milk to pay for my stay and tried my best to thank Ton's family for their hospitality.

It seemed likely that we were in for only a short spell of dry weather so I tried to shoot some photos as we walked. But everything I wore was already covered in the sticky red mud of Montagne d'Ambre and it was almost impossible to keep my hands clean enough to operate my camera. Also, it was so humid that the viewfinder misted over as soon as I raised it to my eye. By 8.30 we were trekking along a high ridge and I shot a last couple of photos as the angry black thunderclouds rolled over us.

As we were wading out of yet another rushing creek, using sticks to balance against the current, I saw a large white snake disappear into the undergrowth. It had been sloughing and left the crinkly ribbon of its skin behind on the track, like a neatly rolled-off condom … a metre-long condom.

It rained steadily for the rest of the day and we trudged for kilometre upon soggy kilometre through sparsely wooded savannah across the western slopes of Montagne d'Ambre. Here we saw herds of zebu standing with their backs to the rain, which turned to sniff at us sullenly, with an air of limitless patience. There was one startling little bird that is rarely seen in the forest and has found its niche on the open grassland, and a flash of brilliant scarlet often alerted me to the low, dipping flight of a *fody* – Ton pronounced it uncomfortably like 'food'. I was aware that, like the panther chameleon, I was privileged to see the male fody in its fleeting rainy-season mating costume. For most of the year this little weaver wears a sombre plumage of dull brown.

For eight long hours we dragged boots loaded with great clumps of mud before finally arriving in Antsalaka – the name of which, according to my Lutheran Press dictionary, could either mean 'Victory Chant' or 'Place of Loincloths'!

'Must visit the *délégué*,' said Ton, as we dropped our bags under a lean-to roof outside the village store. 'Must register one's arrival.'

The délégué is a throwback to the old French system of colonial rule – bringing order to the bush in the name of *la mission civilisatrice* – and is still today the local government officer in charge of all official happenings in regional headquarters. Apparently the arrival of a vazaha in Antsalaka was regarded as an 'official happening' so, after exchanging pleasantries with three old women who were washing onions on the trading-post veranda, we stepped back down to the wide mud street, which was now in full flood. The deforestation of Montagne d'Ambre has seriously exacerbated the problems caused by rainwater run-off.

Under the eaves of the concrete government office three glassy-eyed youths were chewing their way through a large basket of leaves. This was *qat*, a narcotic plant, something like betel nut in that it is a mild tranquilliser with no great effect other than the stimulation of vast quantities of bitter-tasting saliva (in this case green rather than red). The chewing of qat is a habit that has, in the last few years, swept like wildfire through the men of Diego province and is just beginning to work its way southwards.

One of the young men hauled himself wearily to his feet and went into the building to alert the délégué of the visit of a soggy vazaha. The latter, when he eventually called us in, was surly but not overly officious. He checked my passport and Ton's ID card and wrote our origin and destination in a pink exercise book.

'Go to see the vazaha,' he advised me.

'What vazaha?'

'All the vazaha who come here invariably go to visit Monsieur d'Amour.'

'Do many vazaha come here?'

'Oh yes, many. Last year there were two Germans ... in a Volkswagen!'

Monsieur d'Amour, the famous vazaha of Antsalaka, was born in Joffreville during the 'glory days', when the French Legion was still there, and he had married a French farmer's daughter in Diego, in the dying days of the colony. By the time that independence was declared – or 'recovered' to use the words of the Malagasy politicians – in 1960, Madagascar's French population had become so much a part of the country that Philibert Tsiranana, the first president and himself a Tsimihety, regarded the *colons* as Madagascar's nineteenth tribe. But in the early 1970s, the ruling communist regime closed the French base in Diego and the majority of the local plantation owners left with the forces. The d'Amours went to live with friends in Mauritius and continued their self-imposed 'exile' on La Réunion and for few unhappy months in the mother country, or *La Métropole*, as they referred to France. As soon as peace was assured the d'Amours gratefully turned their back on *La Métropole* for the last time and moved home to Antsalaka.

Madame d'Amour said it all: 'We were born here and my father built this house. Of course we had to come back ... for rich or poor.'

Their house was a little bigger than the others around it but in the wide eaves, steep roof and weather-beaten clapboard exterior it was essentially the home of any relatively successful Malagasy farmer. It and the farmland had survived their absence more or less untouched – a testament to the d'Amour's popularity in the town – but the island's main export crops, vanilla, coffee and cloves had all but disappeared, and the education system and transport infrastructure had collapsed.

By the time Madame d'Amour brought the *cafetière* over to the rough-hewn kitchen table I had already formed the impression that although they looked on Antsalaka as home they had lived most of their lives in a sort of limbo. Everyone in Antsalaka knew the d'Amours simply as the vazahas and they were condemned to be the vazahas wherever they lived for the rest of their lives. Monsieur d'Amour stated vehemently that, despite the fact that their three grown children were settled in *La Métropole*, he could never again consider living there. 'One cannot relate to those people,' he said. Yet the Malagasy were clearly even less his own kind and, although we were both served with coffee (to Ton's embarrassment), only I was offered a room for the night. My guide was apologetically sent back to sleep in the délégué's building. M d'Amour went to great pains to explain that this was an unfortunate necessity since there was only one guest bed – but later I noticed an empty bed in a separate room. I considered politely turning down the offer and sleeping on the floor of the délégué's office myself but decided that this would only serve to make everyone involved feel morally (and myself physically) uncomfortable. Besides I had quickly come to like this quiet, relaxed old couple and was looking forward to an evening in their company.

Through the flyscreen on the back door we could see that the rain had eased slightly and M d'Amour offered to show me around the orchard. As we pushed back our chairs I was surprised to see him slap a moth-eaten toupee on his head; it didn't seem to fit with his casual workaday clothes and tough backwoodsman's character.

'I had a couple of horses out here until recently,' he said as he pulled on an old plaid workshirt.

'What happened?'

'Well, you know how it is … It's not a healthy climate.' I recognised, in his sun-wrinkled eyes, the same resignation that I had seen in the Malagasy who had told me about the epidemic.

The rich basaltic soil and the high rainfall had made this place one of Madagascar's premier areas for vegetables, groundnuts and maize and for rich crops of pineapples, mangoes, papayas and even strawberries. I have never liked tomatoes and at first I refused M d'Amour's offer of a double handful of what he called tree tomatoes, but these fruits turned out to be delicious. In taste and texture they were more like kiwifruit than tomatoes.

I went out to pay Ton his wages so that he could enjoy his evening in 'the big city' and found him with his cheek bulging and a thin dribble of jade *qat* saliva running from the corner of his mouth. By the time I got back to the kitchen, the table was laid and a bottle of claret was breathing next to three mismatched glasses.

'There are some things that one should not live without,' smiled M d'Amour.

'We get this sent by the case direct from Bordeaux,' said his wife as she cleared a space for zebu casserole and home-grown *petits pois*.

'Things used to be much better here,' continued my host, looking out of the screen door where fresh streams ran from the roof, glowing gold in the reflected light of an oil lamp. 'That muddy river, running past the front door, used to be tarmac right down to the Route Nationale 6. We had constant electricity and phones and when a storm or cyclone brought the lines down engineers were sent to fix them. After independence when the lines came down ... well, they stayed down.'

This was a story that I was to hear all over the country. Wherever you go in the Third World veteran travellers almost seem to queue up to tell you: 'You should've seen this thirty years ago – there was nothing!' In Madagascar you often feel that you've travelled back in time, against the natural current of progress. In the eastern rainforests I saw a majestic colonial railway station falling into ruin, where now no line even exists. On the west coast I saw the remains of a once important port, now hopelessly silted up and isolated for five months of the year by impassable dirt tracks.

I slept well on a big old mattress and was glad of a chance to repay something for my room with a packet of spare Lariam malaria tablets.

M d'Amour smiled, shaking my hand with that now familiar look of resignation.

'You can get through a lot of these living here,' he said.

CHAPTER 4

THE MAVERICK

Maverick / 'mæverick'/
– *n* **1** an unbranded calf or yearling
2 an independent-minded person; an individualist
– *v* **1** stray or wander like a maverick
[Samuel A. *Maverick* (1803–70), Texas engineer
who owned but did not brand cattle]
– *Oxford English Dictionary*

In Anivorano Nord, my new bovine travelling companion and I
sized each other up. I could tell that he wasn't overly impressed.
I had made some half-hearted charade out of feeling around the
bull's stocky knees, checking for heat that might be a sign of a
sprain, and prodding his back, looking for signs of damage caused
by heavy *charet* yokes. I tried to pick up his hooves, but I had little idea of what one was supposed to look for in a healthy pack-
bull and I was more concerned with keeping a wary eye on the
curling scimitars of his horns.

'He's very healthy,' said the man who was selling him. 'And
very friendly.'

'Mmmh, he looks good,' I replied with faked assurance, praying that this bull would prove to be the 'friendliest' in Diego
Province. 'But will he carry saddlebags?'

'He's very strong and any bull that can haul a charet like he can
will have no problem with bags … Show me them.'

'I'll have to get some made.'

'*Pa't problème*. I have a friend who can make them for you.'

'If I agree to buy him at your price, will you help me to get him
ready for the journey?'

'Okay. I never knew of anybody going so far with a zebu but I'll help you.'

We shook on the deal.

'One question: what does Jobilahy mean in French?' I asked.

'"Jobi" is like *noir* and "lahy" is *garçon* – so Jobilahy is Black Boy.'

I reflected for a moment on the offence that might be taken from a vazaha calling his bull Black Boy, but I need not have worried. Almost everywhere 'Jobi' and I travelled together we were met only with good humour and respect.

He was five years old, 500 kilograms of solid muscle and had a shiny coat of pure black. For a zebu he was on the small side but apart from the mound of flesh that stuck up from his shoulders he looked like a genuine fighting bull. I thought how impressed my Spanish girlfriend would be with him.

Luckily, the man who had raised and trained him from a calf was there to help me, and as it turned out I could have asked for no better-qualified guru in zebu-handling. On the rough compound in front of his hut Christian Michel gave me my first lessons.

'Hold the rope higher. Keep his head up,' he said, as the rough horns grazed my knuckles. All working zebu in Madagascar have a rope passed through their noses and I learned how to run this rope up Jobi's forehead and around the base of his horns so that I had some control over his head if he tried to hook me.

Like his wife and their five handsome children, Christian had an infectious smile, which frequently grew to uninhibited laughter – often aimed, good-naturedly, at the clumsy vazaha who was stumbling around in his front yard.

His father was a German but all he had left his Malagasy son were his deep blue eyes and a twenty-centimetre advantage in height over most people in the village. Christian and his family lived at the bottom of the hill in Anivorano, on a plot of land that he had bought out of the proceeds of several stints as a deckhand on the Japanese fishing boats that sailed out of Diego. He had enjoyed the long voyages on the tuna boats, had learnt the pidgin

Japanese that was the common language among his shipmates and had seen just enough foreign islands to acquire a realistic yet heartfelt appreciation for his own.

Now he made a living by selling the bananas, papayas, cacaos and mangoes that he planted around his hut, and by raising a few head of cattle. Once in a while he could make a bit of extra cash selling an animal to the tour groups that occasionally came from Diego to feed the crocodiles of the sacred lake.

Christian taught me the clicking noise that makes a draught-zebu move on, and the sharp rolled 'RRRRR!' that is supposed to make him stop. I hoped that Jobi would take the quavering, slightly pleading note in my voice for an English accent.

Slowly I began to get more confident and soon Christian's fourteen-year-old son – tall for his age and with smooth, almost Ethiopian features – was showing me how to ride Jobi around the field. Even with me on his back he could get up quite a speed in a straight line but with a rope hooked around the horns under-steering and stopping were problems. Several times I had to bail off, much to the delight of Christian's family. I would never be riding during the journey so – apart from a few cuts and bruises – I wasn't overly worried about my lack of success as a rodeo rider.

That evening as we sat outside his hut, watching the sun melt across the western hills, Christian said: 'I'm taking two zebu to Nosy Be with my brother-in-law in a few days. You want to come with us?'

'How're you getting there?' I assumed that I was being offered a ride and would therefore have to turn it down.

'We're walking. It will take five or six days so you can at least stick with us for the first part of your trek.'

I realised that Christian had held his tongue until he knew that I was serious about walking down the island. I hoped also that it was a sign that he had some confidence in the way I was handling Jobi – but it's equally likely that he thought he'd better keep an eye on me. Apparently, Christian had other sacrifices to make besides baby-sitting a vazaha. He was driving two zebu cows on a 'pilgrimage' to Nosy Be, an island further down the north-west coast. The climax of this trek would be to sacrifice the cows to his grandmother, 'a queen on the island'!

I was intrigued and accepted immediately; I'd find out more about his 'grandmother' when we got on the trail together. It was reassuring to know that I was going to have expert guidance for about the first two hundred kilometres of my journey. We shook hands on our second deal of the day.

'Where will we sleep?' I asked, thinking of my tiny tent.

'Oh villages, along the way – sometimes by the road. We can eat in *hôtelys.*'

Malagasy hôtelys are a major source of confusion for newly arrived vazaha who naturally assume that these establishments will be equipped with rooms for rent. But this is not always so because hôtely is simply the generic name for any local eating house, regardless of whether they have accommodation or not.

In the end it took a week to complete the arrangements for our departure and during that time I stayed at a *hôtely misy fandri-ambahini* (literally a hotel with beds) which, although it had no sign, was known locally as 'Chez Josephine', after the lady who ran it. It was a small iron-roofed flophouse with a two-table bar at the front and two rented cells at the back.

A rickety wooden hut that was collapsing over a putrid pit went by the label of *la toilette*. The floorboards that covered the hole were rotting visibly and one day – perhaps not for two years, perhaps tomorrow – they would crumble and somebody would fall through into the indescribable hell underneath. A rainwater butt, beside the hut, was known as *la douche* but swarms of flies invariably left you feeling ever dirtier and this feeling was emphasised by the need to skate across an expanse of smelly black slime to the hôtely's back door.

My cell was furnished with an iron bed and an electric light bulb that came on when the town's power supply kicked in at 5 pm, and clicked off (whether you wanted it to or not) with the 'blackout' at 11 pm. Every shack in Anivorano owned at least one radio and these were left permanently switched on so that a sudden blast of pop music blared out of each and every building at

5 pm exactly ... and continued, without pause, until a ghostly silence descended upon the town in good time for the witching hour.

Mademoiselle Josephine's brother actually owned Chez Josephine and there were unsubstantiated rumours that he had made his considerable wealth out of various other *hôtely misy fandriambahinis* of a more dubious nature. But he had apparently never re-invested much of his income in Chez Josephine, and his sister – a slim and pretty spinster who struggled to balance her religious tendencies with her brother's infamous reputation – prided herself on keeping a clean and respectable establishment.

At 5 pm Mlle Josephine's battered hi-fi would begin to kick out the boot-scootin' country rock that she thrived on and two ultraviolet tubes would begin to buzz furiously over the tables. It *was* true that a passing bush-taxi driver might stop by on the off-chance occasionally and pick up a girl at Chez Josephine. Or a market stallholder who had had a particularly good day might find himself head down in a pool of THB when the sudden silence shook him awake at eleven. But, on the whole, the pounding speakers and ultraviolet glare made promises of a debauched night-life that Chez Josephine rarely, if ever, lived up to.

The people of Anivorano woke with the sun. I had the drop on most of them since I was invariably woken by the first cockerel which, with full-throated enthusiasm, greeted each day from the step outside my room. I'd lie in bed and read for another hour or so, with a headlamp strapped to my forehead, before getting up at about 6 am. Grating the back door open I'd sit on the stone step and watch the village coming to life. There was a small mango tree just beyond the step and I could see that Mlle Josephine had already brought out her two captive crowned lemurs to their day-time perch. The male was a rich orange-brown with a distinctive black crown and he seemed to devote the first part of the day to marking his territory, by rubbing his scent glands on anything that his tether would allow him to reach – including, most notably, the female.

Unusually amongst primates, it is the females who are the undisputed leaders of lemur groups and this female (grey with an orange tiara) pulled rank mercilessly when Mlle Josephine brought out their breakfast of chopped fruit. An old Malagasy belief says, with delightful logic, that lemurs are perfectly capable of speaking – but refuse to do so for fear of being made to work as men do.

These two prisoners were lodged in the hallway at night and, despite my supposedly superior intelligence as a 'higher primate', the female managed to ambush me regularly as I passed their corner on my way through to my room. One evening she scratched a long furrow out of my forearm with her teeth. Both her mate and myself lived in constant dread of one of her attacks. Crowned lemurs can only be found in this part of Madagascar but – from the pygmy mouse lemur (not much bigger than a 'pygmy mouse') to the indri (like a four year-old boy in a panda costume) – lemurs are certainly the biggest zoological drawcard for tourists to the island.

The Great Red Island is believed to have broken away from mainland Africa long before the first primates evolved and it has always been a mystery how these primitive primates, or prosimians, crossed from the mainland and yet later, more intelligent, primates did not. Some experts now say that they hopped over on a land bridge when Madagascar once again bumped against Africa at a later date. Whatever the answer, most of their predators also missed the boat and lemurs were left in relative peace to occupy the niche that monkeys and apes dominated in other parts of the world.

I would sit peacefully on the stone steps until the morning sun began to steam the damp vegetation, watching the villagers wander past on their morning chores. The water vendor would nod each time he passed, carrying heavy buckets from the well. A small boy drove his father's geese towards the muddy puddles under the mango trees: '*Salut* vazaha'. The lady from the shack next door would drag out her wooden bowl and long pestle to grind rice-flour and I'd shout my order in for breakfast: 'Mademoiselle Josephine! Could one eat milk and yoghurt as breakfast, please?'

Mlle Josephine would call to one of the small boys who were

playing outside the bar and he would dash off up the hill to the marketplace. Ten minutes later he'd be back, flushed with responsibility, carrying a plastic bag full of milk and chilled yoghurt in plastic beakers. The zebu milk had ghostly strands of cream floating through it and the yoghurt, bought before the cool boxes defrosted in the heat of the marketplace, still had crystals of ice around its edge.

I'd always over-order so that I could share my breakfast with Mlle Josephine and the boy. Sometimes he might casually advise me of other delicacies that had appeared in the market that morning: soft sponge cakes with crispy burnt edges or the tangy ginger biscuits that are laughingly known as *gâteaux*. Sometimes there was wild honey to pour into the milk.

After breakfast I'd take a walk around the market myself. In the main square country people from kilometres around sat under the shade of parasols made from nylon rice sacks, selling fruit and vegetables, smoked fish, *gâteaux*, bread, wild herbs and a bewildering assortment of different types of rice. One old man had nothing to sell but a dozen small sand scorpions that crawled over each other in a plastic margarine tub.

'Crush and drink with rum,' he grinned toothlessly, grinding his fist in his callused palm. 'Cure for asthma. Also good for the heart – make you good all night.' The palm wrapped itself obscenely around one stumpy forefinger and the old man winked wickedly.

In the meat market whole sides of zebu hung sweating, like pink and white marble, glittered here and there with swarms of iridescent flies. Tripe, liver and heart hung in bunches above the heads of the butchers and an entire grinning mouth section of cows was lined neatly along the front of the tables. Off to one side, separated by an empty alleyway – in deference to the town's Muslim population – hung the split carcasses of pigs. Dogs fought over the offal.

Everywhere I went the market people in their vividly coloured lambas looked up from their goods to greet me with a friendly: '*Salut,* vazaha!'

As if in reaction to the crocodile curse that had befallen the ancient population of that other nearby village, the inhabitants of Anivorano were even more than usually friendly to a passing vazaha.

The bureaucracy involved in buying a zebu was far more complex than I ever could have imagined and was solely responsible for my unplanned, though enjoyable, stay in Anivorano. Luckily, Christian was ever on hand to guide me past the legal pitfalls and cut through the red tape. Firstly there were vaccination papers to attend to. Then there was the actual deed of sale. Finally I had to visit the local délégué to get passports.

'But I have a passport ...' I began to explain naively.

'No, no. You need a passport for Jobi. There's lots of cattle rustling in the country here and this is the only way that the police can check where an animal came from.'

In an effort to crack down on the cattle rustling that is rife throughout many of Madagascar's wilderness areas, every animal must be issued with a passport before it is moved across the country. The journey of Jobi and the two cows would have to be faithfully recorded in every large town through which we passed. Before I entered the next province to the south I would have to apply for another passport.

Christian arranged for a set of saddlebags to be sewn out of two large nylon sacks. Malagasy eat more rice than any other nationality (half a kilo per person, per day) and it was a sad sign of the times that every rice sack that I saw in Anivorano was stamped 'Pakistan – Long Grain'. My zebu guru also helped me in the perilous task of fitting these sacks and then gently lowering my baggage into them, secured high and tight with a set of bungee cords.

I scrambled around tightening the cinch and trying to dodge Jobi's stomping hooves while Christian, ever cheerful, advised me that I had nothing to worry about: Jobi was 'only playing'. I'd bought a thick saddle blanket to cushion Jobi's back and after some fine balancing and securing we got the load stable. He was able to walk around the yard without any apparent discomfort. I led him slowly out onto the road and we set off down the hill to the vet's office on the edge of town to get him vaccinated and generally checked over.

The vet complimented us on our Pakistani saddlebags and gave some additional zebu maintenance tips: 'Their hooves are quite strong and as long as they get plenty to eat and drink they'll go a long way. I never heard of anyone driving a zebu so far, but as long as you rest him every few days and check for cracks on his hooves or sores under the saddlebags, he should be okay.'

Inspired by this vote of confidence and Jobi's clean bill of health, we collected Christian's two cows and led them back up into the town to get the passports. We had quite a following of bare-foot kids by the time we turned up the track opposite the market-place and tethered Jobi and the cows outside the délégué's office.

We were met by the délégué's teenage son, dressed in a white lamba, like a toga thrown formally across one shoulder. In the style of a typical old-time Malagasy dandy he wore a huge red plastic comb, slipped neatly into a head of tight curls. In towns like Anivorano where the French influence has been felt more profoundly this is a rare sight, but later in my travels I was to see this accessory often on young village bachelors.

'*Je suis désolé*,' said this teenage dandy, gripping our hands in the formal two-handed handshake. 'My father is on business in Diego and is not expected back for two days.'

This young man obviously already felt the responsibility of his position, and promised that should his father appear earlier than expected he would be delighted to pass word to my lodgings personally.

Andrianampoinimerinandriantsimitoviaminandriampanjaka, the name of Madagascar's greatest king, was a mouthful even for the Malagasy so they shortened it to Andrianampoinimerina – 'the Hope of the Merina'.

In 1799 Andrianampoinimerina moved his highly trained garrison of 1,000 soldiers to Antananarivo and set about 'unifying' the whole island. Some claim that Antananarivo means 'Town of a Thousand'. The king was described by a French contemporary as a 'savage of genius'; and he was able to harness the superstition of his warriors so that they became almost invincible on the battlefield.

His most powerful enemy were the Sakalava clans of the west, armed with muskets traded from the slavers of the Mozambique Channel. The spear-throwing Merina soldiers were understandably unenthusiastic about facing the Sakalava's hot lead and their king devised a clever plan to endow them all with a god-given courage. He ordered his priests to distribute powerful charms – crocodile teeth filled with magical substances – and fearlessly stood forward himself to prove their efficiency.

In front of the massed ranks of his army he stood facing a trusted – and carefully briefed – sharpshooter with an Arab musket. There were cries of alarm as the troops heard the shot ring out and saw the smoke blow into the highland breeze ... and rejoicing when Andrianampoinimerina calmly turned and spat a bullet into his cupped hand. Thus inspired the Merina wreaked havoc amongst the Sakalava clans and in a carefully planned campaign of strategic skirmishes subjugated one tribe at a time. Within two years Andrianampoinimerina controlled half the island.

Although there may have been many isolated pockets of Antaifasy ('Sand People'), Antaimoro ('Coastal People'), Antandroy ('People of the Thorns'), Sihanaka ('Marsh People'), Tanala ('Forest People'), Mahafaly ('Taboo Makers') and Sakalava rebels who never realised that they were Merina subjects, they were officially to remain that way for almost a century.

Andrianampoinimerinandriantsimitoviaminandriampanjaka died within a few years of his victory and his son, Radama I, continued his expansion efforts with a highly trained army of 35,000. With the help of Betsimisaraka allies ('Those Who Stand

Together') – descendants, in part, of European pirates – he had taken control of the entire east coast by 1817.

Radama I made war with the princes of the Antàkarana ('People of the Rocks'), who chose suicide or exile over surrender, and he made love to the princess of the Sakalava kingdom of Menabe. Thus he fulfilled his father's dream and claimed: '*Ny riaka no valamparihiko*' – the sea is the only limit to my rice fields. This was the start of Radama I's diplomatic phase and he did a masterful job of balancing power between the European nations who were showing an increasing interest in his island. He appointed a French soldier as general of his armies and an Englishman as his personal advisor. In 1820 the European powers officially recognised the Sovereign State of Madagascar, and Radama I as king.

Radama's death in 1828 led to eight months of dispute amongst his many wives over the right to the throne. After the mysterious deaths of several of her competitors the diabolical Ranavalona I was crowned, beginning the darkest era in Madagascar's history. Ranavalona I was an intensely paranoid xenophobe and she used (and enjoyed) terror, torture and genocide to keep herself on the throne for a hellish thirty-three years. Her first act was to make Christianity illegal and to give all missionaries three days to leave the country; her second was to martyr the two hundred Christians who resisted. All foreigners were evicted and any unfortunate sailor who found himself shipwrecked on Madagascar's beaches would very soon find himself a slave (and occasionally the sexual plaything) of the warped queen.

She was clearly schizophrenic: at one time ordering the construction of a highway to the coast, at the cost of ten thousand lives and then demanding that all roads be allowed to fall into ruin – lest her enemies use them as a route for invasion. She ordered her highly disciplined Hova guardsmen to exterminate or enslave rival tribes but refused to provision them on their campaigns so that, like a swarm of locusts, they swept through the countryside, leaving starvation in their wake.

Contemporary writers claimed that tens of thousands were executed annually, often purely for entertainment, and some historians say that during her bloodthirsty reign Ranavalona may have reduced the island's population by as much as a quarter. Her sadistic imagination knew no bounds. She had pits dug at the base of the cliff in Antananarivo and filled with boiling water so that shackled prisoners could be slowly boiled to death. The Merina nobility attended these occasions as sporting events and when criminals, rebels, traitors or simply victims were thrown from the cliff, a great cheer would go up if they should chance to land in the boiling pits.

Her system of justice was based on trial by ordeal. She knew that a man whom the ancestors judged to be innocent could pick a gold coin out of a pot of boiling water or touch his tongue seven times to a red-hot spearhead without burning. He could swim across a river infested by crocodiles and those earthbound incarnations of the ancestors would proclaim his innocence by refraining from tearing him apart.

Likewise a man who doubted his own innocence could be poisoned by a bowl of clear, untainted water into which a sacred relic (ostensibly made from the gold of the Vazimba) had been dipped. He would be locked up to fast (and think) for twenty-four hours before his trial. The power of autosuggestion, working on the psyche of a 'condemned' man, would mean that if he allowed himself to believe that he had committed some crime, however minor, against the queen, the state or the ancestors, he *would* be proven guilty by the technically innocuous 'gold water'.

Her personal favourite was trial by *tanguin*. Shavings from the poisonous nut of the *tanguin* tree would be wrapped in three pieces of chicken skin and the accused would be forced to eat them. If he vomited in what was judged, by the queen's advisors, to be a propitious manner he would be considered innocent – although he might very likely be paralysed or made impotent by the powerful effects of the poison. If, however, he retched but was unable to throw up the skins, or continued to retch after the skins had been brought up, it would be proved that he was guilty; his body was obviously disgusted and sickened by the treacherous deeds that he had forced it to undertake. Likewise if he only vomited only one or two of the skins then he was guilty and he had better hope that the poison killed him fast, because the queen was not likely to give him a right of appeal.

Should he be found guilty, yet survive, unimaginable horrors would be in store for him. There was no limit to Ranavalona's talent for invention. If he were not boiled alive he might be lucky enough to simply be sawn in half. Or he might be yoked by the neck to a wagon wheel, with three or four other wrongdoers, and turned loose to roam the country until the weight of the dead broke the necks of the others or forced them to starve. Or he might have his limbs amputated and be sewn into a buffalo hide sack until he rotted. Even death could not bring relief because the criminal body was banned from the ancestral grave. His soul would be condemned to perpetual and tormented limbo and his family ostracised – guilty by association.

French estimates claimed that at least one tenth of the island's population (then somewhere under two million) suffered trial by ordeal and about half of them were proven guilty. Thus – if one in twenty of her subjects were undeniably criminals – Ranavalona I's fears were given credence and driven to further extremes. For reasons of security all members of the palace staff, from Hova guards down to kitchen staff, were tested.

Just because you're paranoid doesn't mean they're not out to get you, and amongst the innocent unfortunates there must have been a few brave souls who had tried to put an end to Ranavalona's reign of terror. In 1848 a combined French and British force bombed the port of Tamatave in reprisals for the mistreatment of diplomatic envoys.

But by an awful quirk of injustice in 1861, after thirty-three years of the most outrageous tyranny, Ranavalona the Cruel died peacefully in her bed of natural causes. The whole country celebrated. She had been right all along: they *had* all prayed for her demise.

Her comparatively angelic son, Radama II, at once abolished her slavery policies and her twisted judicial system and re-opened the doors to foreigners. The Christian faith came out from underground and was soon one of the country's official religions. Radama was keen to curry favour amongst the European traders and diplomats who began to pour into the country.

But fate played a cruel trick on the young king. After he'd been in power only a short time a mysterious plague hit the capital and hundreds died. The Merina nobles whispered that it was a curse from the ancestors, brought on by Radama's shameless pampering of the vazahas. He was assassinated by his Prime Minister's brother.

Tradition is an almost sacred concept in Madagascar – irrevocably related as it is to the ancestors – and it now dictated two things. Firstly, that no matter how the king had deviated from what were considered to be the accepted norms, royal lineage must be respected and his widow must be crowned. Secondly, that she must marry the Prime Minister – even if fate (or dastardly cunning) had also made him the brother of her husband's killer.

This state of affairs lasted only until General Hononaire Rainilaiarivony (the Prime Minister's ruthless brother) staged a coup and proclaimed *himself* Prime Minister … and husband to the queen. Rainilaiarivony's hunger for power was to keep him firmly in Madagascar's driving seat through two more successive marriages – to Queens Ranavalona II and III!

However, the Prime Minister did not have it all his own way. In 1890 France and Britain signed 'The Convention of Zanzibar', mutually recognising that island as a British colony and Madagascar as property of France. With no further ado the French sent an envoy to Ranavalona's palace in Tana, as the capital is usually known, advising that they were now subjects of France and demanding the queen's surrender. The envoy was executed.

False reports and spies were circulated to convince the Merina that an attack was imminent from the French stronghold of Tamatave, on the east coast. In fact the attack, when it finally came, came from Mahajanga, on the west coast. The forest and tropical diseases inflicted a horrendous death toll on the French forces long before they arrived in the capital to fight their swift and decisive campaign against the Merina defenders.

The *Menalamba* movement, born just a few months later, is often looked upon as the first flash of the independence struggle. The rebels were known as the 'Red Cloaks' because of their practice of camouflaging their lambas with the red dust of Madagascar. In the town of Arivonimamo – appropriately the geographical centre of the island – a gang of Menalamba rebels attacked a compound belonging to the London Missionary Society. They killed a family of Quakers and an avenging French punitive force was quickly sent from the capital to slaughter 150 Arivonimamo villagers.

General Joseph Simon Galliéni quickly established the mood of his governorship when he was asked when he would like to be escorted to the palace to make the acquaintance of the queen and her family. He replied: 'Ranavalona is a subject of France; I shall expect these ladies tomorrow'.

He banned the English language, all English-based education and even suppressed the Malagasy language itself. He took the decision himself to depose the queen and his *coup-de-grâce* came when she was shipped into exile in Algeria (where she died in 1917) and he ordered the destruction of all records of the Malagasy monarchy.

The enlightened French *colons* abolished the 'benign' slavery of the Merina caste system (in which slaves were considered part of the family) and replaced it with a taxation system under which men could be jailed if they didn't earn money by working for the state. The communications infrastructure, agriculture and business boomed and Madagascar was soon exporting cloves, coffee and vanilla to the world. The French were making a lot of money but health-care and education were also high on their list of priorities – the latter reserved specifically for any one who showed the necessary dedication to the French system.

Unfortunately, one or two of the 'wrong types' slipped through the net. In 1921 the 'Betsileo agitator' Jean Ralaimongo, a schoolteacher who had volunteered to fight in the war in Europe, returned home from Paris (where he had shared a room with another 'young trouble-maker' called Ho Chi Minh) to begin a long campaign against his country's invaders. At his homecoming, Governor-General Hubert Garbit warned him:

'I don't want anyone coming to upset my Malagasy under the pretext that they're unhappy when they are not unhappy.'

Ralaimongo rapidly built up quite a following amongst the Malagasy – who were obviously nowhere near as happy as Garbit led himself to believe – and managed to do a very thorough job of upsetting the French settlers around Diego, where he based his campaign. Although he is commonly regarded as the father of the Malagasy independence movement, world events were to postpone its realisation for a few years yet.

At the start of World War II, on hearing of Germany's occupation of La Métropole, Madagascar's colons were faced with a decision: should they side with the Vichy government and Germany, or join de Gaulle in the fight to free France? Perhaps they were just too far away and out of touch, because they chose Vichy – and so their leaders answered for treason after the war.

In May 1942, after a badly planned landing, the British army occupied Diego Suarez, ostensibly to curtail Japanese plans to use it as a naval base. They marched inland expecting resistance and instead were readily joined by tribesmen who were more than happy about the prospect of marching on French farms and businesses.

The British occupiers made rash promises; and the Malagasy were disgusted when, in 1943, their island was finally handed over to de Gaulle's Free French. The *Fanafahana* (liberation) movement rapidly gained momentum, culminating in 1947 with what was perhaps the most horrifying military action of France's colonial history.

On the evening of 29 March of that year, French troops were surprised by carefully synchronised attacks in key locations all over the island. One of the freedom fighters' greatest successes was to maintain clear lines of communication – not easy even today across the forests, deserts and mountains of the world's fourth-largest island. The rebels hit hard at Diego and captured the army barracks and the port. Their compatriots in Tana cancelled their plans at the last moment – leaving the French government still in authority there, but the Fanafahana fighters took control of about a sixth of the country.

At the army barracks at Moramanga, on the forested slopes of the eastern highlands, scores of sleepy Senegalese legionnaires were hacked to death with *coupe-coupe* machetes or run through with spears. The surviving Senegalese massacred an undetermined number of Moramanga men, women and children in revenge. In October several Foreign Legion units and thousands more Senegalese soldiers were brought in as reinforcements. The Malagasy came to hate and fear the Senegalese, to whom they attributed almost diabolical characteristics. They were certainly involved in many atrocities during the twenty-one months that the rebellion lasted, but the extent to which they practised black magic and cannibalism have probably grown out of proportion, becoming part of Malagasy independence folklore. The insurrection was finally put down but the shock waves that spread back to La Métropole contributed to Madagascar 'regaining' independence thirteen years later.

Both the Malagasy and the French look on the dark months of the rebellion as a regrettable and shameful part of their joint history. It is a wound that needs time to heal and when 'Insurrection Day' was first officially commemorated, on 29 March 1967, President Tsiranana urged his people not to dishonour the dead in acts of vengeance. He avowed that there was still a place for the French in Madagascar: 'You do not kick away the canoe that helped you to cross the river'.

An official Commission of Enquiry reported that while over 1,000 French soldiers and thirty settlers died in the 1947 insurrection, the numbers of Malagasy dead may have been as high as 80,000. Throughout the north and the east there were few families that did not lose husbands, sons or fathers in the rebellion.

Mademoiselle Josephine believed that her father had died as a direct result of the feverish months that he had spent hiding out on Montagne d'Ambre after the collapse of the insurrection. Insurrection

Day is still a day of heartfelt national mourning in Madagascar: when the electricity came on at 5 pm all the town's radios would, for once, already have been turned off and there would be no sudden, migraine-provoking flash of blue neon at Chez Josephine. Since the délégué would be unavailable and the bar would not need tending, Mlle Josephine had agreed that, after church, she would accompany me on a walk down to the Sacred Lake.

As we walked down a rutted cart track that was perhaps once trodden by a thirsty old sorcerer on his way to a condemned village, she recounted her father's greatest memory of his exile in the rainforest.

'He saw a Vazimba,' she said breathlessly. 'He was a small, hairy man with long, dirty fingernails and ... no, not my father – the Vazimba.'

'What did he look like? Was he white?'

'You couldn't say it was white, but it was not really black. He saw the creature only briefly but he remembered it clearly until the day he died.'

Having once suffered bewitching malarial hallucinations in Borneo – where I watched a beach full of 'Lilliputians' in absolute clarity for almost half an hour – I could quite understand the old man's insistence that the Vazimba had been real. But yet again the description differed substantially from anything that I had read about the 'white pygmies'.

'Is a Vazimba then a man or an animal?'

'A Vazimba is an animal, but an animal with magical powers.'

'Do people still see them on Montagne d'Ambre?'

'Every now and then a hunter sees one. You see, they can't resist the burnt crust around the edge of a rice pot and sometimes, although they're very shy, they'll come into a camp to steal it!'

The previous evening's storm had washed across the landscape so that everything appeared clean and bright in the warm morning air. There were just a few perfectly formed puffs of cloud arranged artistically across the deep blue of the sky. The whole country seemed to be swarming with life as if in celebration of the continuing rainy season.

Madagascar boasts over 450 species of reptiles and amphibians, of which only a handful can be found elsewhere and, despite rampant deforestation, new species are being discovered all the time. Of the island's frogs ninety-nine per cent are endemic and between 1990 and 1995 no less than thirty new species were found!

For the amateur naturalist, however, it's not the variety but the sheer abundance that is breathtaking. Everywhere you look chameleons stick up from prominent branches like big green thumbs. Contrary to what I had been led to believe, they seemed to be absolutely hopeless at disguising themselves. Twenty minutes into the walk I had, with the help of Mlle Josephine's practised eye, clocked up a dozen chameleons and too many brightly coloured day geckos to count. The day geckos have been described as 'the living jewels of Madagascar' and if so, the crown jewel can only be the greater Madagascar day gecko – an emerald dagger (growing to thirty centimetres long) sprinkled with a dozen bright rubies.

Wherever two bushes stood close together, scores of golden orb-web spiders were strung out, swaying gently on their tough webs. These ubiquitous spiders alone (they are seven centimetres across) could qualify Madagascar as an arachnophobe's nightmare. I knew that these were all females because the unfortunate male of the species is only about as big as one of his mate's eyes – a trick that keeps him safely beneath her contempt even as a worthwhile meal.

Every strand of the web is as tough as nylon and in the last century an innovative entrepreneur began a silk farm in Madagascar using these spiders. But the idea never caught on with the fashionable elite of Europe despite the fact that Queen Victoria was presented with a pair of stockings made from the silk of the golden orb-web spider.

I was relieved to see that Mlle Josephine was not an arachnophobe because I had already noticed that she had a powerful aversion to chameleons. On one occasion I had seen an extremely large specimen walking along the wall near Chez Josephine and, after photographing its unhurried passage, I mentioned it to Mlle Josephine.

'Oh, *mon Dieu!*' she gasped, visibly upset, 'But, tell me Monsieur Mark, was it coming towards us or walking away?'

In response to my honest – but perhaps thoughtless – reply that it did indeed appear to be Chez Josephine-bound, she became even more agitated. As she hurried away she crossed herself.

When I was setting up my camera to get a shot of the spiders peppered across the sky, I narrowly missed putting my tripod down on an extremely lazy snake, with the dry, dusty look of one about to shed its skin. In that single four-kilometre stroll to the Sacred Lake I saw more snakes than I've seen during whole months in other tropical countries. My pleasure at seeing these creatures was further enhanced by the knowledge that, inexplicably, there are no venomous land-snakes in Madagascar. My favourite (perhaps by association of ideas) was a metre-long reptile that was blessed with richly coloured and tasty-looking chocolate and caramel stripes.

Mlle Josephine's response to them was, by western standards, rather more predictable: a half-strangled scream was closely followed by her crashing into the undergrowth with her skirt clutched around a pair of shapely, coffee-coloured thighs. Her explanation for this fear was more typical of her Malagasy outlook. 'Many people here,' she said (pointedly not including her good Catholic self), 'think that snakes are the ghosts of dead people'.

Out of respect for this belief (and because I was still wary of becoming the unfortunate discoverer of Madagascar's first venomous snake), I contented myself with photographing these brazen sunbathers from a safe distance.

The boa, known here as *dona* (pronounced 'doon'), is the largest of the island's snakes. Its closest known relative is in South America (another mystery) and it occupies a special place in Malagasy belief as an envoy from the spirit world. If a dona is found in a rural village the whole community must turn out to greet it. It may be that somebody in the welcoming committee will notice that this particular dona has a walleye, a wart by its left ear, a hair-lip, or perhaps it is strangely wrinkled around the back half.

'My goodness!' he might then joyfully cry, 'This can be none other than great-aunt Ratanakanjolova come to pay us a visit'.

The dona will then be entertained with a saucer of milk, honey or even rum and the blood of a freshly killed hen. Then the dona's long-lost relatives will make a parting speech along the lines of: 'We are very pleased that you have come to visit us. We hope you are happy with the hospitality we have been able to offer you. Please do not harm us, but give us your blessing and go in peace, oh most beauteous Ratanakanjolova!'

There's actually only one truly dangerous reptile in Madagascar and by now we were nearing the lair of some of the largest and most fearless specimens on the island. Our trail was now walled on the left by the thick curtain of vegetation that grew around the edge of the Sacred Lake and under my landlady's nervous guidance I was treading discreetly. (I was disappointed to note that crocodiles didn't seem to have the effect of making Mlle Josephine pull her skirt up).

'There was a man in the village who used to fish from a boat on the lake,' she said, in a hushed voice. 'One day, as he was pulling his boat out of the water his leg was bitten off by a submerged log. He swore that he would never come anywhere near *Lac Sacré* again, *naturellement*. Finally, even Anivorano was too close and he moved to Diego!'

We walked cautiously out onto a small sandy beach. Through the thinning bushes I could see patches of water but as far as I could make out nothing moved. There was a small compound made from rough-cut branches at the far side of the beach. It was filled with a jumble of zebu skulls, some still mounted on stakes; horns, many half a metre long, probed up out of the sand.

As I peered into this zebu graveyard I had been keeping one wary eye on the lake and now I turned my undivided attention in this direction and, ignoring Mlle Josephine's pleas, edged between the trees for a closer look at the lake. I had attached a telephoto lens to my camera to avoid the need for too close a look and was scanning the shallows with it for 'submerged logs', when I saw the crocodile's eyes. Its Malagasy nickname means 'two little pebbles' and these two little stones sticking up above the surface at the water's edge have often been the only thing that a crocodile's victim remembers. There was a big crocodile about six metres from the bank watching me. I froze and we stared at each other for about five seconds. Then he calmly sank out of sight and I remembered that I was supposed to be taking photos.

Mlle Josephine and I climbed the hill at the back of the lake from where we could get a better and safer view over the foliage. The sunny hillside was like an English meadow, sprinkled with colourful wildflowers, and we had sat there for barely five minutes – scanning the muddy banks of the lake with my pocket telescope – when what seemed to be a brown submarine rose nose-first to the surface. The wide saw-toothed platform of its back showed clearly against the deep blue of the Sacred Lake. Perhaps it was an optical illusion and the lake seen from above was not as big as it appeared but I would estimate that this Nile crocodile – intimidating enough to give me a jolt of adrenaline even at this distance – was no less than four and a half metres long. Within a few minutes this 'master of the lake' was joined on the surface by three other monsters of almost the same terrifying proportions.

The people of Anivorano say that the crocodiles surface when they hear human voices, in anticipation of feeding. This 'feeding' usually takes the form of sacrificed zebu but the crocodiles of the Sacred Lake have had one or two unexpected bonuses in recent years. I remembered the story of a French traveller who made a bet with friends that he could swim across the lake. I couldn't believe that he had taken the time to get a sneak preview from our vantage point: the crocodiles were the only winners in that bet and the Frenchman didn't live to regret it.

In the time that I waited for the teenage dandy's summons to the offices of his délégué father I packed and repacked my bags many times, trying to balance them perfectly. I bought supplies from the market and tried to dry some of Montagne d'Ambre out of my boots.

Now that I was officially a 'cattleman' it seemed that I had risen in the eyes of the village; I got the impression that the ownership of a bull was rated as at least twice as impressive as would be the ownership of twice the bull's worth in cash. As the Malagasy saying goes: 'He who owns zebu, needs not money'.

Only recently has the human population of Madagascar overtaken that of the cattle and amongst most of the country's tribes a man's worth is still measured in head of cattle. There's a particularly poetic Malagasy saying that goes: 'Life is like a unique zebu: if you lose it, it can never be replaced'. Owners have been known to commit suicide after the death or theft of a favourite bull.

Pride of ownership is often the only benefit that owners and villages get from their herds. The slaughter of cattle is regarded as a ceremonial obligation – never to be undertaken simply to ease hunger. Although three hundred zebu may be killed at the burial feast of a headman, during the normal course of a year many subsistence farmers may never even taste beef. It seems devilishly unfair that custom dictates that the burial feast must be marred by continually voiced criticism of the meat – lest it appear that the diners are enjoying themselves too much.

The zebu of Madagascar belong to an Indian strain of oxen. They are known for their strength and hardiness, the fatty hump which can see them through the tough dry-seasons and for the fact that they cannot moo! *Omby*, as they're called in Malagasy, have become such an integral part of rural life that there are more than eighty words to describe them, and an intricate and (to the outsider) hopelessly convoluted system of taboos and rituals has grown up around them.

In the old days, omby were accepted as the tools of destiny, with the power to decide life or death. For instance, a baby that was born on an inauspicious day could be considered a direct threat to the peaceful life of his village. The priests might simply rule that he be placed on an ant heap to be eaten alive so that the evil destiny would pass into the ants or, if it was a 'borderline case', he might be given to the zebu herd to decide his fate. The baby would be placed in the gateway of the village kraal and the herd would be driven over him. If he were not trampled to death it was a sure sign that his evil destiny was neutralised. His rebirth as a useful member of the community would be symbolised by his adoption by new parents, who could not be affected by the old curse.

To many rural Malagasy an all-black bull like Jobi would be considered doubly unlucky: black is universally known as the slave colour and it is also reminiscent of a paddy field after the devastation of a locust plague. Even today, in some areas, Jobi would have been slaughtered at birth and left to rot, uneaten. Christian's cows were also absolutely black so our trek to Nosy Be with three black zebu could be looked upon as the Malagasy equivalent of chasing black cats through a ladder warehouse, wielding an open umbrella.

Every event in Malagasy daily life is governed by taboos: the personal taboos of an individual; family taboos; village taboos; tribal taboos; and many that have become so widespread as to be almost promoted to the status of national taboos. Very few Malagasy would ever risk causing offence by pointing directly at a tomb ('this could make your finger fall off'). At the other end of the spectrum I've heard it said that the rough, fibrous, boiled cassava is 'taboo' for people with sore throats, even if only for a single day. It is impossible to generalise because, even in the realm of well-established tribal taboos, there may be individuals and clans that consider a particular belief to be outdated – and others that may have bestowed it with an even more profound and widespread meaning.

In *Taboo*, Jørgen Ruud described the findings of twenty years of study into this subject in Madagascar, a project that could have broken a lesser man in a quarter of that time. By the end of *Taboo*'s three hundred pages of small type you are filled with admiration for the tenacity of a man who devoted a large part of his life's work to defining the beliefs concerning cattle with white legs; cattle with white hooves; cattle with white humps; cattle with white stripes along their back; cattle with white muzzles; red cattle; white-and-red spotted cattle; cattle of a whitish-brown colour; cattle with a white tail which has a ring-mark …

Later in my travels I visited a Sakalava village where, since time immemorial, it had been absolutely forbidden to move cattle on Tuesdays or Thursdays. Should a cow therefore be lucky enough to find its way into a neighbour's cassava plantation on Monday night would be absolutely free to remain there, feasting unmolested, until Wednesday morning.

When the sheepish farmer finally went to collect his cow he would invariably be bare-chested, since another taboo decreed that it was forbidden to tend the cattle wearing a shirt. A delightful explanation for this taboo was given to me by the headman:

'The zebu know that their owner always comes to collect them without a shirt on. So if bandits come one day to steal them, the cattle will see their shirts – they'll think "oh oh, this can't be right" and run away!'

The Sakalava tribe, whose territory I was to travel through later, is more than usually strict in their observance of zebu taboos. It is forbidden to sell the milk of their cattle, which belongs rightly to the calf, and is therefore not theirs to sell (although they will often, with typical Malagasy generosity, give it away). I once watched a Sakalava cowboy milking, carefully sharing the yield equally between the bucket and the frantic offspring. He would hold the calf back while he pulled off few cupfuls of milk, then he would step back and let the calf barge its way back under its mother for a while.

Christian and I made several unannounced visits to the délégué's office before our passports were finally issued. Our passage through the northern territory was predicted – 'Anivorano – Ambilobe – Beramanja – Antsakoamanodro – Ambanja' – and the passports were prodigiously stamped. I was soon to come to the conclusion that a Malagasy bureaucrat is judged primarily by the amount of rubber stamps (*tampons* in French) that he has hanging from the little tree in the centre of his desk. This was a twelve-tampon délégué.

The last two stamps were added to Jobilahy's passport with particular gusto and we were ready to hit the road. As we stood to shake hands I noticed one prominent word in blood-red block capitals at both the top and bottom of the passport: 'JULIAN.'

I hesitated to ask – might it be the name of the *préfecture* or maybe Malagasy for 'authorised'?

'*Oui, c'est moi, ça,*' the délégué smiled proudly. 'I'm Julian!'

CHAPTER 5

RAWHIDE!

> Once upon a time and a very good time it was there
> was a moocow coming down along the road ...
>
> *A Portrait of the Artist as a Young Man*
> – James Joyce

At dawn on a hazy April Fool's Day – appropriate or not, I'll leave
you to judge – Christian, Landry (his brother-in-law) and I were
on the trail south. Landry had arrived late the previous evening. He
was as short and stocky as Christian was tall and slim and he was
also darker-skinned than his half-German brother-in-law. Landry
was an adventurer. He had decided to come with Christian simply
for the joy of the journey – travel was the second most important
thing in Landry's life:

'Wait 'til we get to Nosy Be, man. You never seen gurrls like
they got in Nosy Be.'

Fiarena, a friend of Christian's from Anivorano, was the last
member of our convoy and he was coming along only for the first
couple of days. Fiarena had been sporadically 'helping' us
through our preparations. I had entrusted him just once to go to
the market with some money to buy a rope and when I bumped
into him two days later he was totally unabashed.

'Oh I ate it,' he said.

'The money or the rope?'

But Fiarena was likeable enough even in his unreliability and
Christian seemed to find hilarity in his every word.

We got off to an inauspicious start. Within fifty metres of
Christian's front gate – from where his lovely wife and kids still

watched – Jobi wrenched the rope out of my hand and shot off into the trees beside the road. He moved surprisingly quickly and when I caught up with him most of my kit was already strewn through the undergrowth. My precious camera equipment, while still half inside the saddlebags, was now strung under Jobi's belly rather than secured on his flanks. As he kicked and bucked to rid himself of the load I imagined my camera being crushed under his pounding hooves.

I managed to grab the rope and calm him by talking soothingly and stroking his muzzle. Within a minute he was his usual docile self and I was able to open my knife and cut the baggage loose. Miraculously my photographic equipment was unharmed and my trusty old metal water-bottle bore only a few more telltale dents. Jobi and I renegotiated our deal and, by the time we stepped back on the road, I was carrying half the baggage myself. This eased my conscience and apparently Jobi had achieved what he wanted – he'd showed me who was boss and established the rules. Now he was content and, apart from a moment's dancing when an occasional truck sped past us trailing a cloud of dust, he plodded along quite happily.

Driving from behind, without the benefit of nose ropes, the others were having trouble keeping the two cows out of the lush roadside grazing. I walked on ahead to give Jobi and me an opportunity to consolidate our partnership. It was a beautiful morning and the countryside was still damp with dew – I could appreciate why the cows were almost frantic to get their tongues around the juicy vegetation.

It was a perfect morning to be on the road and I was full of antic-ipation for what lay ahead. Then – almost as a promise of all the fascinating sights that would fill the two thousand kilometres of my trek from top to bottom of this unique island – I saw something that I'd imagined had probably vanished from all but the remotest cor-ners of modern Madagascar. On a sloping paddock to my right, three men were chasing twenty-five zebu round in circles.

'RRRRR!' I halted Jobi and let him wander into the verge while I shaded my eyes with my hat and watched. As they chased the cattle, a hundred scrabbling hooves chopped up the earth so that the centre of the field was already muddy brown in contrast to its verdant corners. This was ploughing in its most basic form.

I felt incredibly – almost illogically – happy as I clucked Jobi into motion again. The rising sun was throwing its heat onto my face and burning off the dawn mist, and the colours of the countryside were almost shining. I sang 'Rawhide' to myself under my breath as we dawdled along, only breaking the rhythm now and then to murmur reassuringly to Jobi.

If he's really motivated a zebu will maintain a sluggish five kilometres per hour and until you get into time with their footsteps this can be frustratingly slow. By midday I figured that we had done just over twenty kilometres. The blue mountains of the Ankàrana Massif were creeping almost imperceptibly towards us, and dotted here and there across the rolling hillside were villages of stick huts that I can only describe as picturesque.

Rich western travellers (and almost all of us can be considered rich) cruise the undeveloped world in search of the 'picturesque'; and in most cases poverty and hunger lie in its shadow. The inhabitants of these little huts, woven from branches and covered in mud, would gladly have traded instantly for a concrete box with a television aerial. Then I would have had to travel even further off the beaten track, to find huts that threw ramshackle shadows into the dusty playgrounds of naked children in my search for the 'picturesque' … and the impoverished.

Nevertheless, these farmers appeared to be a happy crowd. Everybody we passed on the road greeted us cheerfully – either with the Arabic 'Salàma' or the French-Malagasy 'Salut vazaha' – and then turned to stare until we had entirely disappeared from view. In the villages we became pied pipers, attracting a noisy swarm of kids who laughed and cheered. At first I joked and shouted with these kids until I noticed how nervous Jobi became with the unaccustomed noise. Only once did we have any serious trouble with the animals and on that occasion Jobi came horrifyingly close to demolishing an entire street of market stalls.

In the northern foothills of the Ankàrana Massif was a ramshackle shantytown of miners, built around the spot where some lucky soul had discovered a wealth of sapphires. The town was itself called Saphir and it was growing everyday as new swarms of refugees from difficult pastoral lives all over the island sold their zebu to buy the rudimentary equipment necessary for scouring the red silt of the mountain streams for *vatosoa*, or 'sweet stones'. They built small bamboo or stick huts on the outskirts of the growing *bidonville* and added to the burden on the already overcrowded natural resources of Saphir with its growing dangers of cholera and typhoid.

We had already seen a couple of conspicuously luxurious four-wheel drives on the road. Christian told me that they were owned by Thais – practised in gem trading – whose experience and shrewd business dealing stood them in good stead with the Malagasy '49ers. All along the roadside, as in a Klondike boom-town, stalls had been set up to supply the needs of these refugees and, apart from increasingly rare lucky breaks, it was these traders, and the Thais, who were making a killing. Some sold warm THB and a sickly cream soda called *Bonbon Anglais* to the thirsty prospectors. Others sold brightly coloured plastic buckets in a range of sizes and hand-tools for hopeful hacking into the hillsides. Several more were purveyors of charms and potions that would bring desperately needed luck.

A vazaha, leading a pack-bull dressed in Pakistani rice sacks into this bustling market, was sure to cause quite a stir. We immediately picked up a very large and noisy following and Jobi began to get frightened. He started first to shake his head so that his horns scythed viciously to either side. His eyes were wide, his nostrils flared and his ears twitched at the shouts. I cooed to him quietly and scratched his forehead but he kicked his back legs up at the noisy crowd behind us, who roared with growing delight at this sign that the show was about to get more interesting.

I held the rope tightly and tried to keep Jobi moving forward between the rows of fragile stalls. The more he kicked the more the crowd roared – and when he appeared to calm down for an instant some great wits in the audience roared again to reanimate him. Suddenly I was fighting with all my strength just to keep Jobi within the confines of the street. I wrapped the rope around my hands and dug my heels in to keep him from tearing off through the mob. All the time I tried to make my soothing (now desperate) words cut through the din to reach Jobi's swivelling ears. I managed to glance ahead and saw that Christian and Landry – though making greater headway – were having similar difficulties with the two cows. Fiarena was nowhere to be seen.

Jobi was in absolute panic now and it took every bit of strength I had to hold him. The rope that was habitually wrapped around his horns had come loose and was secured only through the hole that pierced his saliva-flecked nose. Twice he gave up pulling and made a short, treacherous charge at me; and twice I just managed to jump clear of the horns. My fear of being responsible for a crazed bull going berserk in a crowded market-place was greater even than my fear of Jobi's 'pointy bits'. Even in the midst of the fight I drew determination from a picture of what my fate might be, should my terrified travelling companion trample some innocent child into the dust. Even if he only destroyed a couple of stalls, this rabble looked wild enough to lynch me. The mob had almost formed a complete circle around us and I knew that I could expect no help from Christian and Landry, who were busy fighting battles of their own. My strength to resist Jobi's five hundred kilograms of muscle and four pumping legs was quickly waning.

I alternately gave Jobi his head when he made an occasional dash that happened to be directed towards the – still invisible – far end of Saphir main street and then dug my heels in to keep him away from some hastily vacated trader's stall. Then he gave two unexpectedly wild bucks, jerking the rope painfully through my hands and throwing me forward onto my knees. Impotent to do anything I watched the saddlebags tip in teasing slow motion right around so that one swung under his belly.

Irreplaceable pieces of equipment bounced under Jobi's stomping hooves as I looked desperately about for a friendly face. There, in the second row (safer than the front-line of this most unpredictable of bullfights), was Fiarena. He had merged so perfectly into the multitude that nobody but one of his ex-travelling companions could ever have known that he had anything whatsoever to do with this crowd-pleasing vazaha. I suspected that he might have been camouflaging himself even more efficiently with a few carefully subdued bull-baiting shouts!

I fought for a few more stampeding metres of dusty street and then shouted in Fiarena's general direction: *'Aidez-moi! Tout de* bloody *suite!'*

A young man stepped forward instinctively from the front row and I jerked my head furiously at Fiarena: *'Non, mon ami!'*

Sheepishly, Fiarena hustled forward to collect the trail of battered books, clothing, medicine and film canisters, and follow me at a safe distance as I continued to work Jobi towards the last of the huts.

Christian, having tethered the cows under Landry's supervision, jogged up to help me and together we hauled Jobi bodily up the street.

'Ils sont des sauvages,' Christian spat with hatred as he watched me pour cold water over my blistered hands. 'It will be okay after Saphir. They're savages here.'

After reloading Jobi and replacing the broken saddlebag straps, I was glad to move on and let Saphir get back to its usual daily routine. A bush-taxi came rattling towards us, already beeping its horn to clear the road. Two vazaha faces peered out from the midst of the dark beaming faces but I was too exhausted even to take any notice.

Jobi slipped back quickly into his earlier unhurried gait. I walked alongside him now, gently swatting the flies off his shoulders with the end of the rope. To deal with the hot countries in which they live, zebu have evolved an unusual abundance of sweat glands. Sometimes Jobi's shoulders would flicker with a mass of thirsty black flies but luckily only a fraction of them seemed to have any taste for vazaha. After several kilometres we crossed a creek with a wide meadow on the far side. Christian reflected all our thoughts (human and zebu alike): 'We should stop here to eat and rest for half-hour.'

The lime-green meadow sloped slowly into the cool darkness of the trees, which stretched onward towards the almost clichéd mauve of the mountains. Against this beautiful backdrop the four of us sat with our feet in the water and munched on bananas wrapped in bread.

It was now half-past four and we'd been walking slowly, but steadily since 6 am.

'At what hour do we stop to camp, Christian?' I asked

'There's a good village with a room about twenty-five kilometres from here.'

Every kilometre of the road was marked with a small white stone labelled with the distance still to go before Ambilobe, the next town. I was getting weary now but these little monuments to distances passed made it easier to keep going. I could easily inspire myself to walk to the next stone, then the next – and the kilometres clicked over so much quicker than old Brit miles!

Apart from watching up ahead for the next kilometre stone, I passed the hours as we walked in scanning the branches of the low trees alongside the road for chameleons. I still couldn't believe how many reptiles there were. In that climb up onto the Ankàrana Massif even without pausing I could average one chameleon every five bushes!

Many fantastic characteristics have been attributed to these extraordinary animals: to see into the future, to change colour to match their surroundings and even to be able to feed only on air. This last ability was recorded by none other than William Shakespeare. It seems that the Bard's sources had never noticed the occasional lightning flash of a pink, sticky tongue (as long as the reptile's body) shooting out to snare unwary insects that came too close. The characteristic colour change is not, as is commonly thought, an attempt at camouflage but rather a sign of mood or hormonal changes, caused by the opening and closing of pigment-containing cells just under the skin. An angry or distressed chameleon typically opens cells containing melanin that makes it much darker and exaggerates its normal markings. As it calms down and relaxes other cells gradually open, containing yellow and blue pigments, resulting in the chameleon's normal green colour. Later I was to find that chameleons are even easier to spot at night with a torch because in sleep they often lose almost all colour and become ghostly white. During the mating season, however, the hormonal explosion can be powerful enough to create gaudy patterns, such as those of the panther chameleon I had seen in Joffreville.

I had only been two hours in the country when I met my first reptilian local in Tana: a Brookesia chameleon, one of the world's smallest at little more than three centimetres long. He was calmly – chameleons are too sluggish ever to appear anything but calm – making his way along a busy pavement behind the old colonial railway station. I wondered if this diminutive visitor had hitched a ride in on one of the banana stands that were being hauled out of the battered boxcars.

The little volcanic cones of a chameleon's eyes are free to swivel independently of one another, so that the animal is able to look ahead with one and behind with the other. Some Malagasy believe that they have the ability to see simultaneously into the future and the past, and that stepping on a Brookesia will make your arms and hands swell up painfully. A Malagasy proverb says that: 'It is better to tread on a divinity than a Brookesia'. Nevertheless, my tiny friend was lucky to have been avoided for so long on this crowded footpath. Perhaps, like me, he was feeling slightly awed by the dust and noise of the capital and I took great care to find him decent lodgings in a comfortable bush.

Cresting the top of the Ankàrana Massif we entered an avenue that led us into a dry deciduous forest, far removed from the dripping, sweaty montane rainforest of Montagne d'Ambre. In *Lemurs of the Lost World*, Jane Wilson described the several months of study in the 'ecological wonderland' that afterwards (largely through the efforts of Miss Wilson's team of scientists and explorers) became the Réserve Spéciale de l'Ankàrana. That Lost World lay now about fifteen kilometres away to our right and the forests therein, protected by the towering needle-like limestone formations (known in Madagascar as *tsingy*), are said to boast the highest density of primates of any forest in the world.

The sun was rapidly sinking now and it was cool under the trees. I took off my wide-brimmed hat and looked for a place to stow it. It occurred to me that Jobi's hump was about the same size as my head and from then on we took turns wearing the hat. Suddenly Landry grabbed my arm and whispered: 'Fosa!'

The animal had clearly just seen us and was standing in the middle of the road looking back at our strange convoy. With a store of fat to prepare it for the coming dry-season this fosa looked like an oversized, long-nosed cat with a thick, bushy tail. Even in the dappled light of the trees I could clearly see the pattern of black spots on its back and realised that this particular 'fosa' was a Malagasy striped civet. These creatures are rarely seen because they are very shy and strictly nocturnal, but after watching us for a moment this individual calmly trotted over the road and disappeared into the trees en route to its habitual hunting grounds.

Strangely, the eight species of carnivore in Madagascar are all from the family of civets, genets and mongooses. There are three subfamilies of wild cats: the puma-like fosa, the Malagasy striped civet (or *fanaloka*) and the *falanouc*. Jane Wilson also reported rumours of a 'fierce cat', half as big again as the fosa, that had been spotted recently in these forests. The civet's Latin name, *Fossa fossana*, adds to the confusion and just as the amateur naturalist begins to think he has sussed it out, he learns that fanaloka may also be written 'fanalouc' and that *fosa* (pronounced 'foosh') is the generic Malagasy name for any animal of this type!

Jobi and the cows now walked steadily onwards in front of us through the deepening shadows. The older of the two cows constantly leant against Jobi's shoulder and alternately crushed my baggage or shoved it up so that it tipped off-balance. I kept smacking the old cow on the rump to move her over while I rearranged the saddlebags. It was frustrating work.

'Leave them together,' said Christian, 'they're friends'.

'I think she's got the hots for Jobi,' Landry said.

'If you can afford the bride price you can buy her from me,' laughed Christian.

'By the time you get to the bottom of Madagascar, maybe you'll have a little baby Jobi!' Fiarena clapped his hands at his own joke.

The sun dropped quickly onto the western hills and I stopped to take photos while the others drove the zebu onwards. The sky was clouding over and reflected the sunlight from above, so that the ball of fire seemed to be bleeding onto the horizon rather than actually sinking. We had been lucky to get through the first day without rain. I prayed that our luck would hold out.

We'd covered just over forty kilometres when we saw a rickety stick shack silhouetted in the faint glow of a fire. It didn't seem to be a lot of headway for fifteen hours on the road.

'*Voilà,*' said the voice of Christian, from out of the darkness. 'There it is – Mahamasina.'

'Is this the village?' I asked.

'This is it. This is where we'll sleep tonight.'

As we stepped clear of the big roadside mango trees, the moon threw just enough light to reveal two more huts, smaller than the first, and a rough-cut two-bar fence enclosing a small grassy compound. Mahamasina means 'Sacred-making' but nobody was able to tell me if this unimpressive collection of shacks had ever lived up to such a promise.

A group of figures, sitting around the fire, shouted greetings as they heard the clop-clop of our zebus' hooves: '*Ny vaovao?*' – what news?

'*Tsy vaovao!*' – no news – we replied, sticking politely to the accepted formula. I couldn't help thinking, after all that had happened since our departure from Anivorano, that this response was unnecessarily non-committal!

An old man came forward, hauling his slipping lamba up over a sinuous shoulder, to help drag two fence bars out of the way so that we could drive our animals through. He turned and shouted something towards the crowd at the fire. I caught only one word: vazaha.

The night was warm but I could already feel the attraction and comfort of the twisting flames. However, the fire was left momentarily unattended as eight or nine people sauntered over to watch me unload Jobi at the back of the smallest shed. I could almost hear his sigh of relief echoing mine as I dropped my backpack onto the ground. Landry led him away to join the cows in the long grass of the paddock.

A young man picked up my backpack up and, after carefully dusting it off, placed it just inside the door of the shed. Then he grabbed my arm and with an unmistakable eating gesture led me to the fire. Here Christian revoked his earlier claim that we had 'no news' by talking long and animatedly about the day's trek. My couple of French interjections met only with uncomprehending smiles, so I contented myself with a grin that was aimed at the cheerfully benign but which probably wavered, in my tiredness, into the realm of the gormlessly bemused.

As we sat ladling white rice into our mouths with our hands and flavouring it conservatively, a speck at a time, with some sort of salted dried fish from a communal plastic bowl, I scanned the faces around me. I still couldn't tell what sort of place this was and whether we were with a family or at some kind of Malagasy country hôtely. The mix of men and women, young and old, all wrapped in long light-coloured lambas, gave me no clue but all smiled happily when they caught my eye.

At Landry's instigation a few warm bottles of THB were produced and, in the absence of enough cups, the bottles were passed around the group. I noticed that none of the women drank. A loosely woven palm-leaf canopy had been built high over the fire, to keep out all but the heaviest rain and yet still allow the smoke to escape. I pulled myself back so that I was resting against a sturdy log and stared up at the stars while I listened to the murmur of voices around me.

Malagasy belongs to the Austronesian language family with its closest linguistic relative being that of a Dayak tribe from southern Borneo. I had taught myself Bahasa Indonesia (a language that was 'invented' to link all the peoples of the Indonesian archipelago) and had no great problems in communicating with the Dayaks of southern Borneo. I reasoned that after 2,000 years there would have been substantial changes but, although I had never heard of anyone who could speak Indonesian trying to communicate in Malagasy, I hoped that I would at least be off to a head-start. Many nouns share their basic sounds with Bahasa and these usually form the foundations for regular verbs and adjectives in a similar way. But, in the fast rattle of the Malagasy tongue, I found it impossible even to pick out where one word ended and another started. I was never able to make any headway with the language.

A dark shadow slipped across the field of stars so fleetingly and silently that, after the first surprise, I wondered if I'd really seen it. But then another followed it. I sat up and turned to see what looked like a huge tail-less bird swoop up into the blackness of the mango trees.

'What was that?' I asked Landry, who was casting lecherous glances at the young woman clearing away the plates.

He reluctantly followed my stare towards the trees, just as one of the shadows fell out of it and slipped away up the dark canyon of the road. 'Oh that ... I don't know how you call it.'

He leaned forward to confer with Christian and I caught one word that I recognised. *Vorona* – pronounced *voroong* – was one of those words that could only have evolved over two millennia years from the Bahasa *burung*, meaning bird. But these weren't birds, I now realised, but Madagascar fruit bats, or flying foxes.

'Good meat,' said Christian. 'Tender and sweet at the end of the mango season.'

The Antàkarana people of this area have been known to smoke

flying foxes out of their vast roosts in the caves of the massif and to batter them down with clubs as they swarm out into the daylight. In the south of the island the bats, with their cute puppyish faces and hideous Dracula-cloaks for wings, are forcibly plucked from the ceiling using vicious burrs fastened to the ends of long wooden wands.

Madagascar flying foxes are amongst the biggest of all bats, weighing a kilogram and with a wingspan of over a metre. Strangely for a mammal that is capable of covering great distances these creatures have never penetrated mainland Africa and, although they exist in slightly differing forms on other Indian Ocean islands, they are yet another mysterious Asian phenomenon. The ghostly forms continued to drop out of the trees and to swoop quickly across the compound as we trailed down to the creek. One of the girls showed us down a track that ran along a dyke to a spot where a wooden bathing platform had been built over the swampy river. She held the lamp while we stripped down to our underwear and took turns to fill the bucket and wash ourselves. I tried not to think of the crocodiles that might be anxious to grab a last morsel, before retreating into the underground rivers of the Massif when these swamps began to dry up.

I was almost asleep on my feet when we got back to the shed. There a set of sleeping-mats had already been laid out. The hut was raised about a metre off the ground on stilts and, apart from these mats, it was furnished only with a clay slab on which a small fire could be built – for long-term residents. I made a space against one wall and was asleep even before the others had lain down.

I was woken – seemingly moments later – by the sound of Christian and Landry rolling up their mats. I rolled over and held my watch under the ray of moonlight that shone through the door. It was 3 am.

'*Salut* vazaha,' said Landry. 'Did you sleep well?'

'We've got a long way to go today,' said Christian. 'We can make some distance before the sun rises.'

Landry went to fetch the zebu. By the time I had bundled my kit together, Jobi was tied to a post by the doorway, patiently waiting for his saddlebags. It suddenly occurred to me that I hadn't yet paid for the lodgings.

'Christian, how does one pay for the food and sleep?'

'I will leave money at the hut of the *patron*.'

'No, no, it is for me to invite for the first night,' I said. Including food, board, beer and 'lodging' for four of us and the zebu, the bill totalled just over US$6!

As we walked out beyond the last of the huts I was brushing my teeth and Fiarena seemed still to be in the process of waking up. He shuffled along the street with his sheet wound around him – like many rural Malagasy Fiarena was in the habit of 'wearing his bed' for the first couple of hours of the day as a sort of surrogate lamba.

Christian was his usual cheerful self.

'We should be able to do about sixty kilometres today,' he said with obvious anticipation and Landry whistled a tune that cut through the stillness of the night. It would be a couple of hours before the sky began to pale, and I too was looking forward to another day on the road. It was still cold enough for a jacket and my hat protected me from the settling dew. In the murky woods the silence was broken only occasionally by the cry of a hunting animal, or its victim. Twice we walked like spectres through sleeping villages where not even a dog was awake to notice the clop of our zebus' hooves. Even the flying foxes had retired to their caves.

My backpack was not uncomfortably heavy but, although I had balanced them as well as possible, the saddlebags were still slipping and I often had to hike one side or the other up. This invariably came as a surprise to poor old Jobi who was momentarily thrown off balance by the sudden shift in his load, but I didn't want him to strain himself by having to lean against any extra weight on one side.

I voiced my worries to Christian: 'Do you think that Jobi is okay with these bags? He stumbles when I take the weight.'

'Don't worry – this is nothing for him,' Christian shrugged confidently.

In the first silvery light of dawn we wandered down off the Ankàrana Massif towards an immense plain that stretched as far southwards as the eye could see. Related rainforest species have recently been found on Montagne d'Ambre and far to the south in the forests of the Tsaratanana Plateau, leading some experts to claim that this entire area was one vast jungle before human arrival in Madagascar. Now only a single bottle-green hummock broke the uniformity of the plain. The rising sun was already sending out a steady heat that was no more than a forewarning of what would hit us on the flat reflective surface of that plain within a couple of hours.

'In Africa a thing is true at first light and a lie by noon,' wrote Hemingway, 'and you have no more respect for it than for the lovely, perfect weed-fringed lake you see across the sun-baked salt plain. You have walked across that plain in the morning and you know that no such lake is there'.

Within an hour and a half we were pointed towards the southeast and an awesome expanse of shimmering plain that sprouted with the tousled heads of palms. This landscape was a far cry from the forests, hills and *tsingy* of Ankàrana or the rolling fields around Anivorano. Dotted across the plains were the regimented peacock tails of traveller's palms and the sight struck us with the power of a brave new world. There is nothing that can put a spring in your step like the gentle whispering of the wind through a thousand traveller's palms.

These trees are so named because it is believed that their two-dimensional plane points east and west (false) and because there is a reservoir of water at their base that has comforted many a thirsty wanderer on plains like these (true, if they were prepared to pick the mosquito larvae and beetles out of their teeth afterwards). Even so, 'traveller's palm' is technically a misnomer because it is actually a type of fruitless banana tree rather than a palm.

Known locally as 'ravinala' – 'the leaf of the forest' – these evocative trees have pipped even the famous baobabs to the position of honour as the national tree. The mighty baobab – fifteen metres tall, and almost that around its swollen paunch – is one of the most impressive and endearing trees in the world. In Malagasy myth it is 'the upside down tree'. They believe that the baobab angered the gods with its vanity.

'I know I'm the tallest tree in Madagascar,' said the baobab, 'but why can't I have beautiful flowers like the jacaranda or sweet fruit like the cherry?'

Malagasy gods don't take no lip from no one: they pulled the baobab up and replanted it, roots upward!

The potbellied baobab tree may be a celebrated African icon, but Madagascar boasts seven species to the mainland's one. Africa is justifiably proud of its fifty species of palm trees; Madagascar has an estimated one hundred and seventy!

By the time we'd been walking for six hours the sun had become a searing fireball and the bottle-green hummock was looming out of the burnt savannah. Fiarena had already given in to the 'hardships' of the pilgrimage and had managed to flag down a passing bush-taxi. He had taken Christian and Landry's bags and we would meet him in Ambilobe later. Occasionally we passed the crumbling huts of mysteriously abandoned hamlets where nothing moved but starving pariah dogs.

I had smothered all uncovered flesh with sun block and was grateful for the protection that my hat gave me. We stopped at every trickling stream to let the zebu drink, and I refilled and sterilised my water-bottles. One big benefit with this dawdling zebu-pace was that I was able, whenever I saw a likely subject, to tuck the end of Jobi's rope into a saddlebag and leave him, probably unaware of my absence, in the care of Christian and Landry, while I went to take photographs.

If I kept up this steady regime I hoped that, even with a few rest days for Jobi, I could cross the high plains of the Tsaratanana Massif into central Madagascar within three weeks. On the other side of those mountains I'd *surely* be walking into the dry season. Then, edging down the western flank of Madagascar's highlands, I hoped that by varying my altitude on the gentle hills of the savannah I could find the most comfortable climate and the richest grazing for Jobi. The trail would take in a fair sample of Madagascar's terrain, although little remains of the deciduous forests that once clothed those hills. Less than twenty per cent of the forest that once covered Madagascar is left today, and most of that is along the island's eastern edge where the hills are too steep to be farmed. The countryside would become steadily drier as I walked through the region of the great baobab trees. By the time we crossed the Tropic of Capricorn, into the southern cactus forests known as the spiny desert, Jobi and I might be thanking our lucky stars that the rainfall had lasted so long.

I was just catching up with the others after photographing a large hawk on the top of a particularly majestic traveller's palm, when we overtook an old man whose walnut-brown face nodded as he stepped aside to our chorus of: *'Azafady'*.

I unhooked my water-bottle from the saddlebags and walked back to the old man.

'Misaotra,' he said – thanks – and then, as he raised the bottle to his lips, he echoed our 'azafady'.

Azafady is perhaps the most useful word in the Malagasy language. It can be used as 'please', 'excuse me' or 'I'm sorry' but literally it translates as 'if it is not taboo' and reflects the power of *fady*, taboo, in Malagasy culture. We had used it to excuse our breaking of an old taboo that forbade the impertinence of young people overtaking an elder on the road. The old man's own 'azafady' was ensuring that it was not taboo for him to drink directly from my bottle.

In the late morning we passed the first of Ambilobe's vast sugarcane plantations where regimented stands of two-and-a-half-metre canes whispered together in what little breeze there was. Sugarcane is Ambilobe's main industry and, besides being the biggest market and the regular refuelling stop between the northern 'metropolises' of Diego and Ambanja, there is little else to recommend the dusty town.

We began to see more and more people, many with huge bunches of sugarcane on their heads and by the time we shuffled past the first hôtely, on the furthest outskirts of Ambilobe, the thought of an ice-cold Coke was almost a torment. But Christian pulled rank and, though Landry and I found renewed energy in daydreams of wilful mutiny, we accepted his decision to keep walking past the sun-bleached tin signs on the crumbling concrete walls that read 'THB' and 'Fanta'.

I was happy to see that Jobi was still going strong and, shoulder-to-shoulder with the matriarchal cow, he seemed now to have settled into his stride. He had, however, learned to recognise the occasional bamboo platforms in the villages on which fruit was sold and he now knew that, when I stopped to buy some, a couple of the bananas and at least the stones of the delicious mangoes would be invested as zebu fuel. He would chew these stones blissfully until, every last strand of sweet flesh shredded off by his rough tongue, he would spit out a naked wooden pip ten minutes later. I thought that with a constant enough supply of mango stones Jobi would happily walk all the way to Cap Sainte Marie.

Christian had made this journey many times, although never on foot, and he had remembered exactly the position of the first refrigerator for sixty kilometres. At an unusually well-built and furnished hôtely I ordered three big bottles of Coke. They were so cold that the ice that had formed inside them clunked as we filled our glasses.

I wandered outside to sit on the veranda at the back of the bar. A group of old men were sat in a circle around a *bao* board, moving handfuls of pebbles in rapid and complicated jumps through a series of cups carved out of a hardwood platform. Bao was a game that brought back vague memories of my childhood in Nigeria; I had once been taught to play it amongst the concrete shacks that backed onto our house – technically forbidden territory to an expatriate of seven years old. But that was a long, long time ago and there are said to be as many versions of bao around the Indian Ocean and African mainland as there are languages. I couldn't recall a thing about my Nigerian bao sessions beyond the typical childhood memory of a large jar of boiled sweets that our cook kept in his hut.

We waved across the road to a police roadblock and two sweaty-looking *pôlisy* waved back; they were busy arguing with the driver of an overloaded bush-taxi and didn't bother to check our papers. There was money to be made from the driver. With Saphir still fresh in my mind I was a bit worried about having to walk Jobi through a town as big as Ambilobe. But Christian led us down a near-deserted back street that ran parallel with the main road and we slipped through with a minimum of noise and excitement to a small meadow on the far side of town.

This meadow formed one edge of a roundabout in Ambilobe's southern district. There were no trees to use as hitching posts so I pulled a thick bunch of grass together and knotted Jobi's rope around it. I had learnt to get the saddlebags on and off as smoothly and quickly as possible, so that Jobi was soon happily munching away on succulent grass side by side with the two cows.

Fiarena was nowhere to be seen.

'I'll keep an eye on the animals,' volunteered Landry. 'You two go and eat.'

We wandered down into the market, past the usual collection of stalls, selling towels from India, plastic goods from China and lambas in bright colours with Malagasy maxims along one edge – 'Don't worry about girls: if you have zebu, you can have all the girls you want'. A boy in a *Titanic* sweatshirt was blasting his favourite theme tune through a pair of crackling speakers. Madagascar was *Titanic*-crazy. Even here, in Ambilobe, a short search through the market would reveal the same collection of *Titanic* regalia that could be found in every market in the country: T-shirts, handbags, shorts, posters, watches, purses, bracelets and key rings. In Tana I'd even seen 30-litre backpacks emblazoned with a picture of Leonardo and Kate in heart-rending embrace.

We left the marketplace, crossed a street that was strewn with paper and plastic bottles and went into a hôtely. It was so busy that the diners at the long table had to move along to let us perch on the ends of the benches. This was a typical bush-taxi 'service station' and the food would be simple, plentiful and cheap.

Jugs of water and stacks of plastic cups were laid out down the middle of the table. Christian helped himself to water and I ordered a Coke. There would be plenty of rural hostelries where I would be forced (either by necessity or politeness) to take whatever was on hand. After the usual preliminary bout of 'hôtely belly' that had me dancing the Antananarivo quickstep, I hoped that a steady intake of Coke and yoghurt would turn my intestines into a relatively inhospitable environment for all but the toughest of local parasites.

A blackboard listed the menu for the day (and for yesterday and tomorrow). Since the fare in these roadside hôtelys rarely changes, my Malagasy was already up to translating this unimpressive *carte*: *'hen'andrano'* (fish), *'hen'akoho'* (chicken) and *'hen'omby'* (beef). These would invariably form only a small part of a meal that would be in great part boiled rice. The fish was often bony and the chicken was usually stringy but I had found that the zebu beef could be delicious. We both ordered 'hen'omby' and it came with a complimentary dish of young cassava leaves, prepared like spinach. The beef was good and there was just enough sauce to moisten the rice.

Landry was dozing on a heap of bags near the tethered zebu when we got back.

'Fiarena's already been here, man,' he said. 'He asked me to tell you: *"Adieu et bon voyage"*. He's going to stay here with relatives and take a bush-taxi back to Anivorano tomorrow.'

Across the other side of the roundabout was a small clapboard bar with a veranda that would give a clear view of the zebu.

'We're over a third of the way to Nosy Be,' I said to Christian, as Landry trotted away to the hôtely. 'I think we should celebrate a little.'

Although I had the feeling that Christian had already considered the benefits of this vantage point, it was obvious he was glad I had suggested it. We sat on rickety chairs around a low table and watched the citizens pass by, going to and from the market. My saddlebags were piled against the wall of the bar and across the road our zebu grazed. In an ideal world Three Horses would always be drunk chilled enough to give you an ice-cream headache, and by the time we had finished the first two frost-beaded bottles Ambilobe had begun to look faintly like the run-down and beat suburbs of a 'perfect world'.

All was well with the world by the time Landry hurried up to join us. 'I wish we could come along with you, after Nosy Be,' he said as he raised his glass. 'We could travel together all the way to Cap Sainte Marie, man.'

Christian echoed his thoughts: 'I'd come if I didn't have to go back home'.

'I couldn't afford for the three of us to travel all that way. We'll go together to Nosy Be – I have to send some things from the post office – and then I should move on alone.'

Jobi seemed to be holding out well: his hump was still big and firm and his coat was glossy. There were no sores under the sad-dlebags and his hooves showed no sign of damage. I was grateful for Christian and Landry's help, but felt that I'd served my 'appren-ticeship' and was looking forward to going on alone with Jobi.

A crowd of spectators gathered while I was getting Jobi loaded and he began to shake his horns and jab. Heat and a full stomach had made him lazy and slow and I easily managed to keep him at the end of the rope. I hauled on my backpack and our little convoy hit the road again, dodging through the dusty backwater traffic of Ambilobe: a few old French trucks, a dozen Peugeot pick-ups and a motley assortment of motorbikes. Market-bound women with stands of bananas or baskets of *baguettes* on their heads stopped to stare as we passed by – and then quickly disguised their surprise with beaming smiles.

Barefoot school children in starched blue-and-white uniforms greeted me as they skipped home from their classes. There was nothing precocious in their shouts, just a friendly: *'Salut* vazaha'. They brightened my day even more as the sun blazed in the perfect blue of an African sky.

An old man in a white lamba and a battered Homburg stopped to lean two-handed on his knobbly walking cane. *'Bon voyage monsieur,'* he nodded in proud, careful French, showing the children that he too was educated.

Within a few minutes we were on the northern bank of the mighty Mahavavy River, a wide rusty torrent that in the rainy-season takes on the appearance of a river of jungle, washing large quantities of vegetation into the Mozambique Channel. The big white concrete bridge looked conspicuously out of place and it was not surprising that the animals showed their suspicion of it. But the only alternative was a tiny wooden ferry, moored to the big trees and dwarfed by this expanse of rushing current. Since my suspicion of this flimsy craft was even greater than Jobi's of the bridge, I managed to bully him across.

From the centre of the bridge I gazed upriver towards the Tsaratanana Massif and Maromokotro, the island's highest mountain, where the Mahavavy was born. It crossed my mind that a psychologist should be able to draw revealing conclusions from the way in which a person is inclined to view a river. I was naturally intrigued by what lay in the remote country where the Mahavavy was young and raging. I wanted to see from whence these floating trees and islands of vegetation had been torn. An equally – or perhaps more – romantic witness might have been inclined to look downriver to where the already ageing Mahavavy would shortly spread out into a massive delta of mangrove swamps, settled here and there by Sakalava fishermen. Or even further, out into the glittering reefs and islands of the Mozambique Channel.

Jobi's hooves pounded hollowly on the tarmac and I guessed that his mind was concentrated neither to the right or left, but simply on the abyss that lay a metre below his hooves. He almost sighed with relief as he hit terra firma on the southern bank of the Mahavavy. It was the still, sultry part of the afternoon and even the birds were stunned into silence by the heat, but a hundred metres further on Christian directed us into a narrow tree-shaded trail. It looked like an English nettle-lined bridle path, as a deep canal swept along its right-hand side. An angler, sitting smoking on the other bank while his float bobbed on the water, reminded me even more of England.

I drove Jobi ahead, keeping him moving by tapping the knotted end of the rope across his rump. If he slowed too much, a hand on his tail was enough to worry him into a momentary trot. I had no room to overtake him and, aware that the cows were right behind me, I used this trick now to get clear. I had seen the cows take vicious, scything swipes at both Christian and Landry, and knew that every year people are killed by supposedly tame zebu. But the cows hurried to keep up with 'the herd' and I held onto Jobi's tail so that he would pull me along, clear of the horns, as we rushed between a bank of thorny bushes and the steep drop to the canal. The mad rush up that trail reminded me less of Old England and more of early Pamplona mornings.

A crowd of naked kids stopped leaping off a stone bridge to squawk: 'Vazaha, vazaha!' Christian pointed to a dusty patch of scrub where the trail widened.

'We'll leave the animals there while we wash.'

Near the road, wherever the slippery bank gave access to the water, men and women were unashamedly stripping off for their afternoon bath. As I walked over the bridge the children began shouting with renewed excitement: *'Salut vazaha, salut vazaha!'* A naked old man who was carrying out his afternoon ablutions nearby rebuked them sternly.

All eyes were on me as I strode along the bank looking for a vacant bathing position. I still hadn't decided whether it would be more appropriate to bath in my underwear or, like everyone else, naked. I came to a spot where a treacherous mud slipway led down to the water and began to take my shirt off. As I unbuttoned my shorts I looked self-consciously along the bank to the bridge and realised that, miraculously, I was being totally ignored. It suddenly dawned on me that this was the first time that I hadn't been watched in public since leaving the regular tourist hangout of Diego. I stripped off and washed in the cool river and even the little kids on the bridge managed to resist the temptation to take a peek to see if I was *fotsy* (white) all over. It was a valuable lesson:

the only way for a vazaha to feel invisible in rural Madagascar is to get naked!

Cool and refreshed we set off again, with Jobi dancing nervously to a high-pitched chorus of: *'Au revoir* vazaha! *Bon voyage* vazaha!*'*

Thanks to Christian's welcome cross-country detour we had cut a wide curve out of the highway. We rejoined it at a long straight section along a dyke above a wide plain of emerald rice paddies. We passed a meadow where a herd of zebu grazed while their calves frolicked happily against a backdrop of smoking trees.

A marching line of tall grass was fluttering gaily with flags of orange flame and behind it a black dusty desert lay in readiness for the rice farmers. The flames were already licking at a stand of trees – some of the few left in this man-made landscape. As we drew level we could see men with lambas pulled up over their faces 'guarding' the fire, but it seemed that we could already hear the leaves boiling and the trunks cracking.

We drove our animals down off the dyke to a small lake, where they could again slake their thirst. Large frogs (there are no toads in Madagascar) plopped off the bank when the three big black beasts waded gratefully belly-deep into the cool water. The sun began to set as we watched the fire. It was hard to tell if the flames were growing out of control or if they were just enhanced by the orange glow that spread across the plain behind them.

I was to see deforestation and burning on a small rural scale throughout all my travels in Madagascar and in even the most uninhabited areas the denuded landscape bore the deep scars of ancient erosion. Yet I was never able to fully comprehend the awful truth of what it really means when seventy-five per cent of the world's fourth largest island is officially classed as 'severely degraded' and an estimated twenty-five per cent is deliberately burnt off every year for rice or to provide a 'green bite' for cattle.

Madagascar even has even introduced to the world its own 'endemic species' of land-degradation. I had first seen the horrible, cancerous sores of *lavaka* from the flight deck of an Air Mad 747 as it began a bumpy descent over the island's north-west coast. They are formed where the denuded earth along the edges of the valleys finally loses the wherewithal to hold itself together and collapses in spreading landslides into the rivers. From the air they looked like a bad joke: like a child's drawings of blooming, storybook trees carved in blood through the green skin of the land.

The Great Red Island becomes poorer every year and crimson rivers continue to haemorrhage ever more of the thinning laterite soil into the sea. Astronauts have reported that Madagascar appears to be bleeding to death. With more than half of the island's inhabitants under fifteen years old, the population will have doubled within a quarter of a century: by then Madagascar may already have bled dry.

But a hungry farmer, whose sole concern is to feed his family *today*, can't afford the luxury of worrying about even such 'distant disaster'. A bitter term has been coined for that hungry farmer and the great dilemma of one of the world's poorest countries: 'conSTARVation.'

The sun had set on another day's travel when we reached the far end of a long village, stretching two kilometres along the roadside and yet never exceeding two huts in depth. The headman's front yard was crowded and noisy with women, children, dogs and ducks. At our appearance there was a yelling of women, a scattering of children, and the headman, podgy torso sagging over the waistband of his pinstripe trousers, came to offer us a solemn welcome.

This was the only concrete dwelling in the village and it was a source of great pride for Monsieur Rabearison who with no further ado ushered us, and our footsore zebu, around to the back door. We waited while M Rabearison dashed back through the house, issuing hushed commands to its female occupants, to re-emerge moments later buttoning a white shirt across his sweat-glistening belly.

The back room was the dining room but a rusting filing cabinet betrayed the fact that it also occasionally masqueraded as an office. Having sat Christian and myself – Landry was seeing to the animals – along one side of the table, M Rabearison removed from the cabinet a pink exercise book, a pen, an ink pad and the prized regalia of his rank – the stamp tree. (M Rabearison was an eight-tampon délégué). For the first time since leaving Anivorano our zebu passports were checked and their details logged in careful script. M Rabearison's tongue protruded with concentration as the information was committed to history on the pale blue grid of graph paper.

He now rose to his feet with great formality: 'Welcome to my village. If you would do me the honour of being my guests for the night, we'll move this table against the wall and my wife will bring in some mattresses.'

M Rabearison's house was perfectly positioned for the village water supply. It occurred to me that, in a two-kilometre-long Malagasy village, it would be possible to be a very long way from the nearest tap. We held the hosepipe for each other while taking turns to wash in our shorts. Then I searched through my pack for the least dirty of my dirty clothes and 'recycled' them – it was a process that would have to be repeated several times before I found a laundry service in Nosy Be.

There was a knock at the dining/reception/guest room door and Madame Rabearison appeared with two heaped plates of rice. A young girl followed her with the third plate and a bowl full of greasy water with boiled chicken legs and three spoons sticking out of it.

'Misaotra!' (Thank you) we chorused as the pair laid the food on the table and left with silent smiles.

Back on the veranda at the front of the building a powwow was taking place between M Rabearison and three other men. M Rabearison sat with his back against the wall and when we arrived, two of the men got up to leave. The remaining one, in his late teens, wearing a grey suit jacket with no shirt, moved over to make space for us. M Rabearison introduced him as his brother Jean.

I sat next to the délégué with my back against the cool breeze-blocks and watched the lightning flash above the treetops. Beyond the oil lamp, crackling with suicide bugs, the night was pitch-black, but in the stroboscopic flashes I saw black-and-white stills of the children playing by an old Renault 5 in the yard. I wondered out loud if we would be walking into those storms.

'It must happen soon,' said Christian. 'We've been very lucky so far.'

'It's moving this way, man,' affirmed Landry. 'We'll get it either tonight or tomorrow.'

M Rabearison stifled a yawn: 'If you like, I can arrange to take you to a bar this evening – in the car?'

Brother Jean shrugged with elaborate casualness and I felt sure that this proposed sortie had already been fully considered and discussed at length. But if that's what they want, I thought, it would give me a chance to repay the headman's hospitality.

'Okay,' said our host, happily dropping all pretence at casual suggestion. 'My chauffeur is on his way here now.'

The 'chauffeur' turned out to be a third brother and was a very different character from the slovenly elder, M Rabearison, or the quiet young Jean. Olli (Olivier) was the biggest Malagasy that I had ever seen: a tough-looking man with jailhouse tattoos (an unusual adornment for a Malagasy) on his forearms and a scar that ran down the left side of his face to trail off just on the edge of his moustache. I wondered what the man who gave him the scar looked like.

Olli shook our hands and, with a commanding *'On y va,'* led us to the Renault. The children scattered squealing to regroup quickly for the thrill of watching the machine actually *move*. Christian, Landry and I sat in the back seat. M Rabearison and Jean shared the front passenger seat while Olli craned his neck, checking for errant kids and dogs in the darkness behind the car.

'We go to Ambilobe,' he said.

He was official chauffeur and unofficial 'bodyguard' for his brother, but I soon got the idea that it was Olli who made the decisions. He was one of the few unpleasant Malagasy that I ever met.

He leered at the bar-girls in Ambilobe's 'Bar Oklahoma', with the look of a man who knew what he wanted and would not be adverse to applying 'political pressures' (or worse) to get it.

The owner of the Oklahoma, a wide-boy in a red satin shirt, came over to welcome us with a tray of beers. But the beers were *petit modèle* Queens and Olli sent him scurrying back to the bar with the accusation that he only served Queens rather than good ol' Three Horses because it was easier to dilute.

Not surprisingly, we didn't see the owner again and Olli leered at the young waitress who returned with a tray of THB (*grand modèle*) so blatantly that even Landry was embarrassed. I paid for the first round and tipped the waitress enough to guarantee that she would at least come back to serve us a second time.

The tip was not lost on Olli.

'You like?' he grinned.

'I like!' I confirmed, holding my sweating glass up to the sick blue neon lights, deliberately misunderstanding him.

We clinked our glasses and Christian, Landry and I sat back with the contented sigh that is a natural effect of the first beer after a long, hot day on the road. But, even as I relaxed back in my creaking bamboo chair and let the neon flashes and wailing Malagasy pop music wash over me, I felt a slight tension from the rest of our party. Olli was watching me. He tried a strained grin and raised his glass in an almost imperceptible salute. I nodded back.

The evening went on and the THB went down. From across the table I felt the easy companionship of my two fellow wayfarers and the sleepy pleasure that comes from knowing that you are with friends who don't need constant conversation as proof of that friendship. It had been a long, hard day on the road and we were happy with the numbing ache in our legs that bore testament to kilometres-past.

Before we finished our bottles Olli had already raised his hand to the waitress and another tray was brought over. There was an uncomfortable moment when the bill was laid on the table. After a pause, only Christian reached into his pocket – so I paid again.

My two friends leaned back in their chairs and Landry drummed his fingers on the table in time to the music. Yet from my right I felt the strain growing slowly with the realisation that the evening was not going to develop into the night of glorious excesses that had been planned. From Olli's stare I could see that he had hopes that the young waitress would turn out to be a part of those excesses and it looked fairly certain that the content of a certain vazaha's wallet was destined to be another 'trophy'.

Jean had said nothing all evening and Olli and M Rabearison now had their heads together in muttered conversation. Even from their body language, I could tell that it was Olli who was the boss. It was clear that anyone who opposed or threatened his brother's power as headman would also have to face up to him. With his jailbird looks and hoodlum attitude Olli could not have lasted long himself as a headman – he was simply too blatant – but with his elder brother as a 'front' he would still be free to reap certain benefits. He would have been what the French describe as a *petit coq du village* … if it weren't for the fact that he looked so unpredictably dangerous.

As I paid for the fourth (and, I decided last) tray – this time loaded with one large bottle of white sugarcane rum and two of Coke, at M Rabearison's request – Olli leaned towards me across his brother.

'I think you don't like me!' he shouted above the wailing music.

M Rabearison looked away, embarrassed or nervous.

'What? … Can't hear!' I shouted back, trying a smile.

'I said, "I think you don't like me!"' Across the table I sensed Landry move his chair back slightly as even he heard this time.

'I don't know you,' I answered.

Olivier rested two huge tattooed forearms on the table and tried to stare me down.

It wasn't out of the question.

Although I had never enjoyed using it, my battered old alarm clock was a sentimentally treasured item of my travelling kit. The battery cover had long ago been lost and the flap over the face had broken off (they were replaced with insulating tape and a Super-Glued denim patch respectively). But this clock had been responsible for early starts on what had – later – developed into happy days in many different parts of the world.

When it woke me at 2 am the next morning, however, it was roundly cursed and rendered smartly unto the floor. Christian had declared a 3 am start, but Jobi's saddlebags were still slipping and I was determined to sort them out once and for all before we hit the road for another day.

I lay in bed thinking about the night before and feeling happy that we would be out of the village before anyone awoke. M Rabearison's disgusted 'chauffeur' had driven us back home about eleven o'clock after stopping on the Mahavavy bridge to have a smoke and watch the river. The rushing current reflected the sheet lightning that was coming in from the sea and Olli's mood seemed to darken with each crash of thunder. On a dark, narrow bridge twenty metres above the muddy river he was not good company. I made up my mind that at the first sign of a threat I would try to hit him as quickly and as hard as I possibly could. But he brought us back to the village and settled for merely trying to crush my hand when he wished us a tense: *'Bon voyage'*.

I was grateful for small mercies.

By the time the others had rolled their mattresses up against the wall I was confident that Jobi's saddlebags were as secure as they were ever going to get. I had also managed to rig up a system, with lengths of parachute chord woven tightly into the nylon straps, that would allow me to load and unload in half the time and so minimise the stress that this procedure caused to Jobi.

It took us another ten minutes, moving at zebu pace, to get out of that immensely long village. It seemed that the animals knew what was expected of them now and the cows no longer tried to break away into the dewy grass. The storm that had been threatening the evening before seemed to have dissolved into occasional patches of angry cloud that blocked the stars. I checked our position on my global positioning system and logged it in a notebook. Although it could only measure distance in a straight line, the results were not pleasing: we had covered only 68 kilometres, in 26 hours of walking, for an average of 2.6 kilometres per hour! Slow even for a zebu. Blame it on the moonlight, if you will, but I also recorded that I was exactly 8,008 kilometres from my girlfriend, and home in Madrid.

Even in those silent hours before dawn we occasionally passed people on the road. The Malagasy are by nature incredibly friendly, gregarious people: a chance meeting between any two Malagasy will invariably become a friendship and a queue of more than three (waiting for anything at all) will become a party.

Yet, occasionally, as if by common consent, neither my friends nor the passing stranger would utter a word of greeting. At first, I pointedly made my own salutes and the passer-by would then respond. But later, out of curiosity, I too kept my silence and not a comment or a glance would pass between the three Malagasy walking within metres of each other on a dark and otherwise deserted country road. It was strangely out of character and I could never predict which meeting would be greeted with a chorus of well-wishes and which with mutual ignoring. There were times in my journey through Madagascar when I would cultivate new questions quicker than I could ever harvest the answers to old ones. The Vazimba mystery, for example, was no closer to being solved. Christian and Landry had only muddied the already murky waters by agreeing with Mlle Josephine's description of the Vazimba as a hairy dwarf with a penchant for burnt rice!

At 6 am, when it had been light for half an hour, we passed through a tiny hamlet. The sounds of arrogant cockerels and grumpy, bickering dogs – mixed with the painful sound of human throat-clearing sessions – told us that all was well on another village dawn.

Plumes of smoke, lavender-coloured in the weak light, rose from behind some of the huts and presently we saw a family reaping the comforts of their breakfast fire. We waved our greetings and drove the animals down the bank towards them. A middle-aged couple and two young girls squatted around the fire, still wrapped in the floral sheets that they had slept in.

Landry and Christian tied the cows in a small patch of road-side grass and I tethered Jobi to a bamboo platform, which would invariably be stacked with local produce – cassava, yams or bananas – by the time the day started in earnest. I pulled the tin of coffee and my large aluminium mug from Jobi's right-hand saddlebag and pulled my hat down over his hump. The watching group by the fire laughed. The father nodded a cheer-ful greeting to let me know that we were welcome and I smiled and bowed slightly to shake hands in the polite two-handed style. We sat down close to the fire and held our hands out – less against the cold than from some ancient feeling of well-being that a camp fire brings. A tin bucket, like an old paint pot, was hung over the fire and bubbles of boiling water peeped out from under the lid.

'Ask him if we can have some water, Christian,' I said. 'And if they would like coffee.'

Within a minute the three of us were taking turns to slurp sweet, black Nescafé from my battered mug and our hosts were raising their own tiny enamel mugs in a happy, toasting gesture.

Suddenly and unexpectedly Christian jumped to his feet. I turned to see him rushing to where Jobi was dismantling the bamboo stand, in his desperation to reach grass that he obviously considered was sweeter than that which was under his nose. Our hosts laughed at the capriciousness of this vazaha bull and I teth-ered Jobi further away while Christian rebuilt the stall.

One of the young daughters was mixing batter in another 'paint pot'. (Where all this paint had been used I couldn't see.) From inside the mud hut her sister produced a small tray, dented with eight shallow cups and raked out a flat bed of embers. Oil and bat-ter was ladled into the cups and the satisfying sound of early morning frying rose to our ears.

The mother took control now and, after a moment, expertly tipped the swelling white balls over so that the crispy golden crust was on top. This was *mofo gasy* (literally Malagasy bread) and although I knew that it was only made from sweetened rice batter my stomach began to rumble in appreciation. The father tested the first mofo gasy that was ready and nodded his approval to his wife before she passed the tray around. They were sweet and soft on the inside and crunchily caramelised on the outside.

I pulled a note from my pocket. With a smile, and pointing to my friends and myself I passed it double-handed to the man whose breakfast we were sharing. Even if the thing that was being passed were physically as small as a banknote a polite Malagasy would always grip his right wrist with his left hand to simulate a two-handed pass. When we started walking again my aluminium water-bottle was full of coffee and we were carrying a bunch of tiny sweet bananas to munch on the road.

By half past eight it was already powerfully hot and the countryside was steaming with the downpour that had broken here the previous night. Golden orb-web spiders, dotted across the spaces between stunted trees, were unmoving in the sultry heat. What is referred to in Spain as 'the sun of justice' blazed down upon us; the pressure seemed to be building to a bursting point and a growing stain in the western sky told us that it was only a matter of time before something blew.

The land here was far more populated than the less accessible country of the Massif. We walked through a chain of villages where children rushed into the flooded compounds in front of their huts to shout at us. Their parents waved from the rice paddies that formed a swampy malarial cordon around each little settlement. We shuffled on steadily all through that day with only two hours break from the midday sun, beside a meadow where the zebu found rich grazing. We scraped back the leaf-litter under the roadside bushes to evict scorpions and centipedes and crawled into the shade to doze.

This was the great orange-growing region of Madagascar and every village that we passed through seemed to be dedicated to the sale of green oranges. The harvest had only recently begun and when the roads into the south reopened, after the rainy season, oranges would be transported for sale all over the island. The fruit was not yet ripe but the crop is so huge and distribution so unreliable that the locals have to pick and sell the bitter green oranges long before the main harvest is ready. We bought some of these dark green fruits from roadside stalls and sucked on them as we walked; Jobi much preferred the bananas and the rarer mangoes.

By mid-afternoon the heat seemed already to have passed bursting point and the angry clouds and bursts of lightning looked unavoidable. Our trail curved now towards the coast and pulling out my map I saw that we must have been about twenty kilometres from the Mozambique Channel. The landscape was becoming more dramatic as we climbed from the plains once again into a chain of low, rolling hills. The road wound alongside steep valleys forested with traveller's palms. This countryside is known as *savoka* in Madagascar: secondary forest where the rainforest has been burnt off but cultivation has either been abandoned or was never attempted. Here it was too steep even for rice terraces.

Around the towns on the central highlands, where the population is denser, I saw valleys so concentrated with terraces that a special digging implement has evolved for the cultivation of strips of land too narrow for even a spade! But here in the rain shadow of Tsaratanana, traveller's palms, with their private reservoirs and fire-resistant seeds, had become the great colonisers of the steep savoka.

Suddenly, and completely unexpectedly, a bicycle came racing around the curve towards us. The cyclist was going hell for leather, pumping his legs hard to drive up the beginning of the hill. Two large silver bundles, hanging from his handlebars, flashed in the sun. Another two bicycles – again standard black 'sit-up-and-begs' burdened with shimmering bundles – came tearing after him. I saw my own amazement reflected in the faces of each of the cyclists as he found himself face to face with a vazaha and a bull.

'Fish,' said Christian, laughing at my surprise. 'They're taking fish to sell inland.'

Twenty bikes later we met an unfortunate who was struggling to fix a puncture in a muddy pond by the side of the road. We gave him the last of our cold coffee and some oranges and he told us his story. Every day he would ride twenty kilometres from his village to the coast to wait for the Sakalava fishing boats. He could get the fish much cheaper if he waited longer but it was crucial to buy two good bunches from the first of the day's catches. He would then string them on the handlebars and pedal off as fast as possible, his success depending on whether he could get back with fresh fish before his competitors arrived.

Today he was out of luck and seriously doubted whether he'd be able to sell the bunches of glittering fish at all. I thanked him for his story and we bought as many fish as we could carry for our evening meal.

By sunset the countryside was steaming like an overworked launderette and ominous clouds had gathered, fusing into a single thundery mass to shut out the sun. As I watched the building storm, two phantom-like silhouettes, backlit through their wings by the last of the dying sun, sailed towards us out of that smoky sky. More followed and within minutes there was a stream of hundreds of flying foxes, flapping steadily on mighty metre-long wingspans. It was one of the most spectacular natural shows that I have ever seen. They swarmed out of the bruising sky of the west, heading in a nightmarish horde towards their night feeding grounds in the mountain forests. Some almost skimmed the traveller's palms and I was struck by their cute, puppyish faces, clashing so bizarrely with the awful bony 'fingers' on the front of their wings and their vampire image. I had never seen such an impressive exodus and I stared upwards until my neck had began to ache *almost* as much as my legs.

Christian had also stopped shuffling his tired legs and broken sandals.

'Good meat,' he said again wistfully.

The rain hit us about an hour after sunset. First the road began to blister with fat raindrops for a few short seconds and then it drove down in an oblique silver wall. In other places the rain was a blessing: gently sprinkling crops and watering livestock. But here it hammered down ferociously and the people's heart sank with it as it flattened the young rice and swelled the rivers, rushing the earth away in Bloody Mary rivers.

There was nothing for us to do but keep moving. I followed Christian and Landry's example, took off my shirt and stuffed it into a plastic bag in the top of my backpack. I pulled my hat tight down on my head and felt the water running through my shorts and boots. It seemed that the whole countryside was flooding. Even the road, with steep banks running off to its sides, was centimetres deep in water; the rain was coming down so fast that there was no time for it to wash off.

Our greatest danger was the few bush-taxis that were still occasionally passing. Their visibility would be almost nil but they would be sure to maintain their usual cruising speed, regardless. Even under good conditions they were usually far below Madagascar's lax safety standards. It is not unknown for the owner of a fleet of bush-taxis to be in possession of only one satisfactory brake system or a single good set of tyres. These precious items will usually be out of circulation, however, because they are temporarily installed on whichever of his vehicles is currently due for its annual safety check!

A set of headlights flared in the waterfall ahead of us as they screamed around the corner and I prayed that their pilot would see us. Jobi was safely on the verge behind me but the cows were walking side by side and encroaching onto the road. Christian and Landry shouted and waved their sticks, trying to drive the cows closer in but the stubborn animals refused to move over. The lights were bearing down on us, as I dropped back behind Jobi and gave the old cow a hard shove in the shoulder. She shoved back as she turned to swing her horns at me, moving even deeper into the road.

Christian shouted, *'Attention!'*

I ducked in behind the cow as the pick-up truck shot past. It must have missed her head by about a foot! I quickly fished my caver's headlamp and the Maglite from my backpack and gave one to Christian so that we could show our position. The rain continued to fall in unbelievable sheets and all we could do was to trudge onwards. We saw the lights of a village sometime around nine o'clock – just as the rain turned off like a tap.

The windows of the guest hut were filled with dark smiling faces and the rain dripped lightly from the palm roof. When Christian finished 'giving the headman our news', I was on my third cup of coffee-coloured rice-water, which is almost the national drink of rural Madagascar, often jokingly referred to as 'whisky Malgache'. After being boiled for a couple of minutes with the burnt rice in the pot it is not only surprisingly tasty but also reassuringly sterile.

'If you need to make water in the night,' said the old headman, perhaps thinking of the amount of whisky Malgache that I'd drunk, 'you should go to the northern edge of the village and never into the wasteland here'. He pointed to the rioting vegetation outside the door where our zebu grazed. 'Here you would be making water towards the south and this is fady in our village.'

Even a Malagasy travelling through the island could never be expected to know all the rules of every village through which he passes and, contrary to the reports of some writers, there is no great danger for the vazaha who unwittingly breaks a fady. However, great care should be taken around tombs in all areas and using them as photographic backdrops can be regarded as a dangerous sport. Having been told, however, that it is taboo to urinate to the south of the village and then to do so would be looked upon as intentionally inviting a curse onto the village. It would be met with, at the very least, by immediate expulsion.

While the headman was talking I had been slapping and scratching at the scores of mosquitoes that had been driven inside by the storm. I was glad to see the fat pink forms of geckos in the corners and along the bamboo rafters of our sleeping quarters, but defence against this swarm of invaders was obviously going to require stronger measures than a few tiny lizards. Breaking out one of the little bottles of mosquito repellent from my pack I slapped it around the back of my knees, tops of my feet and ankles, around my neck and over the backs of my hands. The headman and the crowd in the window and doorway watched this bizarre vazaha ritual with fascination. I finished by dabbing a little bit of the repellent into each ear – to try to keep out that maddening nocturnal whine – and my audience roared with laughter.

I couldn't behave as if mosquito bites were more intolerable to me than they were to my hosts, even if it was true that the resultant malaria would overcome my flimsy resistance to far greater effect, so I passed the bottle, double-handed, to the headman. By the time the giggling congregation left us to our boiled fish and the delicious sleep that followed it, the bottle was empty and the whole hut reeked of that sweet, citric odour. My hips and knees had already moulded themselves into the shape of the bamboo slats under my sleeping-mat and I was in deep and grateful sleep when our passports were returned by the headman's son.

We had been walking for over two hours when an unseasonably hazy sun began to rise into a bleak gunmetal sky. The morning mist lay in thick cold blankets in the gullies and swirled like ghosts across the rice paddies, but as the sun climbed higher the early freshness became sultry and we could smell a hot storm in the air.

Beramanja was just another sleepy roadside town with a couple of bars and a few bamboo stands selling the usual bananas, mangoes and endless piles of green oranges. At a paint-flaking concrete hut I unloaded Jobi and tethered him with the cows in the long grass. A large woman hurried out into the yard, wrapping a lamba around her ample bosom:

'*Salut* vazaha! *Ny vaovao?*'– what news?

'*Tsy vaovao!*' – no news!

She roared with hearty laughter.

Helena was a widow and she owned what was probably the friendliest (and certainly the most sparsely stocked) bar in northern Madagascar. Despite numerous battered tin signs promising refreshments, we were invited to buy THB or *Bonbon Anglais* at another bar around the corner and bring them back to drink in comfort at 'Chez Helena's'. It seemed a strange way to run a business.

We spread a blanket in the compound under the shade of some papaya trees, bearing swelling rugby ball shaped fruits that were tantalisingly close to ripeness – but the gathering storm-clouds soon drove us into an empty storeroom. I was woken once by a strange rhythmic thump that I didn't hear so much as feel through the stilts of the hut and the split bamboo floorboards. It wasn't until I rolled over and looked out through the doorway, wondering what had woken me, that I actually heard the thud and then saw Helena pounding cassava under the sheltering eaves of a neighbouring hut.

It was already raining heavily when she woke us again with an afternoon snack. In Madagascar, cassava is often considered the poor man's rice because it is relied upon as a staple in years when the locust swarms have decimated the paddy fields. It is like stringy, tasteless, boiled potatoes (in the West cassava is used, fittingly, to make glue) but it is palatable enough if liberally sprinkled with sugar. We sat cross-legged on the floor eating sugared cassava and watching the bouncing puddles in the compound as they joined together under the steady bombardment of rain.

Helena sat watching us. Something seemed to be on her mind.

'Where's your tattoo from, vazaha?' she blurted out suddenly.

Neither Christian nor Landry had ever asked me what the tattoo around my left biceps signified. An old fady states that one should not enquire into the fadys of others; this had been the primary reason for my own reticence concerning the customs of the communities we had visited. This custom apparently stems from the fear of evil witchdoctors who, the folktales say, travel the country usurping the powers of the people through knowledge of local fadys.

Helena had quite simply not been unable to contain her curiosity and now my travelling companions also listened carefully as I explained that it was a tattoo from a tribe in Borneo. The circle of dotted tramlines was a tribal motif and the feathers were hornbill tail-feathers from the sacred bird – 'the fady bird,' I said – of the Iban tribe. The headman of an Iban long house had spent one long afternoon performing the operation with three needles dipped in a mixture of sugarcane juice, water and soot from the rice pot.

'You think it protects you, like a charm?' asked Helena with obvious distaste.

'How can I tell? ... So far it seems to have done.'

'Then I'll pray that it continues to do so, vazaha,' she smiled, as we began to prepare for the afternoon's trek.

The road was a creek of rushing water and within minutes my hat was so drenched that the rain filtered through it in another steady stream. The animals plodded onwards, head down into the silvery wall and we trudged after them for five sodden hours, rarely even glancing up from our squelching feet.

Jobi's major morale boost came from the old cow; she walked stoically shoulder to shoulder with him and even Christian mentioned that she seemed to be giving him strength. The young cow was wide-eyed and scatty – a bit of a bimbo, I thought – but, call me romantic, I thought Jobi should have shown a bit more interest in her. I knew that when Jobi and I finally hit the trail on our own he'd miss his bovine travelling companions. I would have to push him hard until he forgot them and resigned himself to the habit of travelling alone with me.

We shared the responsibility for the whole 'herd' now and if I saw one of the cows swerving into the grass I would follow, clucking my tongue, to drive her back onto the road. As I walked beside them, kilometre after kilometre, I had begun to recognise very different characters in these three animals. The old cow's nose had never been pierced (a sure sign that she had not been used as a draught animal herself) but in her old lined face I imagined that I could read the sad story of a lifetime of acquiescence. I was haunted by the part I was playing in leading the cows towards their executioners and Jobilahy towards whatever difficulties lay ahead.

The next few days continued in a similar vein. The sun came up to find us already on the road and within an hour the clothes that had been soaked by the evening's storm would be steaming dry across Jobi's saddlebags. I looked forward to stopping for breakfast in some nameless village amongst yawning curs and drowsy-eyed Malagasy families shuffling around their fires, still wrapped up cosily in their 'beds'.

A bottle of syrupy-sweet black coffee and some *mofo menakely* – the sugared doughnuts, made from deep-fried rice flour, whose name translates as 'little reds' – would provide sustenance for the morning's walk. The countryside was becoming increasingly populated as we neared the coast and one group of rickety roadside shacks after another appeared on the horizon.

I checked Jobi's hooves for cracks and his back for saddle-sores every morning without finding the slightest signs of discomfort. His hump was as big and meaty as ever and I was confident that he wasn't losing weight. I hoped that, if we kept up this travelling pace and I gave Jobi a few days rest every fortnight or so, he might be able to make it all the way down the island with me. I would scarcely be able to afford the loss in time or cash that would be the price of trading him for a fresh pack animal. Also I had grown attached to him and didn't relish the thought of trying to get used to another bull.

Over the last couple of days, however, Jobi had developed an increasingly persistent 'cough.' It was actually not so much a cough as a grunt – he sounded like he was continually clearing his throat. Being a zebu, Jobi was unable to 'moo' and in the grunt, the 'language' of his kind, he was becoming ever more outspoken. I hoped that a short period of 'R & R' on the mainland near Nosy Be would get him back in fine fettle.

In preparation for our impending break from 'the herd', Jobi and I walked ahead of the others as we set off on our penultimate morning. The silence was broken only by the steady clop of Jobi's hooves. Even the birds had not yet begun their dawn chorus when an unexpected sound drifted down to us, from the darkness of a wood on the hill ahead: the deep booming of drums and the eerie mumble of chanted voices from somewhere within the trees.

I waited for Christian and Landry and, as we drew level with the noise, we saw a tiny chapel, not much bigger than a suburban garage, with a light shining out through the open door. Although it was still long before daylight, a congregation was crammed down either side of the aisle and rows of candles reflected from the sacred gold against the far wall. Only then did I realise that it was Easter Sunday. The Christian faithful from kilometres around had congregated in this lonely chapel to worship as dawn rose on the Day of the Resurrection!

We moved on and were in open country when the rising sun began to paint a rosy wash across a landscape in which everything seemed exceptionally bright and clear. Under the shade of some mango trees a tiny hamlet was waking, with occasional flutters of floral lambas as women stoked breakfast fires. Pale blue smoke spiralled into the bottle-green canopy and even the dried palm roofs of the ragged huts looked fresh and new. Spiders' webs were threaded with glittering dewdrop diamonds and roadside flowers opened in the first heat of the day. The countryside seemed to be coming to life around us, freshly washed by the evening's storm and repainted by the peachy sun. This would be my last full day on the road with Christian and Landry and it was a fitting farewell.

As a crowded bush-taxi came around the bend towards us, wallowing dangerously from side to side, an animal burst out from the roadside cover. Then, seeing us on the far side, it tried to cut back across the road. There was a sickening crunch and the pick-up rushed onwards, heedlessly Diego-bound. Christian ran towards the twitching body in the road and picked it up by its long tail. It was a large, well-fed tenrec – like a long-legged hedgehog – and he tied its dripping carcass by the tail onto Jobi's saddlebags.

Though not the largest of Madagascar's tenrecs, this creature weighed close to a kilo. Some tenrecs fatten themselves up to aestivate ('hibernate') through the dry season and Christian explained that, like flying-foxes, they make particularly good eating right at the end of the rains, when their flesh has been sweetened and tenderised by a concentrated diet of mangoes.

Later in my travels, in a village in the eastern rainforests, I saw children playing with three luckless individuals from what is perhaps the most remarkable tenrec species. Streaked tenrecs are just slightly bigger than a common mouse but they are covered in prickly black fur and long yellow spines. A specially adapted set of dorsal spines vibrate together to make a threatening rattle that deters attackers or a supersonic whine that serves as a locating call.

The village children had tied strings around the hind legs of these three little animals and were playing with them as western children might play with a wind-up toy. The streaked tenrecs would try to escape and the kids would let them reach the ends of the strings before hauling them back, always wary of the detachable spines on their heads with which their victims would try to butt them. I knew that sooner or later the kids would tire of these toys or a village dog would make a snatch at them and I yearned to buy them and let them go in the forest. But I was close to Madagascar's well-touristed Périnet Reserve and I couldn't risk teaching the children how to make such a living from the local wildlife.

I had to turn my back and abandon the streaked tenrecs to their fate. As I walked away I tried to console myself with the thought that there would always be more where they came from. The streaked tenrec has won a place in the *Guinness Book of Records* for reaching sexual maturity in a precocious thirty-five days, and a larger, tail-less species is capable of giving birth to over thirty offspring at a time!

Luckily for them, tenrec are a common fady animal for many people throughout Madagascar. The meat is taboo for pregnant women because it is believed that the baby will not only have dry, prickly skin but the foetus will curl itself up in a ball and provoke a difficult birth. It is also a universal fady animal for warriors because it instinctively rolls itself into a ball instead of fighting. Many believe that this cowardly characteristic can be passed on through the meat.

Most fady are so old that their origins have been forgotten and they are now explained only by a shrug and the ubiquitous phrase 'it's always been this way'. However, as the tenrec's blood dripped down Jobi's shoulder, Christian explained the origin of the Betsileo's most famous tribal fady.

'French soldiers trailed a group of Betsileo rebels to a highland cave. But just as they were about to enter they saw a *tandraka* – a tenrec – trot out into the sunlight. They were sure that an animal that was so good to eat could not possibly wander out of a cave in which a whole group of Betsileo was hiding, so they moved on to search elsewhere. The animal had saved their lives and to this day any Betsileo would rather die than eat a tandraka.'

There seems still to be no shortage of people who are only too happy to risk the dangers inherent in such deliciously sweet meat. Our own luckless roadkill was destined to be baked that evening in mud, to remove the spines, and shared hunk by tender hunk amongst our hosts. The large cheek muscles are a particular delicacy saved for the elders.

The road crossed a creek and we entered a long straight avenue passing through a forest of palms and wild orchards, heavy with green oranges. This stretch of road ran for seven kilometres without the slightest kink or hill so that we could see, in uninterrupted perspective, where we would be walking, at monotonous zebu speed, for the next two hours. It was halfway along this stretch that we passed a small, whitewashed marker that said: 'Ambanja – 20 km'.

Jobi's 'cough' seemed to be getting worse. I was anxious now to give him his rest but I was sad to think that we would soon be delivering the cows to the butcher's knife. They still had enough energy to make a dive for the grassy verge occasionally and I would call them with a loud 'clucking' sound. They would usually ignore this and would have to be driven back with a stick. But I would feel like a heartless traitor if by chance my call should happen to bring them obediently back onto the trail that would inevitably lead to slaughter. It went against my carnivorous instincts to feel this way but somehow I had developed an affection for the cows, after all the kilometres we had travelled together. I took refuge in the fact that the feeling was unlikely to be mutual.

'We'll stay tonight in my home-town,' Christian said suddenly. 'I haven't been in Antsakoamanodro for over twenty years but I still have family there.'

'The Queen is in Nosy Be so we can stay at her house,' put in Landry. *'Pa't problème.'*

'So the Queen lives in Nosy Be or in … this village?' I asked, not attempting a name that sounded difficult even for a Malagasy.

When Radama I ruled that Malagasy would first be written in Latin script he also decided, with great diplomacy, that his English advisors from the London Missionary Society would be responsible for consonants and the French for vowels. The undisputed champion for the English language was Welsh missionary David Jones. Raised amongst villages such as Llanfairpwllgwyngyllwllllgogerychwyrindrobllantysiliogogogoch (Consonants – 47, Vowels – 14), one feels that he had an unfair advantage. But the French put up quite a fight (most Malagasy words end in an obsolete vowel) and it is easy to imagine the free-for-all that finally degenerated into the Malagasy dictionary of today.

'Antsakoamanodro,' repeated Christian. 'She is the queen of both Antsakoamanodro *and* Nosy Be.'

During the conquests of the warrior Sakalava and the later period of Merina expansion, many of the minor royalty of less powerful tribes were forced into exile among the islands of the Mozambique Channel. There are people on Nosy Be today who claim descent from Sakalava queens who were themselves driven to a watery refuge by the Merina. So it was possible that the

Queen of Antsakoamanodro was *simultaneously* Queen of Nosy Be's Antàkarana settlers *and* 'Grandmother' to Christian, Landry and the rest of her subjects.

The first thing that I noticed about Antsakoamanodro was an immense mango tree whose thick canopy threw a shadow in a vast circle around the gnarled trunk. The ground was deep with mango stones and a loose picket fence marked the forbidden zone under the tree. Christian explained that it was fady for anybody to enter there and that even the abundant harvest of the sacred tree must never be eaten. A missionary explorer who travelled through western Madagascar in 1875 described such sacred trees: 'under which a hundred oxen are accustomed to shelter and not a horn of them feels the sun'.

'We'll go now to give the news to my uncle, who's also the headman, and check that we can sleep in the Queen's house,' said Christian.

I had seen the capital's impressive Rova Palace, once home to Ranavalona the Cruel, the roof of which – before arsonists destroyed it in 1995 – had been supported by a 39-metre rosewood tree trunk, apparently transported from the eastern rainforests by 10,000 slaves. But not for a moment did I expect anything more from the Queen of Antsakoamanodro's house than the unremarkable, if slightly larger than average, stick shack in which the three of us were within minutes billeted.

An old man, who lived alone in the next hut, was reputed to have once been Antsakoamanodro's most celebrated hunter. He owned a young black lemur that was so confident in the presence of humans that it immediately leapt onto my shoulder when I offered it a chunk of banana. This female was reddish-brown with white ear tufts and, apart from her name and her hands and face, there was nothing black about her whatsoever. It is not unusual that the sexes appear entirely different: the male black lemur has a glossy jet black coat and shares with the female only a pair of brilliant amber pennies for eyes.

When I first arrived in the capital I had visited Tsimbazaza zoo, an institution that received considerable support from Gerald

Durrell's Wildlife Preservation Trust. I don't know if somebody had been shuffling cages (or occupants) but my notes on lemur identification read like this: 'red-bellied lemurs have white bellies'; 'blue-eyed black lemurs are brown'; 'white-fronted brown lemurs are indeed brown – but they're devoid of white fronts'; 'red-fronted brown lemurs are entirely pale chestnut' … and so on.

As with the nomenclature of Malagasy carnivores – fosa, *Fossa fossana*, 'fanalouc' and 'falanouc' – the names of many lemur species seem to have been deliberately thought up to throw the amateur naturalist into utter confusion. Some of the most respected authorities on Madagascar's wildlife have at times voiced their own thoughts on this subject.

Jane Wilson wrote, in *Lemurs of the Lost World*, that sportive lemurs are 'amongst the least energetic of lemurs' and, in fact, described them rather un-sportingly as: 'a pot-bellied, Fozzie Bear of a lemur'. Gerald Durrell himself testified to the fact that the sweetly-named gentle lemur is capable of giving a rather nasty nip.

At Antsakoamanodro's clapboard bar that evening I made another wonderful discovery. Djamandjary rum (natural sugar-cane rum, flavoured with vanilla) is a delightful beverage made on Nosy Be, which should rightly by now have ousted rice-water for the title of 'whisky Malgache'.

The next morning we would arrive in Antsahampano port. I could secure lodgings for Jobilahy with Christian's friends and accompany the others on an excursion to sample the joys of Madagascar's premier holiday resort and 'paradise island'.

We dragged a table and a set of oil-drum stools out into the evening breeze near the fady tree and the barman joined us to drink to the successful completion of our pilgrimage together.

'If you like, I'll go south with you,' said Landry, 'I'll take care of places to stay … I know some gurrls … you just buy food and rum!'

By the time I awoke at three o'clock the next morning, with my head throbbing and the wickerwork sleeping-mat imprinted into my face, I had renewed faith in the health-giving properties of rice-water. With cautiously fluid movements that were devoid of abrupt, head-jerking motions, I loaded Jobi and trudged out of town between two equally repentant Malagasy pilgrims. We covered the last twenty-five kilometres of our trek in total silence.

Soon after we left the darkness of an extensive pine forest to enter a plantation of curiously stunted trees, we were blessed with a cool, clear dawn. The trees were twisted and tortured but they had yellow-green, juicy-looking leaves growing straight out of their gnarled ancient branches. These were the first of the region's ylang-ylang plantations, another Indonesian success story – albeit imported much more recently by the French. The flowers would be harvested by hand to produce essential oils for the perfume manufacturers of the west and as soon as we walked into the plantation I understood why Nosy Be had earned the moniker of the Perfumed Isle.

Christian's friends lived on the road to Antsahampano, in a sturdy compound with four well-built timber shacks on stilts and a small but promising forest of budding papaya trees. At first glance the compound seemed deserted, then a teenage girl, with her hair oiled and bound African-style into tight clumps, came from the back of one of the huts carrying two buckets of water. She saw us standing by the wooden gate and dropping the buckets came running over to greet Christian.

Christian hugged her and they exchanged some words in rapid-fire Malagasy, then he turned to me:

'There's not much time. The boat to Nosy Be leaves in just over an hour. Brigitte will show you where to put your bags and she'll get somebody to look after Jobi. Then you follow us to the port – *tout de suite*.'

'It's only a few more kilometres,' Landry cut in. 'We'll leave our bags for you to bring along, man – so you better catch a bush-taxi.'

'Okay. What should I pay to leave Jobi and my bags here?' I

asked Christian, who was already driving the cows back out of the damp grass.

'Don't worry – we can arrange that when you come back,' said Brigitte in a cultured French that somehow I hadn't expected.

I tied Jobi loosely to a branch that overhung the spot where he was already grazing. He seemed not even to have noticed that the cows were gone and was only irritated by the interruption to his feeding when I divested him of the saddlebags.

'When you come back from the island you can rest here,' said Brigitte, as I shoved our baggage into a truck that was heading for the port.

'*Merci beaucoup*, Brigitte. Please thank your family for me.'

Only as the truck grated into gear and began to rattle towards the port did it strike me as incongruous to suggest that I would need a rest after a few days on a paradise island!

CHAPTER 6

ROUTE NATIONALE: THE ROAD TO HELL(-VILLE)

TOUR COMPANIES exude such cloying terms as 'Tropical Island Paradise' and 'Jewel of the Indian Ocean', in much the same way as a carnivorous plant exudes the stench of rotting flesh, to attract swarms of more than 15,000 tourists a year to Nosy Be. In fact, most of Madagascar's visitors are in Tana only long enough to allow another Air Madagascar jet to waft them onwards to 'The Perfumed Isle'.

Christian, Landry, the two cows and I, made the last stage of our journey to the island in a British World War II landing craft that had been adapted for the (relatively) easy dockside loading of animals and cargo. The crossing took two hours and as we passed the tiny island of Nosy Komba, where a volcano cooled its lushly forested heels in an aquamarine reef, I had to admit it was possible that the tour companies were not being overly effusive after all.

Architecturally, and atmospherically, it's doubtful whether much has changed in Nosy Be's capital since the French left. The concrete promenade of Avenue de la Libération, leading from the port into the town, has perhaps crumbled slightly but its squat iron cannons still stare pugnaciously towards the mainland. Colonial buildings with dangerously sagging balconies overlook a small overgrown park where Avenue de la Libération becomes Cours de Hell.

Though officially called Andoany, Nosy Be's capital is still known universally by its French name. 'Hell-Ville' is (to an English-speaker at least) guaranteed to conjure up a whole kaleidoscope of ghastly images – none of which complements the tour companies' propaganda. It seems incredible (again to an

English-speaker) not only that the name ever stuck, but that there could ever really have been an Admiral de Hell.

Let us go back in time, way back, to a time when ships were made of wood, men were made of iron and Admiral Anne-Chrêtien-Louis de Hell was the governor of La Réunion. When, in 1839, the good admiral received word that a certain damsel was in considerable distress on Nosy Be he was only too anxious to lend assistance. The fair damsel was none other than Queen Tsiomeko of the Sakalava tribe and she had taken tentative refuge on 'Big Island' from the wicked King Radama I of the all-conquering Merina. She now considered herself, quite literally, between the devil and the deep blue sea. Admiral de Hell gallantly sent French forces to protect the goodly Queen ... and two years later the Sakalava ceded both Nosy Be and Nosy Komba to the French crown.

We turned into Hell-Ville's main street, Boulevard de l'Indépendance (why did they re-name it in French?), and walked in the shade between the sun-bleached two-storey town houses. I was pleased to leave the handling of the two cows to Christian and Landry and to become almost anonymous, for the first time since I had frequented the backpacker dives of Diego.

Shops and bars had their doors swung wide open onto the street and their wares spilled out over the pavement. Lambas, carvings, baskets of sea-shells, illegal turtleshell trinkets and carefully chalked blackboards – *musique vivante*, *plats du jour*, *karaoke* – called to scantily clad tourists with pink thighs and red faces. Indian, Arab and Somali traders hawked fake Levis, carpets and cheap jewellery, and at Hell-Ville market Malagasy women haggled for pineapples and mangoes.

Nosy Be has no shortage of tourist accommodation. Airconditioned beach-side bungalows and luxury hotels, complete with casinos and swimming pools, are an integral part of that much-touted 'desert island dream holiday'. But I wanted to stay where Malagasy traders would stay when they came to the Big Island. Also, I would be here only a couple of days (long enough to get replies to some faxes) and would have to stay in town. Also, I was very poor.

The others were going straight to the 'Queen's' village, high in the island's centre. After the sacrifice Christian and Landry would head back home again to Anivorano. We shook hands and uttered those few inane stock phrases that mar every important goodbye.

'Well, take care,' I said. 'It's been good travelling with you.'

'Yeah, and you. Be careful on the road.'

'Be more careful of these Hell-Ville gurrls, man. They eat vazaha for breakfast, lunch *and* dinner!'

I shot one last guilty look at the old cow that had helped Jobi, and the bimbo cow with the big brown eyes, as they were already moving away …

'Hey Christian, write when you get back and give me the news.'

'Of course!'

A year later I received a letter from Anivorano, probably dictated through Christian's eldest son, in which he 'gave me the news' with the only words of English that we ever shared:

Monsieur MARKY

13th Juillet 2000

I was very glad to write this letter for you. I brought this letter since month of ~~No~~ november but I sorry for the answer this letter for you. I made the answer of the letter for your contente and courage.

Marky, please give my souvenir for you.

I stop this letter because I go to the market.

bye!

Michel, christian

Transit Malaky was an ugly block of pale green concrete with iron-barred windows, a typical cold-water flophouse, looking more like the town jail than a hôtely. It was Landry's recommendation.

Pink plastic letters above the door – TRANSIT MALAKY – seemed to advertise the short-term nature of this particular establishment. *Malaky* is a Malagasy word meaning quick, or prompt – as in 'short time'. The letter 'T' hung by one loosening screw;

it wouldn't be around much longer either. Another sign on the flaky green wall inside read '*Chambres à louer*' and prices were chalked underneath for weekly, nightly and hourly rates.

I decided I'd try a single night. A quick exchange of pleasantries and banknotes with a sleepy-eyed 'receptionist' got me a bed and a squeaking ceiling fan. A shuttered window overlooked the swampy shantytown that makes up the suburbs of Hell-Ville.

That evening I ate an expensive and ordinary meal of zebu curry at an Indian restaurant and paused to check out the little cinema that showed an endless run of kung fu films to the shoeshine boys and taxi drivers. The storm that had threatened all afternoon from beyond the mangrove swamps (known locally as Horaka Atsinanana – the Eastern Rice Paddies) broke at dusk and within moments the streets were rushing with water. I took shelter in a palm-roofed bar next to the market and found solace in several glasses of Djamandjary and Coke. I watched the rainwater pouring through the roof and dripping off the electric light brackets, and tried to keep my feet back from the advancing puddles.

A Malagasy wide-boy (with his cap on backwards) asked where I was from, then – without even waiting for an answer – asked me if I wanted to buy grass.

'… Not wan' grass? Okay, you wan' a girl then? … a boy?'

'Look, if I need anything I'll come and find you. Okay?'

'Okay. Okay. You do that, man. Jus' ask for Jean-Claude. Ev'ybody knows me, man – I can fix anything.'

Hell-Ville was sad and lonely. Too many people trying to live up to a Las Vegas hustle-town attitude that they could never realise and that would only, in the end, lose them the happy-go-lucky ways of their own people, just a boat ride away on the mainland. Soon the puddles creeping in from the walls would meet in the middle and the whole place would go up in smoke.

Hell-Ville was a moral time bomb – one big accident waiting to happen.

I breakfasted on *café au lait* and a croissant at a *boulangerie* next to the Catholic Church, while I wrote a fax to my girlfriend. Spring would be in full blossom in the Spanish capital by now and the Parque del Retiro would be filling with holiday-makers moving through the ranks of mimes, puppet shows, fortune-telling gypsies and Ecuadorian musicians. It seemed a world away from this sad and sunny, morning-after terrace, where every other table was occupied by a dishevelled but pretty Malagasy girl and her yawning French client.

I realised that what I needed was the beach. The first few bush-taxis were full and it took a while before one slowed down.

'Run vazaha. Jump!'

The pick-up braked just enough for me to leap onto the running board at the back and grab onto the roof-rack. I rode all the way to the beach like this, with three of us swinging out over the road as we shot past banana and sugarcane plantations, and fields of gnarled ylang-ylang bushes where the perfume hit us like a warm wave.

Twenty minutes later I was walking down a track through the sugarcane to a group of fishermen's huts beneath cyclone-ravaged palms. The huts too had seen better days and were raggedly patched with driftwood. The fishermen answered my greetings only with stares as I walked self-consciously between their upturned dugouts and through the last of the palms. Absent here was the light of friendship that shone in the eyes of their mainland compatriots. But then I was just another vazaha – looking for the 'picturesque'.

The sea was still a long way out down the shallow slope of rippling sand and a large, brightly painted outrigger fishing boat was stranded just above the line of polystyrene and plastic bottles that marked high tide. These boats, known here as *pirogues*, are descendants of the craft that brought the first Indonesian pioneers to Madagascar. They are rarely seen elsewhere in African waters.

A group of children who had been playing on the sand charged over to me. But here the cheerful '*salut* vazaha' calls were replaced by others, learnt from a constant run of tourists.

'*Donne moi bonbons,*' they shouted, tugging my shorts. '*Donne moi un stylo.*' Give me sweets – give me a pen – anything at all.

A little girl – maybe four years old – came towards me, lent courage by her older brothers and sisters.

'*Don don bonbon,*' she said, holding out a chubby hand, and the others laughed happily.

It was all she knew for now, but she would learn. The other children or the rich French tourists would soon teach her more. The wheels had been set in motion. The time bomb was ticking away on another small corner of the island.

The children (and the fact that this bit of sand was obviously the village toilet) drove me onwards towards the western end of the beach, shimmering far off in the heat haze. But halfway there I found another sign of the time bomb. What had once been a sort of freshwater lagoon, with a complementing fringe of vegetation, had become nothing but a sterile bed of clay. The rampant defor-estation that has stripped the island in the name of sugarcane, vanilla, coffee and hardwood, has led to massive silt build-up around estuaries and beaches and finally to the destruction of almost all of Nosy Be's once magnificent coral reefs.

It didn't take me long to get disgusted with Nosy Be. Doubtless the island deserved its oft-repeated reputation as a paradise when Admiral de Hell came to 'rescue' the Sakalava Queen. Probably it was even an Indian Ocean idyll when the first few backpackers arrived looking for beaches on which to wash off the red dust of Malagasy overland travel.

Today, Nosy Be is so busy celebrating its reputation that few seem to notice that the warm, friendly attitude with which Malagasy people meet you on the mainland has been replaced here with children begging for sweets and young girls selling themselves for the price of a bottle of rum. Nosy Be rum might be the best in the world but even so ...

The Ministry of Trade and Commerce hopes very quickly to triple visitor numbers to Madagascar and the trend is that most of them will end up in Nosy Be. In the few days that I waited for faxes to arrive I saw that, thus far, the tourist boom has made very few islanders any richer and even fewer happier. Ten minutes after receiving replies to my faxes I checked out of the Transit Malaky, thinking that my own transit had been rather less fleeting than I would have wished and that the capital's name, if slightly harsh, was not *totally* inappropriate.

As I passed the last of the posturing cannons on Avenue de la Libération I was informed by a lad who earned commission from the skippers that a boat was just about to leave for Ambanja.

'To Ambanja, how much?' I asked a Malagasy passenger as I dropped my pack into the bilgewater. She replied without thinking and was angrily rebuked by the tout, who obviously worked on the theory that a vazaha in a hurry could be very close to laying the week's golden egg.

The bow rode high above the water as we roared out of the bay and fishermen shouted furiously at our baseball-capped pilot as their little outrigger dugouts bucked dangerously in the speedboat's wake. In just forty minutes we were skipping alongside the steep, green walls of the outcrop that shelters Ambanja from the sea.

Ambanja stretches along the last strip of tarmac before the Tsaratanana Massif. In fact the town's notability comes primarily from the fact that it lies on the Route Nationale 6 from Diego and is the provisioning point for all expeditions heading south – and any journey southward from here could, by most definitions, be described as an expedition.

Ambanja is also the 'border town' for Maevatanana region, so I made a bee line for the imposing concrete government building (a veritable monument to *la mission civilisatrice*) to apply for an ongoing passport for Jobi. The bustling *Bureau des Permis*, with wooden filing cabinets, rattling ceiling fans and regulation beige paint-work, looked like it hadn't changed since the French walked out. A young bureaucrat in a pinstripe shirt paused in hammering at an ancient electric typewriter to ask what he could do for me. My hushed announcement that I needed an ongoing passport for my zebu caused great hilarity amongst his administrative comrades when he repeated my request in astounded French.

'*Mais c'est pas possible* – one cannot cross *those* hills with *these* animals.'

'One can walk from Anivorano with these animals.'

'Anivorano … *vous êtes sérieux?*'

I assured him that I was *'très sérieux'* and handed him my expired zebu passport as evidence of the fact.

A burst of wholly unexpected efficiency followed and barely half an hour later I walked out with a new passport (stamped this time in red by 'MOHAMAD'). It listed – perhaps somewhat prematurely - the towns through which I would pass during the next stage of my journey: Maromandia – Antsohihy – Port Bergé – Mampikony – Maevatanana.

It was the evening 'rush hour' at Ambanja market when I jumped into a little Renault 5 taxi that was bound – *'tout de suite'* – for Antsahampano. Two Indian women were sitting in the front passenger seat with small children on each of their laps so I slid into the back in luxurious solitude.

By the time the long-suffering Renault rattled out of the marketplace, with its exhaust pipe grating on the road, it was carrying eleven of us. There were six adults in the back, so tightly packed that an errant buttock bulged out of each window. When forced into such intimate contact with one's travelling companions, it was difficult to maintain that old cold-shouldered London Underground aloofness. The little car rang with laughter and goodwill despite the discomfort, and I was glad to be back on the mainland.

Jobi's eyes didn't exactly light up when he saw me but he did seem quite pleased with the bananas that I brought him from the market. I had come to realise that zebu are only ever driven long distances if they are going to slaughter (in which case, few tears will be shed over their declining health) and I had been worrying about that worsening cough. I noticed as I led him around the compound that his breathing was still slightly laboured but he looked strong enough. Brigitte assured me that her brother Patrick had been looking after him well and had got quite attached to him.

Brigitte's mother, Mme Ana, worked as a midwife in Ambanja General Hospital and her sister Louise worked in the big ylang-ylang distillery down the road. Louise was a pretty refugee from a short-lived marriage with a Frenchman and readily agreed that the best thing to come out of this bitter experience had been her beautiful little girl. With big black eyes and little multicoloured bands in her clumps of fine hair, Tanya became the star of my favourite Malagasy portraits. I wondered if her vazaha father knew what he had left behind in Antsahampano.

I was anxious to hit the road again and had decided to depart at 4 am the next morning, so that I could pass Ambanja while it was still quiet. For now, I was content to sit back peacefully and listen to the clatter of Malagasy voices – and think how wonderful it was to be back in the company of such relaxed and happy people.

By dawn the next morning it was all over. Jobi was sick and weak. He stumbled continuously and twice he almost collapsed. He coughed and grunted his way along the road with a blind, almost fatalistic, obedience that was heartbreaking. Near the outskirts of Ambanja I stopped on a grassy meadow to unload the bags. I couldn't see any sores on Jobi's back or around his belly where the double nylon girths were knotted, but he was clearly in great discomfort. A couple of days of this, never mind the entire mountain crossing, could be enough to kill him. With a sinking stomach I turned back.

I knew without a doubt that I would abandon the trek immediately if I thought that it would lead to the death of my bovine travelling companion, but I had to balance the chances of this against my commitment to the expedition. If I sold Jobi I would perhaps be able to buy a fresh animal, but I would lose a considerable amount of my dwindling funds in the transaction, especially since I would be choosy about whom I sold to. This first, relatively easy part of the trail, had obviously been much tougher than

I'd thought and perhaps the ongoing mountain crossing was asking too much of a zebu. If I could reduce my baggage – get rid of the medical kit, reference books and the heavy photographic equipment – I could carry the pack myself. But without photographs I would have little chance of publishing the articles that I had promised my sponsors.

By the time I arrived back at the waking compound I was feeling heartily sickened with the whole trip. Perhaps I'd been overly optimistic or stupidly naive in the planning, on which I had spent more than a year. The guidebooks had reported confidently that there were horses in northern Madagascar but the only place that I knew for certain that they survived in any quantity was on the highlands south of Tana. If money was no object ... but, as always, money was very definitely 'an object'. With a heavy heart I unloaded Jobi for the last time and put him out to graze. Without the saddlebags he walked comfortably and I prayed that with rest he would soon make a complete recovery.

Patrick promised to help me find a buyer for Jobi and to look out for another likely pack animal but in the next three days I became increasingly jaded with the prospect of press-ganging another animal into a forced march. A butcher in Ambanja offered 300,000 FMg and I politely but resolutely turned down the offer. I warned Patrick: 'No butchers for Jobi'.

I tried to find out what I could about the route to the south and in a dusty hôtely I met a bush-taxi driver who had made the run to the south many times. He was a middle-aged man with a face that showed lines beyond those of his years, and he wore a dusty denim jacket over a plaid shirt.

This modern day Wells Fargo stagecoach driver of the Malagasy wilderness told me how it was. In the dry-season Ambanja is connected with the entire central part of the Great Red Island only by the red dust track that is the lower half of Route Nationale 6. It runs for almost five hundred kilometres in a rutted chain of deep dust bowls and craggy hills. Occasional flat sections crossing the desiccated savannah allow a motorbike or a four-wheel drive to get up to a galloping forty kilometres per hour.

At either end of the rainy season the track becomes an obstacle course of blood-red mud. Cambered sections, taking confidence and care to drive across even in the dry, become treacherous slides that invite vehicles into the depths of swampy gullies. The RN6 becomes a veritable graveyard for trucks: crippled on the sump-cracking boulders that lie like assassins just below the thick red mud. For up to four months of every year, in the middle of the rainy season, Ambanja cannot be reached overland from the south by any means at all.

The RN6 is one of the legendary road trips of Madagascar and at any time of the year it's a gamble at best. There are always desperado truckies or kamikaze bush-taxi drivers who over-play their hands one too many times. Their bogged-down vehicles can remain for months as a monument to their audacity. Two four-wheel drives, travelling in convoy, had just got through from the south, but their drivers told me that it would be impossible to cross on foot for at least another month. A zebu with baggage would be unlikely to make it even as far as Antsohihy, they warned, and it would surely die before reaching the highway near the port of Mahajanga (almost five hundred kilometres away). Some painful soul-searching led me to the inescapable conclusion that I could not let this happen.

I'd had an offer for Jobi for half of what he had cost me but, having taken him from Christian's Anivorano homestead, I was more concerned now about finding him an equally good home where he would be given time to rest. I knew that Mme Ana and her family had formed a genuine fondness for Jobi – based partly on the novelty of his arrival and partly on his own natural charm – and I reduced the price still further and asked Mme Ana if she would buy him. She accepted and I was delighted that Jobi would spend the rest of his days in retirement as a herd zebu – pride of ownership being the only service he would render his new owners

My trek had been cut short but I had after all seen a large strip of northern Madagascar at relatively close quarters. It had been a great experience and as long as Jobi made a full recovery I would have nothing to regret. I wanted to see another part of this vast and diverse island before funds and time ran out. I decided to make my way back to the capital on the first available transport and then try to follow the trail that the Vazimba kings may have taken on their mysterious exile into the west.

The wisdom of my reluctant decision not to tackle Route Nationale 6 with a pack animal was quickly confirmed when I saw how the last potholed strip of tarmac crumbled into a sticky red swamp a few kilometres south of Ambanja.

'Whoooo-Hooo! *Ça commence, la aventure!*' Arno our driver whooped as he hurtled the four-wheel drive Toyota pick-up into (not *onto* but *into*) the RN6. The passengers laughed and whooped back, none of us yet realising what was ahead. Arno's boss rode shotgun, keeping a beady eye on his investment and with him, on the front passenger seat, was a young woman who was going only as far as Antsohihy (about two hundred kilometres/thirteen hours away). Squashed along the back seat were a honeymooning couple from Diego, a Catholic nun heading for a highland mission school and myself, facing the long retreat to the capital. The young honeymooners were going all the way to Toliara on the south-east coast, an overland journey that could – even without breakdowns – take them an entire week of rough travelling. The girl was big and buxom with chipped nail varnish of a different colour on each fingernail. Her husband spent the first part of the journey in blissful reverie, chewing handfuls of narcotic qat leaves.

'Try 'im,' he slurred. 'Best katz in Mag-assar, from Diego.'

But the leaves were dry and bitter and produced sickening quantities of green juice. The nun, a sweet little bird-like lady in a long white habit, offered me an orange to neutralise the taste of the qat.

I couldn't understand the logic of starting such an expedition with only two hours of daylight left but I was soon to see that neither dark nor rain nor fire nor flood would halt Arno in his 'aventure'. Riding in the flatbed of the pick-up were eight lads with their lambas pulled over their heads to keep off the constant drizzle. They were travelling for free, since their help would be needed to get the Toyota out of some of the pits in which it would surely find itself, despite Arno's skilful driving.

Sometimes the road was swamped for long sections, even beyond the reach of the headlamps, and one of the lads would jump down to wade carefully across, probing with a stick to find the firmest footing for the Toyota. Arno watched with the concentration of a snooker player analysing a difficult shot and directed the man in a weaving path until he had built up a picture of what lay under that red lake. Two hours after darkness the rain was slanting steadily in front of the headlights and the blood of the Great Red Island deepened in the ruts of the RN6. Often the trail had sunk so low that the slimy bank was level with the windows and twice we had to get out and scramble across the deep, soup-filled gullies.

My thighs already felt bruised from the strain of gripping onto the seat and my ribs were bashed by the elbows of the back seat passengers. Several times we had literally hit the ceiling, once throwing one of the lads right out of the flatbed. To much hooting and laughter he had come running up, muddy and wet but unhurt, to climb back into his place.

With the possible exception of Arno, who was riding in the un-cramped front seat luxury, and Boss-Chief, who would presumably have to foot the bill, we were grateful for our first puncture on a dark, drizzly ridge just before midnight. The 'economy class' passengers were soaked and shivering miserably but for the lucky ones, cramped in the back seat, it was luxury to be able to stretch our aching bodies. I found it almost inconceivable that there might be no improvement in these travelling conditions for the next three or four days!

Seven hours after leaving Ambanja we were greeted by the noisy canine population of Ampotaka. This row of concrete cells had probably been built as a French outpost for those who were given the thankless task of 'civilising the interior'. Arno and Boss-Chief immediately laid claim to the car seats, leaving the rest of us to bed down on whatever dry patch of Ampotaka's long concrete veranda we could find. It was a cold night and as I wrapped a lamba around me and thumped my backpack into shape as a pillow, I envied the people who were cosy and secure in their concrete cells.

We lay stretched out along the wall, a chain of battered and bruised southbound refugees amongst the curled forms of the village curs. I was grateful for the few minutes of sleep that I managed to win, between airborne onslaughts of whining mosquitoes. In three short hours Arno roused us with, I thought, unnecessary chirpiness and the announcement that it was 4 am and time to hit the road again. I thought that, tired as I was, I should be able to doze in the pick-up but the continuing torment of the RN6 soon proved this to be impossible.

Six nonstop hours of spine-jolting mud-plugging followed. We gripped the front seats to stop ourselves from being thrown into each other and clenched teeth to keep from biting on our tongues. The nun complained about getting splashed through the window, so I offered to change with her. This good turn bought me a blissful seven centimetres of extra shoulder space if I draped one arm outside.

Only three economy class passengers were left in the flatbed now, the others having mysteriously disappeared (or given up) in Ampotaka. Despite Arno's care the Toyota got bogged several times and we were all, with the obvious exception of the nun and the young wife, called upon to push it out. The first time the road had been just a thick, sluggish river and we scrambled around to the back of the vehicle without letting go, like swimmers in a current. One rear wheel had dug itself deep into the mud but the other was barely touching the road. We braced our shoulders against the slippery tailgate and searched for some traction under our feet.

At Arno's command – *'Allez! Pousse! Pousse!'* – we shoved with all our strength. Rusty mud flashed through the air, showering over me, but the other wheel clawed at the edge of the sump and we had to keep the pressure on. After a moment the Toyota spun away from us, side-winding crazily, leaving us windmilling our arms and fighting for balance.

I wiped the mud out of my eyes as the others began to roar with laughter, clutching each other in helpless hilarity. I was covered from head-to-foot in splotches of thick red mud and Mr Katz came dangerously close to choking on his leaves as a squirt of green juice jetted out of his burgeoning grin.

I formulated a new rule for the rest of the journey: four-wheel drives and zebus – don't stand behind either when they've got one foot off the ground.

When we eventually caught up with the pick-up the female passengers failed to see the funny side of the situation and did their best to evict my filthy attire – and myself – entirely from the back seat. I began to seriously doubt the nun's Christian outlook when she suggested to Arno that I ride from now on in the flatbed!

She had done this trip before and knew every trick in the book for maximising her comfort. Every time an unexpected bump caught me unawares and launched me into the air she shamelessly shifted her buttocks over to grab a few extra centimetres of the seat. If I leaned out of the window to look at something she would instantly jam her body up against my back to gain yet another precious centimetre. Then she would steadfastly refuse to relinquish her ill-gotten gains when I tried to pull my head back into the car. If, perhaps an hour later, she inadvertently slid back on one of the steep right-hand cambers I would recover my previous position and she would dig her bony elbows into my ribs, shoot me an angry glare and sigh loudly at my lack of respect.

We didn't pass a single lonely dwelling or another vehicle for six hours until we reached the town of Antsohihy where the girl from the front seat and our three remaining flatbed passengers left us. Antsohihy was really no more than a 'wide-spot' in the road, offering food, repairs and a minimum of comfort to wayfarers. I was surprised to find even this much, since for several months of every year this whole region would be utterly cut off from civilisation in any direction. While Arno got the puncture repaired, we found a hôtely where a limited menu offered only boiled chicken and rice. I spent a leisurely hour wandering around the market, trying to get the kinks out of my legs.

In the mid-afternoon drizzle we pulled up by the carcass of a northward pointing truck. The drivers, camped under the canvas, were awaiting spares from some mysterious and unlikely source. We gave them fresh water, some fruit and rice-cakes that we'd bought in Antsohihy and drove on. I would have imagined that it would be impossible to get a truck even that far up the road but Arno complained that within two or three weeks there would be no shortage of people who were willing to test themselves against the RN6 with all sorts of vehicles. Sometimes they would get bogged and it may take three days to get them out or to clear a bypass around them.

By now I was immensely glad that I'd heeded local warnings and hadn't tried to walk over this sodden trail. I could fully appreciate why neither locals nor foreigners often venture long distances overland in Madagascar, preferring instead to rely on the inexpensive and time-saving internal flights. I was sweaty, muddy and bruised when we roared into the dusty main street of Mampikony at sunset, scattering chickens and dogs before us. The timber buildings were lined with boardwalks where old men smoked wild tobacco and chatted sleepily. I needed a shower desperately and a good sleep even more and the hôtely where we stopped was four star by Malagasy bush standards. The rooms were simple clapboard bungalows in a courtyard behind a 'restaurant' (offering THB and rum as its only forms of nourishment), but they were equipped with both electricity *and* running water. Cockroaches dashed for cover as I propped my pack against the wall, switched on the fan and pulled out my towel and soap. I shaved off several days worth of mud-encrusted stubble and stood, motionless and entranced, under the spluttering pipe that served for a shower.

We waited with baited breath for salvation in the form of the strip of blue metal that connects Mahajanga with the capital. Arno had estimated that – punctures permitting – we would spin out onto the silky comfort of that road around eleven in the morning.

During the first hours of daylight we climbed away from the swampy coastal lands. We had to walk at the steepest, most unpredictable sections but, although the track still battered us mercilessly as it bucked and bounced across the hills, at least it was now less liquid. At one point, black specks were sprinkled thickly over the red dust like droplets of oil sprayed from the cracked sump of a truck. Everyone in the Toyota was spurred instantly into excited discussion. Wondering drowsily where the crippled truck was, I leaned out of the window for a closer look. The road was peppered with thousands upon thousands of little black grasshoppers. This abundance was obviously a source of worry for my companions and when farther up the road we stopped to have a look at a larger swarm, their fears seemed to be well-founded. Even the usually silent Boss-Chief was moved to comment:

'Every year they come – after the rains. But I never saw so many. If they get hungry …' He allowed his sentence to trail off.

I estimated that even on the bare red dust there would have been fifty grasshoppers for every square metre. In the lush grass it was even worse. I grabbed my camera and walked back down the road to snap a couple of photos with the pick-up as a backdrop. These creatures were bigger and more developed than those in the last swarm, at about four centimetres long. They were coppery-brown and in such vast numbers that it was impossible to walk without crunching them underfoot. As I walked they fluttered around my legs in a copper-coloured blizzard.

The cute little solitary grasshopper, which small boys and puppies love to chase, is prone to furious and unpredictable bouts of schizophrenia. It happens occasionally, perhaps as a result of over-crowding, that these charming little bounders become obsessively gregarious. Nobody is certain of exactly how it starts but suddenly, out of the blue, a million and more grasshoppers get together in one spot. Then a bizarre hormonal change begins to pass through the crowd and they start to mutate into a hoodlum horde of literally Biblical proportions. Within a very short time that little garden grasshopper, relative of Pinocchio's dapper companion, has turned into the Mr Hyde of the insect world. An English missionary in this same area wrote in 1883:

> The scourge came on like driven smoke, and the hearts of the people sank with them ... The whole atmosphere was locusts, a veritable devouring element and man's only revenge was to strip off the legs and wings off a handful of the invaders and fry their fat bodies as a relish for his supper.

The Toyota moved on and that afternoon, on the blissful tarmac of the highland road, we rounded a bend and Arno hit the brakes as we skidded into what seemed to be a solid wall of locusts. This was a small swarm by some standards but for a second, as it rolled over us, the countryside was like a television picture with the aerial disconnected. Some of the insects blew in through the half-open windows and Mrs Katz picked one up to show me.

This creature was lighter-coloured than the younger generation of its tribe but he was now almost ten centimetres long from nose to tail. It was astounding to think that just a short while back he was just a sweet little black grasshopper. Mrs Katz was now gesturing impatiently for me to take him for a closer look and, although I did my best to deliberately misunderstand, she finally shamed me into catching hold of the repulsive armoured body. The long legs with their sharp spurs gripped my fingers and bulbous eyes stared defiantly into mine. 'What do you think I've got to worry about,' I imagined he was thinking. 'It doesn't matter what you do to me, I've got several million buddies out there.'

Locust swarms can increase incredibly quickly because they breed several times a year and lay up to a hundred eggs. In recent years the locust population has steadily increased in Madagascar and some sources say that as much as two-thirds of the island is regularly infested. They break branches off trees with the cumulative weight of their bodies and sweep over the rice paddies like a bushfire, leaving them black and bare. With a favourable wind locust can travel huge distances: swarms (often kilometres across) that were formed in India during the monsoon have been seen in Arabia during the autumn and in East Africa during the winter.

After asking Mrs Katz if she wanted the brute back, I wound down the window and let him go. The swarm had already passed on – half-flying, half-flailing in the wind – and I wondered if, out of reach of the bad influence of the gang, he might somehow get back to his peaceful solitary life. The close proximity and the urge for society that triggers the swarms so too brings about their demise. Diseases spread quickly through the horde and soon it comes about again that there is not a single locust in the entire world: only the cute little garden grasshopper ... waiting patiently for the next party.

It had taken us twenty-three hours of driving to cross the 463 kilometres from Ambanja to the highway junction near Mahajanga (at what Arno considered to be a very respectable average of just over twenty kilometres per hour). The soothing ribbon of sun-softened tarmac floated us across the extensive malarial-man-grove lowlands of the Betsiboka River and wafted us swiftly into the highlands. Other than locust swarms, convoys of charet-hauling zebu and hamlets of bricked, balconied two-storey houses, there was little to slow us down on the final seven-hour run into Tana.

Just over a century ago the French expeditionary force, travelling over this same route, had found considerably more to hinder their progress. Almost 15,000 soldiers began the march from Mahajanga and by the time they sighted Tana six months and four hundred kilometres later 'General Tazo' (fever) and 'General Hazo' (jungle) had already distinguished themselves in their defence of Madagascar. Dysentery, heat exhaustion and the dreaded Malagasy Fever had already accounted for almost two-thirds of the invaders. Before Tana fell to France the defending Merina army – making their last stand under the command of Major Graves, former British artillery officer and veteran of the Zulu wars – managed to account only for another fourteen of the weakened survivors.

I didn't yet realise, as I pulled a jacket around my shoulders to protect me from the surprising highland chill, that I was also suffering from the first symptoms of Malagasy Fever. Thankfully it was not the cerebral malaria that killed so many of the invading force – and continues to kill almost two million people a year worldwide – but my second case of the recurring *vivax*. Despite the powerful and controversial Lariam prophylactics that I'd been popping religiously, the cold chills that wracked me during my few days in the capital were symptoms of the first explosion of the malaria parasite into my bloodstream. One morning in Tana I woke to find that the fever had broken in the night and that – even as a huge rat lay dying by my bed – I had been unconsciously drenching the sheets in sweat. I felt immediately stronger and put the fever down to just another one of the mysterious maladies that hit travellers in the tropics. It would be five more months before I went into hospital in Madrid to defeat the malarial tremors that shook me periodically.

Tana is an enchanting sprawl of colourful buildings, teetering at impossible angles across the slopes of twelve hills. Terracotta roofs, crumbling brickwork and rickety wooden shutters seem to be clambering recklessly over one another in an attempt to keep from sliding down the slopes. Pegged onto the facades of these fairytale houses are wooden balconies that throw precarious shadows into narrow cobblestone alleyways. These labyrinthine corridors and stairways are more reminiscent of an ancient, sprawling hotel than any western conception of a city, but to Mr and Mrs Katz they were like a first view of the Champs Elysées.

I was charmed by the honeymooners' excitement when the freshly washed Toyota (Arno was hoping for a night's *'aventure'* in Tana) roared them past the modern office blocks around Place de l'Indépendance. I was sorry to say goodbye to them and the others (even the seat-grabbing nun) after all we'd been through together but I was happy to be back on familiar ground and made resolutely for the backpacker's Mecca of Analakely (Little Forest).

Separated from the more dubious comings and goings of the Hôtel Lambert only by greasy curtains, the basement bunks were the cheapest in Tana and, although not actually advertised to first-time arrivals, they were available to those 'in-the-know' for US$3 a night. My old friend Claude – eminently 'in the know' – was still in residence in the basement and we tripped out down the steep and shadowy Analakely stairways for monstrous zebu steaks at Tina's and numerous THBs at Bar Glacier.

PART II

CHAPTER I

INTO THE LONG VALLEYS

> I left my home at Ambòhibelòma on Friday, June
> 11th, 1875, with sixteen men; eight, bearers of lug-
> gage, and eight to carry the owner thereof. Soon
> after getting fairly on the road, one of the eight with
> the baggage began to show signs of breaking down ...
>
> *From Twilight to Gross Darkness*
> – Reverend William Clayton Pickersgill

In remote areas of Madagascar there are few options left to a wayfarer who wishes to travel through the countryside rather than fly
over it. In the mid-west there's only one. So, at Tsiroanomandidy,
when the potholes of Route Nationale 1 finally crumbled into a
dirt track before fading away altogether into the tall grasses of the
savannah, I made plans to set out on foot.

The bush-taxi had rattled westwards out of Tana through lush
green shelves of rice paddies. Within a couple of hours we were
hauling a cloud of dust through a system of long sweeping rift valleys, through a landscape that I could only describe in my notes as
'Immensely African'. For forty minutes a soaring outcrop hovered
on our horizon, patched here and there with the dark green of trees
and looking exactly like a landlocked Rock of Gibraltar.

Oral traditions of the Merina tell of wars that the kings waged
to evict the Vazimba population from their capital at Analamanga
– 'The Blue Forest' – on the spot where Antananarivo stands
today. The 'white pygmies' then supposedly went into exile in the
west, where as a tribe they mysteriously disappeared. I was setting

out with no further plan than to try to follow the route that they might have taken.

Lying directly west of Tana, in almost a straight line, are the towns of Tsiroanomandidy, Ankavandra, Tsiandro and Antsalova. My maps gave few clues as to what lay between them and my guidebooks were absolutely blank for the entire region from the Central Highlands to the west coast – an area of roughly the same size as El Salvador. This was what the Reverend William Clayton Pickersgill had called in 1875 'the land of the fighting Sakalava', and as the bush-taxi staggered beyond the five-hour mark I could fully appreciate how the island's most fearless tribe had come to be named 'People of the Long Valleys'.

In the spirit of great Victorian explorers, Reverend Pickersgill ventured forth: 'to find entrance for light among the darkened Sakalava'. In the pursuance of said aim he became, as far as is known, the first European to see the land west of Tsiroanoman-didy. Amongst the formal journals of his contemporaries Pickersgill's delightfully tongue-in-cheek writing, published in the *Antananarivo Annual* well over a hundred years ago is like a breath of fresh air.

In addition to being a respected member of the London Missionary Society, Pickersgill was an avid hunter: 'rejoicing in bloodshed,' as he said, and 'cherishing slaughterous intentions res-pecting all wild-cattle, birds, and skulking beasts'. He travelled with a Quaker surveyor, Joseph S. Sewell (Mr S.), who carried strapped to his palanquin 'a small tripod and a trap to catch mountain-tops with'.

I had spent several days in the capital shaking with fever and planning my onward trek but strange as it may seem, I had still not heard of anyone – other than Pickersgill and Mr S. – who had even been as far as Tsiroanomandidy. Yet within ten minutes of dragging my backpack off the pick-up roof I was learning about the forbidden bandit country of the mid-west. I stopped in a chicken-wire grocery store to cut the road dust with a *grand mod-èle* THB, and the barman shocked me with his horror stories of cattle rustling, murder and torched villages in what he called the 'Zone Rouge'.

A political meeting had just taken place in Tsiro, as the town is locally known. The busy streets had a feeling of border town tension, as khaki trucks and jeeps bristling with armaments bleated their horns amid the market-going masses. I followed the direction of the crowds down the red dust street, between two-storey brick buildings and, by simple good luck, found a room in the unmarked Hôtel Iarivo Andrefanana ('Best Western' as it came to be known, although it translated literally as Western Arrival). My room was papered entirely with tarnished sheets from the *Midi Madagasikara* newspaper. The noise of children playing in the yard drifted through two box-windows, made homey with plants and lace curtains.

'So, where do you go from here?' a young lady with unmistakably Chinese eyes asked me, as she poured coffee from a huge aluminium flask in the 'hôtel's hôtely'. Tiana was a teacher at Tsiro's primary school and she was the first English-speaking Malagasy I had met outside of the capital.

'Well, first to Ankavandra and then hopefully further west,' I said, thankful for a chance to take a break from my clumsy French.

'No problem – there's a plane in two days.'

'But I don't want to fly. I want to travel by land.'

'You can't. There're no roads through the Zone Rouge and few villages. People are moving into Tsiro all the time. It's too dangerous to live in unprotected villages in the country.'

The army has established lonely military posts of three to five men in outlying villages and has even on occasion made helicopter raids into the centre of the Zone Rouge. But the bandits, known as the Dahalo, knew the terrain and were forewarned and hidden by villages believed to be under their protection. Their leaders – brigands with names like Ratsibahaka (Bad Lemur) and Menasanga (Red Hair) – were famed for the weapons that they carried. It was rumoured that, in the early 1980s, the South African Government or the CIA (or both) had supplied them with automatic rifles in an attempt to destabilise the socialist government. Some had risen to the status of minor kings primarily because of their ownership of an AK47. Yet the bandits were never revolutionaries or guerrillas: they lived primarily from terror and their own ruthless brand of cattle rustling. Every week hundreds of humpbacked beasts are driven from the vast savannah of the western valleys to Tsiro and the country's biggest cattle-market, the *raison d'être* of the Zone Rouge.

Taking full advantage of a rare chance to practise her English, Tiana agreed to guide me to the dust bowl on the edge of town where gangs of Sakalava cowboys leaned on their spears and watched over about 300 head of cattle. There are few guns in the Zone Rouge but the cowboys who herd their cattle on foot – often pushing 250 head for two weeks – do so with their assegai stabbing-spears always at hand.

'Many of the cowboys who bring their cattle to the market have to fight to get them here,' said Tiana. 'They can sell them here for a good profit but often people are killed on the trail.'

It was impossible to judge how much of what I heard was fired by townspeople's paranoia of unknown communities in the bush and how much by actual fact. I tried to find out just how serious the situation in the Zone Rouge was and at the police station a rather excitable desk sergeant warned me: 'You can't go there! Even the army won't go there! The Dahalo have magic powers *and* AK47s. They are raping and killing and they can torch whole villages in the Bungolava Mountains and nobody will even know for days that it's happened.'

I had the impression that the Tsiroanomandidy boys in blue were not shy about pointing out to a vazaha that they were engaged in a tireless war with all the combined forces of the darkness.

I have always been sceptical about those much-publicised cases of travellers who found themselves in trouble after entering 'no-go areas'. When I was a young 'nomad' – migrating to warmer climes through London's long winter months – I never thought much of dangers. I had suffered the minor degradation of robbery that afflicts every traveller at some time and I'd had a fistfight with a gang of teenage muggers in the doorway of a downtown South American hotel (only afterwards did I think of knives). I refused to let myself consider that there were worse dangers in the world. I had faced what I thought was certain death twice, in a Venezuelan cable car and with malaria in the Borneo jungle. It had only inspired me to see and do all that I could before The Big Man called: 'Time!'

Now I thought differently. My attitudes had changed and my sedentary life, as a freelance journalist in Madrid, was now as appealing in its own ways as that old travelling urge had once been all-consuming. Perhaps it was a sign of age (and impending marriage) but I had begun to think of risks, of what I could be giving up if the Zone Rouge stories turned out to be based on fact. Under normal circumstances, I might have hightailed it back out of the Zone Rouge. But sponsorship – along with delightful benefits in funds and equipment – had brought with it an enhanced sense of commitment. I had failed in my 'packhorse' trek down the island and now having just arrived in the west, I was being told that I could go no further overland. Ignoring an increasingly uneasy gut feeling I stuck around Tsiro, making a nuisance of myself with anyone who could tell me anything about the Zone Rouge.

I loitered in the cattle-market and around the grisly abattoir by the creek. I spoke to the cowboys, the hôtely owners who fed them and the traders who came eastwards in convoys of brightly painted charets, but I was unable to tempt anybody into guiding me across the Zone Rouge. As soon as they'd sold their animals and had money in their pockets the cowboys would be jumping on an Air Mad bush-hopper back to their villages in the far west.

The vet in charge of the abattoir told me about the plague that had stricken the black Malagasy pigs: 'Seventy per cent of the pigs here have died of *Peste Porcine Africaine* (PPA). One family had one hundred pigs – they were left with two! It has been tough to kill those hundreds of sick pigs … Yes, I heard about the horses, but I don't think there's a connection.'

I knew that Tiana's three pigs had died of PPA but, nevertheless, back at the Best Western, pork was still the only thing on the menu. Her husband, Mick, worked in the evenings as a DJ for

Radio Bungolava. Tiana and her mother, whom I was invited to call Maman Suzanne, waited on my table and drank coke, refusing rum, as we listened to Mick's crooning voice (punctuated with Boney M and UB40) drifting out of a well-used radio. Suddenly Maman Suzanne blurted something in rapid-fire Malagasy.

'She says, "Don't go to Bungolava",' Tiana translated. 'It's very dangerous.'

Bungolava (Long Mountain) is the range that lies between Tsiro and the town of Ankavandra, in the vast Manambolo valley. The Bungolava Mountains are the very heartlands of the Zone Rouge.

'If you must go west to Ankavandra, take a bush-taxi south first to Belobaka village, then north *around* the Zone Rouge.'

Looking at Maman Suzanne's troubled old eyes, I changed the subject for the time being and asked about the Vazimba. As usual, the ladies were unable to agree on the exact nature of the 'white pygmies' but the general consensus of opinion was that there are three types of pygmies in Madagascar:

1. Vazimba, who have magical powers and live in the forests of the west.

2. Regular Pygmies, who live in villages in the far south.

3. Kalanoro, a spirit with long hair and long nails – answering to the same description as Vazimba in the north.

Despite their tact, the ladies of the Best Western managed to give the impression that there was one spirit (apart from rum) against which I should be particularly vigilant. Lolo Vakotro apparently takes the form of a beautiful girl who tries to lure susceptible young men back to her boudoir. A lolo, it seems, is the lonely, wandering spirit of one who has died away from home; the ghost cannot rest until it has returned to its tribal homelands and its ancestral tomb.

'There's only one way to tell if a girl is Lolo Vakotro,' advised Tiana, 'you have to make her eat: Lolo Vakotro cannot eat, the food falls onto the floor, under the table. But if you go home with her, when you wake in the morning you will see that she has taken you to sleep on a tomb and you'll be cursed forever – like a lolo yourself!'

I pulled out my charts to investigate the Belobaka route but it cut such a wide circle around the Zone Rouge that it could not relate to the old Vazimba trail I wanted to follow. Nevertheless there was a rumour of a guide who might be able to lead me that way and this raised my hopes slightly. If anybody at all would agree to guide me even that close to the Zone Rouge then they could not be the Apache badlands that rumour held them to be. I decided to wait for a guide price to be mentioned, reasoning that it would to some extent reflect the dangers of the trek. Then word was left at the Best Western that the guide had backed out without even mentioning a price!

I was aware that my situation was potentially getting worse with every day that I waited in Tsiro and with every person I spoke to about my plans. I paused one day to talk to the rickshaw boys, hanging around the market, with their brightly painted *pousse-pousses* – so-called because when hauling a load up a steep hill the boys will sometimes call for assistance from a passer-by: 'Push! Push!' I was surprised to hear that they already knew about my plans and even foresaw the route that I was likely to take.

Even if the Zone Rouge was not as bad as local hysteria made it out to be, it seemed very likely that a well-loaded vazaha, whose movements were being predicted before he even knew about them himself, could be viewed by a resident bandit as the proverbial gift-horse. Then, just as I was beginning to despair of ever finding a guide, Mick introduced me to Eloi Razafimandimby. In his late twenties, Eloi had the coffee-coloured good looks and powerful build of the Betsileo tribe, coupled with a deep love for his island and a determination to see as much of it as possible. The Betsilco are the most widely travelled of Madagascar's eighteen main tribes and, perhaps for this reason, their dialect is the most universally recognised. Eloi, formerly a schoolteacher in an isolated Zone Rouge village, astounded me with his excellent English and showed an immediate interest in my quest for the Vazimba trail.

'It could be dangerous if you were alone,' he shrugged, 'but I know many people in the Zone Rouge. They won't hurt you if you're with me.'

These were the first positive comments that I had heard since I arrived in the west and I latched onto them. I had learned to my cost how fast a local guide can travel if you arrange to pay for an entire trip rather than by the day and – balancing Eloi's muscular frame against the honest look in his eyes –I offered a daily rate. This way I would also be free to spend time anywhere that interested me along our route. Our little two-man convoy would be unlikely to attract the attention that Pickersgill and Mr S.'s earlier caravan did – at one point numbering nearly seventy and looking 'like a guerilla band, bristling with guns and spears'. It wasn't until two days later, on the edge of the Zone Rouge, when Eloi started to strap himself into what he called a 'homemade bulletproof vest', that I began to wish I could have recruited such an army.

CHAPTER 2

KALASHNIKOV RIVER

> Thus there are kingdoms to be won in the wild-
> hearted west, and no lack of men on the Madagascar
> field who are ready to lead the first assault.
>
> *From Twilight to Gross Darkness*
> – Rev. William Clayton Pickersgill

The road shook the battered old pick-up truck like a dog mauling
a rat. It could only have been because the passengers were so
tightly wedged inside that nobody was thrown completely out of
the flatbed. I zipped my jacket up high and pulled my hat down
low as the sun withdrew its blessing from the wide savannah, with
what seemed like ruthless deliberation. Eloi sat opposite me with
his fiancée Poussy leaning against his shoulder. Our plan was to
stay with Poussy's family tonight and set off into 'the wild-
hearted west' the next morning.

Eloi and I had studied maps, made calculations and bought
provisions in Tsiro: rice, coffee, sugar, minute-noodles, tinned
sardines and milk and packets of biscuits, for gifts. I entrusted
Tiana with letters advising my family of our planned route and
destination, telling them not to worry if they heard no more
news within the next six weeks. Maman Suzanne gave me a
watery-eyed hug and tried to prevent me from paying for my
room: 'I'll pray for you *mon fils*,' she sobbed, in a rare attempt
at French.

The track was so rutted that the twenty-kilometre drive
northward to Poussy's village took us over three hours – and that

without a single puncture! Thus it was already dark when we pulled to a grateful halt at Borikely. But this was not just darkness. It was an impenetrable pitch-blackness that could have been the 'Gross Darkness' of Pickersgill's journal. It didn't stop after a kilometre or two but stretched impenetrably across the Bepoaka valley and the mysterious grasslands of Bezavona (Place of Many Mists). In a heavy blanket it spread onwards across the Bungolava range and the granite-and-quartz peak of Vatosira Mountain. A few ineffectual electric lamps, powered by the generator of a solitary missionary, managed to fray the thick fabric only slightly in Ankavandra. Then it swept onwards across the wide rush of the Manambolo River and up onto the Bemaraha Plateau. It rushed, as if with renewed determination, through the forests and rock needles of the Tsingy before finally being torn apart by a veritable plantation of a dozen buzzing streetlights above the marketplace at Antsalova. There was also a grand total of four vehicles whose errant headlights might, by chance, also be rending that blanket of darkness somewhere between Borikely and the other side of the Zone Rouge, but three of them were in Antsalova.

Thus the arrival in Borikely of a double set of headlamps, only one bulb of which was broken, was an occasion of great excitement and a crowd gathered to greet the pick-up. A gang of children screamed and leapt, throwing demonic shadows onto the red mud houses. They cavorted with such demented joy in the twin pathways of silver light that I feared that they might be driven literally insane by the sight of a vazaha in their village. Under cover of their noise and dust I pulled my pack out of the pick-up and followed Eloi and Poussy silently through the blackness to one of the buildings.

At Eloi's hammering a door was opened by a man whose face was carved into deep relief by flickering lamplight: *'Tonga Soa!'* – welcome!

He shook hands, his right wrist wrapped in the long fingers of his left hand, and pulled me into the house as if he had been waiting for my arrival. Although he could not possibly have known that we were coming, he refused to betray any surprise.

The room was furnished only with a rough wooden bed and an old homemade storage box. From the doorway to the other room three women, Poussy's mother and sisters, made us welcome with quick head-ducking smiles. A woven mat served as a dining table and Poussy swept it off with a brush made of dried grass stems, thirty centimetres long. This brush was a clever device that I saw in every village in the west; when the crumbs were brushed into a pile Poussy pulled the brush open and let it flick together so that the litter was picked up by the closing stems. Then it was simply a matter of banging the brush on the wall outside to make it drop the sweepings.

Since none of Poussy's family spoke any French, Eloi was able to prove himself a careful and thorough translator during our meal of boiled rice, flavoured sparingly with little pieces of plain omelette pulled from a communal plate. This was washed down with *café au lait* but, in the inexplicable absence of milk, an egg yolk made for a surprisingly good (though hardly cost-effective) substitute. I decided to leave them a couple of our – devastatingly heavy – tins of Lucky Cow.

'You want to drink rum?' asked Eloi, as he sat back contentedly to pick his teeth.

'Yeah okay, if we can get it.' Rum was actually the last thing I wanted but I had a feeling that Poussy's dad would appreciate it. 'Try to get coke too.'

I handed over a few thousand Malagasy francs. A shapely floral lamba and a pair of honey-coloured calves skipped out into that formidable darkness to return, moments later, with two bottles of coke (*petit modèles*) and one of local firewater (a decidedly *grand modèle*). As Eloi poured the drinks into some enamel cups – the coke went mostly to the ladies, who refrained from tainting it with rum – Poussy's father stepped casually out into the night. He threw his head back and began to shout into the darkness! His voice rang out, calm and clear through the village, like a town crier's 'Midnight and aaaaaall's well!'

Seeing my look of surprise, Eloi explained: 'Two years ago bandits raided this village at night and there was a fight. Two villagers died and several were hurt. Now it's a rule in Borikely that every visitor must be officially announced so that there can be no strangers who haven't been accounted for.'

I realised with a shock that we had already entered bandit country. Out there, in that Gross Darkness, lay the Dahalo. It was a threat that was real enough to have given birth to a brand new fady. It was strange to think that peace may eventually come to the Zone Rouge and in another hundred years a vazaha might stop in Borikely for a night and express his surprise at the announcement fady. The locals would shrug and say:'It's always been this way.'

Next morning bright and early, we moved on. If it hadn't been for the official announcement, most of the inhabitants of Borikely might never have known that I'd been there.

Poussy's father tilted his straw hat to a rakish angle and flapped the reins until the little charet creaked into reluctant motion. His wife sat in the blue-and-white striped box clutching a gigantic golf umbrella, itself segmented into red, yellow, green and blue. All of the womenfolk, crushed into the box, were able to shelter under this impressive awning and Eloi and I propped ourselves on the back. In this manner the two lazy zebu hauled us across a vast rolling grassland that could have formed the back-drop to a scene straight from *The Little House on the Prairie.*

In the 'frontier town' of Fierenana I bought breakfasts of mofo menakely ('little red' doughnuts) and black coffee as Eloi and Poussy whispered their goodbyes. Leaving the dusty market-place we stopped at the square concrete block of a tiny mission school, where a young Malagasy nun ran off to collect some assorted items of Eloi's travelling equipment. For a time Eloi, the son of a successful doctor from the Central Highlands, had con-sidered taking vows as a Catholic preacher. (Who can say that, in the history of the Malagasy church, there haven't been many other stalwart young Elois who have been won away from the cloth by a Poussy?)

My optimism was increasing with everything I learned about Eloi, but he was about to do something that would make it plummet to an all-time low. Eloi Razafimandimby (in whose hands I had placed the future of my expedition and perhaps – who could tell – my life) was carefully strapping himself into a shiny black leather body-pad! Two plates of stiffened leather covered his chest and back and knotted straps held them in place on his shoulders and waist.

'Uuh, Eloi,' I began reluctantly. 'What's this?'

'Bulletproof vest.'

'What! You didn't tell me anything about this.'

'Well, it might not be necessary … prob'ly won't, in fact.'

'You think they might shoot us then?'

'They won't shoot me,' he laughed, thumping his chest with a solid thwack. 'No, don't worry … might not need it at all.'

It didn't look like it would stop a bullet anyway but, like a Malagasy *ody* (a charm or talisman), it would at least give a little confidence, if you were the superstitious type. I brooded on this as we marched out of Fierenana and into the waving grassland that would be our home for the next month: 'You couldn't make me a bulletproof vest, I s'pose?'

The grasses, growing to knee-height after the rains, stretched away from us over what appeared to be an endless chain of low, humpbacked hills. We walked onward through the morning along ridges covered with swaying grass, dropping occasionally into densely wooded valleys. In six hours we did not see a single sign of humanity and this, Eloi said, was a very good sign. The trail led us along a riverside ledge, eaten away with blossoming amphitheatres of lavaka, then dropped down into a densely wooded valley, the name of which Eloi translated as 'Place of Many Snakes'.

I took off my boots on the gravelly riverbank and unclipped my pack so that it was loosely draped over one shoulder and followed Eloi to the other bank with the current wrapping around my thighs.

'This is the Bepoaka River,' he said, without looking back. 'It's called after the sound of an AK47 – Be-Pok!'

He sat down on the cracked mud to lace up his canvas basketball boots: 'Manambolo River will be the big problem. If it's high we'll have to cross with ropes and floats for the packs.'

In the early afternoon we stopped at a tight bend in the Bepoaka where we gathered driftwood to boil some rice, into which we mashed a tin of sardines. I scrubbed out the billy can with sand, collected some water for coffee and sat back in the shade. Eloi was obviously struck, as I was, by the feeling of hypnotic well-being that comes from a campfire and was dreaming happily, slumped against his pack – a rather lurid, but well-travelled piece of kit with the signs of numerous reinforcing operations at the tops of the straps. The billy can lid began to flap gaily in the steam and all was well with the world ... until Eloi said:'They call this stretch of the river Analaturk. It means "Ambush" because it's a good place for attack – you can't see anything, 'til you're already down here.'

'Well,' I said, casting about for a silver lining, 'that also means that nobody will see us until they're already down here.'

'Exactly!'

We were indeed at a secluded section of the valley, where 'Kalashnikov River' crooked itself around to the left. As we stepped dripping onto the wide sun-cracked mud beach on the inside of the curve, Eloi pointed out the tracks of three crocodiles. Their bellies and tails had pasted the mud where they crawled out of the water to sunbathe and I guessed that the biggest was no more than 1.8 metres long. These tracks had probably been left about a fortnight ago (shortly after the last heavy rains) but I realised that the crocs were almost certainly still in residence and had probably slipped quietly into the water when they saw us coming.

The humpback hills became steadily bigger as we marched through the hot afternoon towards a lonely hilltop hamlet that went by a delightfully peaceful name that meant 'Bellevue'. In the paddy fields below the village we met two friends of Eloi's with the even more unlikely Malagasy names of Victor and Cyril.

Victor held his iron-tipped assegai in the crook of his arm as he leaned forward to shake hands; Cyril gesticulated excitedly with his *coup-coup* (machete) as he gave us the news of recent adventures in Bellevue. Only two months ago a band of Dahalo had attacked the village at dawn, when the zebu were still in the kraal. But the defenders had a couple of guns amongst them and had not lost a single animal. Because of this victory, reprisals were feared and nobody dared walk even as far as the paddy fields alone or unarmed.

'We wait now for the sound of the whistle,' Victor said enigmatically, as he turned to lead us into the village.

'Sometimes the Dahalo send a messenger,' Eloi explained. 'Or they blow a whistle just before they attack. Then if the people escape – leaving their zebu and rice – there will be no killing. But the people of "Bellevue" won't run away.'

Pickersgill had written, about just such a hamlet as Bellevue:

> The inhabitants of these desert villages must surely lead a wretched existence. Not a soul dare venture out of this enclosure unarmed, and hunger and thirst are enemies ever within. A day or two ago a man and his wife went down into the fields to look after their rice. They were pounced upon unawares by a prowling gang, and the woman carried off. The husband only escaped with his life through a gun missing fire.

Pickersgill and Mr S. had visited this region (long before the term 'Zone Rouge' had ever been coined) when it was the pastures of Merina lords, who mistakenly imagined themselves masters of the 'fighting Sakalava' clans who roamed the sun-scorched grasslands.

> Several such hamlets are to be met with at far-off intervals in this stretch of country known as desert. They are chiefly inhabited by slaves in charge of grazing cattle, are difficult of access, and serve as places of safety for the

> herds when threatened by thieving Sakalava ... This is
> the Màvohàzo country [Yellow Forest], roamed by rest-
> less Sakalava, of whom every mother's son is armed, and
> will fight – on very slight provocation.

The Bellevue villagers were Betsileo from the Central Highlands. They were all young married people who had come to the Zone Rouge to build a village and eventually, if left in peace, a community. Their only defensive advantage was their hilltop position and the determination of people who were fighting for all they had in the world. They were united in the pioneering spirit that had brought them to this lawless country, where there is an abundance of good, rich land – if you are prepared to fight back.

Bellevue was a collection of eight huts, woven from saplings and plastered with the mixture of zebu dung and mud that hardens to red concrete within days under the African sun. Poor as they were, we could not be allowed to pass through without partaking of a plate of boiled cassava and beans. These handsome people were living every day under a very real threat of massacre yet their obvious companionship and ever-present laughter seemed to take them a world away from the 'wretched existence' that Pickersgill had witnessed.

It was already clear to me that most, if not all, of the Zone Rouge horror stories that I'd heard were founded on truth. As we abandoned Bellevue to its state of siege I was already scanning the savannah ahead with greater concentration. The 'yellow forest' stretched away from us in a series of gently rolling hills. If this had ever been more heavily populated, as is believed, one would have expected to see at least a few of the sturdy stone tombs that stand, apparently forsaken, on hillsides all over the rest of the island. But there were very few signs of life – or death – here at all.

Even the birds and the chameleons that I'd seen in such numbers in the north were strangely absent. The relative paucity of plant life – with most of the land colonised by just a handful of grasses – has led, in turn, to a minimal number of creatures that can glean a living in these plains. Although experts now believe that much of western Madagascar may have been savannah even before the arrival of humans (and cattle) these plains were once able to cultivate far richer vegetation. Two thousand years ago they were the domain of flocks of elephant birds (up to a dozen species), pygmy hippos and slothful, giant lemurs.

We waded across the murky red current of the Kalashnikov River four more times without seeing a soul, then, as we dropped down to a creek-side ledge, we found ourselves suddenly on the edge of a rice paddy! Here, inexplicably – and, one would have thought, dangerously – a family was camped in a tiny thatched shelter remote from any village. The father explained that this was the locust season and they were camping here to be ready to drive off the swarms with smoke and noise. Even here it was almost impossible to leave without eating a token amount of the family's precious store of rice. A common Malagasy saying states 'our fore-fathers cursed him who hid food from a stranger' and another says simply 'the food which is prepared has no master'.

I didn't want to eat their supplies and Eloi explained that we were in a great hurry to get to Soa Rano. They only let us leave with the promise that next time we would eat with them.

We were already watching anxiously for the first signs of bruising in the afternoon sky when the thatch roofs of Soa Rano (Sweet Water) came into view in the bowl of the valley. A Malagasy saying warns against arriving in a village after dark: 'You will be met only by dogs'. But in the Zone Rouge this no longer holds true. To walk straight into a village in the dark is to risk being shot.

'If we arrived much later we would have had to make a signal fire on the hill here,' said Eloi. 'And wait until the guards came out to find us.'

With its solid, two-storey mud houses, sturdy kraal for night-time lodging of valuable zebu and a fighting force of about fifty warriors (including many Sakalava), Soa Rano was a veritable bush fortress and a natural place for any Zone Rouge wayfarers to pass the night. Six young men met us at the edge of the village and marched us to the headman's house. Their display of smiles and bows almost (but not quite) offset the intimidating effect of so many bristling assegai. We took off our boots and climbed to the main living quarters up an extremely narrow, twisting stairway, virtually impregnable to attack ... unless the thatched roof was set ablaze.

The headman was a Betsileo, slimly built in the Indonesian mould of some of the most handsome of his countrymen. In Soa Rano tradition dictated that the leading men from each family welcome visitors personally, a custom that may have had its basis in the same fears as Borikely's 'announcement fady'. They came, one at a time or in pairs, each leaning their spears by the door and offering their hands formally so that within minutes there were eighteen men seated around the walls of the headman's quarters.

I sat cross-legged, and massaged my weary feet while Eloi 'gave the news' and explained our mission. The men were all work-hardened and their own bare feet showed the cuts and calluses of years trying to raise beasts and crops in this harsh countryside. They were all clothed in white lambas and four youngsters had big, brightly-coloured plastic combs wedged into their tight curls. All but two of the men wore simple necklaces made from a leather cord decorated with a few beads and pieces of wood. Three women bustled in the next room and, through the doorway, I saw shadowy forms dip water from a bucket and scoop rice from a huge woven basket. These people, lucky enough to have two-storey houses rather than a simple mud floor, slept with their precious rice harvest for security.

The headman's two young sons sat with their father. One was grave and serious and, at twelve or thirteen years old, obviously already felt the weight of his future position in the community. The other, a few years younger, squirmed with boredom where he was propped on his father's lap – he was most remarkable for his shock of sun-bleached, almost blond, hair. A village fady prescribed that every baby boy be committed to a course of obscure, but apparently harmless, medicine for an unspecified time after his birth. Until the boy stopped taking this *fanafody*, it was also fady to cut his hair and this cool, surfie hairdo was the happy result!

The headman's wife stuck her head around the door to announce that dinner was ready. The visiting men rose to their feet to shamble out, in an interminable dance of bows and double-handshakes, collecting their spears as they went. We ate boiled rice with a few beans as *laoka* (the name given to whatever comes with rice) and drank several cups of the surprisingly refreshing rice-water. By now it was dark outside and the evening chorus of frogs drifted up to us from the small 'Sweet Water' lake in the bowl of the valley. I rummaged through my pack and offered the headman milk and sardines – grateful again to lessen the load – and taking a photograph of the proud father with his sons I promised to send him a copy via Eloi later.

There was a guestroom downstairs and it was here that Eloi and I were invited to lay our weary heads. As we rolled out the sleeping-mats a crowd of young men drifted into the room to stand, silently watching, against the wall. Each of them leaned on an assegai and three were also armed with coup-coups. I nodded 'hellos' all around and they bowed silently back. Eloi opened the shuttered window to let some air circulate and, as the shutters swung back, the gap was filled with three more curly heads and gleaming smiles! When I lay down to sleep there were a dozen armed 'warriors' watching us yet, strangely, there was no feeling of tension. They were merely curious to see how a vazaha slept and I decided – also out of curiosity – to lie perfectly still, feigning sleep, and see how long it would take them to get bored and drift away.

I must have 'feigned sleep' for a considerable time because the next thing I knew a shaft of bright sunlight was creeping down the mud wall and the room was empty.

The whole of Soa Rano turned out to see us on our way, as we walked in convoy with three Sakalava men who were driving some zebu to be sold at Tsiro. They were tall and dark-skinned with hard features and athletes' bodies. Their black curls, stacked high on their crowns, made them look taller still. They had been on the trail for ten days, had rested for two in Soa Rano, and expected to arrive at the market in four more.

Their leader balanced a rifle of indeterminable vintage (and efficiency) across his shoulder and the other two carried assegais; all had coup-coups in the wide belts that secured their lambas.

Unlike most of the fresh-faced youngsters in the village these were tough, battle-hardened men who looked like they would be fully prepared to fight for their animals. It was a strange thought that they had certainly, at some time, been involved in spear battles and perhaps knew what it was like to kill in hot blood with cold steel.

Reverend Pickersgill had been similarly impressed by a 'noble savage' from the Sakalava town of 'Ambongo':

> A piece of dark-blue calico is tucked about his loins and relieved against the swarthy skin by a careless fold of white. All the rest is bravery. His leathern belt and shot-pouch are heavy with studded brass nails. A brass-bound powder-horn swings therefrom at the end of two short chains. Surely Fortune favours the brave! And I was not sorry, O barbaric friend, to find thee guiltless of human blood, – though Heaven alone knows what deeds thou hast allowed that old French musket to do, and on what errands though hast sent thy shafted iron since first they became thine inseparable familiars.

Dahalo-ism was first recognised as a manhood initiation rite associated specifically with the Sakalava and the Bara, who live further south: a boy could only become a man after he had stolen zebu, often as a gift for his future father-in-law. It is believed that the organised Dahalo raiding-parties of today are made up mostly from these two tribes.

The Norwegian missionary Arne Walen spent what were, one would guess, two very unpleasant years among the Sakalava in the 1870s:

> … with supercilious airs and bold appearance, having good mental power and strong and easily excited pas-

sions, making them rude, wild, and often raging in their conduct. On the whole, the Sakalava are a sly, perfidious, brutal and arrogant people, given to stealing, drinking, fighting, and plundering at every place where they make their appearance. A more thievish people than the Sakalava can hardly be found anywhere.

Our companions walked ahead, silent and aloof. Warriors like these had once made the Sakalava the most powerful tribe in Madagascar and even the highly organised Hova guard of the Merina had never been able to subdue them. It was only the Sakalava's own fiery independence and clannishness that could sap the power of their own greatest kings. In 1965, Arthur Stratton wrote, in *The Great Red Island*: 'Sakalava, "Dwellers in Long Valleys"; formerly the most powerful of the tribes, their lands used to include the western half of Madagascar … they are on the decline because, it is said, they have chosen to reject modern ways'.

But it was perhaps only their aloofness, and the wild tracts of land across which they were dispersed, that has historically made the Sakalava 'an unknown quantity'. Ruling them was always, as the Merina proverb says, like carrying mud: if you hold it lightly in your open palms, it spills over, and if you close your hands firmly, it slips through your fingers. Some researchers now claim that the Sakalava may even be the largest Malagasy tribe. Nevertheless, their lordly pride still makes them the least approachable and most mysterious of all the eighteen tribes. Certainly, in the short time before our paths diverged I was unable to make any headway into understanding these three stern individuals.

The first leg of our own trek that morning would take us to the town of Bepoaka, five hours away, deep in the Zone Rouge. Here we would be able to buy provisions at the only store before Ankavandra, three or four days further on, beyond the Bungolava Mountains. Eloi told me the story of Bepoaka: 'There are two quarters in the town – one "black-skins" and one "white-skins" and they used to be always fighting. One day, in the middle of a big fight, the Dahalo arrived with about twenty men. Their leader was Zaza Mola – Crazy Baby. He stopped the fight and said to both the whites and blacks "bring all your animals here", and he killed every one of the zebu with his machine-gun.

'Then he said, "There are many cocks in the compound and they all want to crow, still men are like the rim of the rice pot – all part of one circle. You are all equal and you shouldn't fight each other anymore."'

In a country where landmarks were named for ambushes and gunshots and peopled with brigands like Crazy Baby or Red Hair – who, Eloi said, was 'a *giant* with a wisp of red hair on his forehead, scarlet clothes and a submachine gun' – my imagination was running away with me. I couldn't picture these Dahalo as anything other than Mexican *bandidos*, roaring with bloodthirsty laughter as they fired their rifles into the air from the backs of foam-mouthed horses. Of course, I knew from bitter experience that there were no horses within hundreds of miles. I was sure that should we run up against any of these brigands I would soon realise that they weren't the romantic figures I had imagined.

'Where do they live – these Dahalo?' I asked Eloi.

'Aah, the Dahalo ... they lived in camps in the valleys. Before they were heroes here – that was the best part. They had strong magic and protected the villages.'

'But not any more?'

'The parents of Ratsibahaka – Bad Lemur – still live in Bepoaka. Once the army tried to ambush him there. But they didn't want to walk all this way so they flew the soldiers in by helicopter. Bad Lemur knew they were there of course so he stayed away! All the famous chiefs – Zaza Mola, Menasanga, Ratsibahaka – all dead. The Dahalo are too much like bandits now – not heroes. There's always people they wanna fight. The villages don' like them anymore.'

Bepoaka, when we arrived, was still evidently a town of two halves. We walked straight through what Eloi called *le quartier noir* where the dark-skinned people of the Bara tribe lived. It was early afternoon and most of the inhabitants were sleeping in their red mud huts. The lighter-skinned Sakalava and Betsileo residents of *le quartier blanc* were likewise dozing away the midday heat and we reached the army post on the far side of the village almost unnoticed. A ramshackle bamboo stockade surrounded the two-room concrete block where, in the absence of any all-powerful headman, we reported to the guard.

Only a single soldier, asleep on the dining room table, was in residence – the rest were apparently 'on patrol.' Antsi was the guard's name and he welcomed us with a bleary-eyed smile. He was dressed in washed-out camouflage fatigues and his battered AK47, with most of the paint worn off the clip, was propped against the corner. Antsi spoke good French and we talked in the compound while Eloi went to find out if the store was open. He was a Central Highlands Betsileo and had spent two months in this outpost. It was a peaceful enough life, he said, and there had been no trouble here since he arrived.

A Bara woman, more essentially 'African' in her appearance than the women of other tribes, brought us a huge pot of rice with two boiled eggs on top and a plastic jug of hot rice-water. It was 'feeding time for the vazaha' and all the village children came to press their faces against the bars of my bamboo cage. I wondered if they would be disappointed when they realised that I ate rice in exactly the same way that they did.

As I scooped up the rice with a rusty spoon that seasoned it with the flavour of old coins, I asked Eloi to explain the Dahalo's magic.

'The Dahalo have sorcerers called *mpanandro*, who can read signs … For example, a mpanandro can tell you the best way and time to build a house, from reading the moon or the trees or from speaking with the spirits. Sometimes, the mpanandro, he uses special materials or pieces from inside an animal. Every one works different, but we call every person – a chief, or a priest *or* a Dahalo – who can read these signs mpanandro.'

'The Dahalo chiefs you told me about – Red Hair and Crazy Baby – were they mpanandro?' I asked.

'That I don' know. I can't tell – they were shot about five years ago.'

'Do the Dahalo have many fadys?'

'Very many. It depends on their ody – the charms – that they wear around their neck or on their waist. I wanna tell you some powers of the ody.'

Eloi always liked to give examples and he cast about for one now: '... For example, it's night-time and somebody tries to break in your room but, no matter what they do, you can't hear any noise. This is because they spread oils in your bed or they can make a fire from special wood and put it under your bed.'

'Not like gas?'

'Yes, not like gas,' Eloi affirmed. If there is any way to avoid it, a polite Malagasy will never answer 'no' to a question. 'You can't wake up and you can't hear a thing – they have power over you.'

'Do they always get the power from substances? ... Or is it more like a spell?'

'They get the power maybe from some roots, water, smoke – something like this. But they carry it with them. They wear it ... For example, the Dahalo often carry their fanafody medicine in a zebu horn around their neck and this is called *mohara*. Here there are many different charms.'

'The necklaces that people wear here. Wood and beads and pieces of glass. Is this also ody?'

'Yes, but this is good medicine – for protection, not attack. It's to protect him from bad medicine. Enemies can bury a piece of wood in your path and if you step over it without this ody it will break your leg or kill you.'

'And where do they get these things?'

'From someone with power. You can buy it from a mpanandro.'

'So the mpanandro has the power to kill people if he wants?'

'Yes, but it's not so easy because many people have the protection. Like having a gun, you don't have to shoot it but it protects you just by having it.'

The store was the only other concrete building in Bepoaka so, being cooler than any of the huts, it was a natural place for the village elders to gather. Not surprisingly – since there was not even a charet track leading to the village – the store was almost devoid of stock. We bought what we could: a few packets of noodles, coffee, two rusted tins of sardines, six eggs (which we wrapped carefully in a bandanna) and some limes, to take away the flavour of my chlorine water-purifying tablets.

Though I had no taste for warm beer, the smiling eyes of four old men who were seated against the cool stone walls shamed me into buying six of the eight remaining Three Horses *grand modèles*. An old Michael Jackson tape was reverently slipped into the battered ghetto-blaster that was the store owner's pride and joy, and the party was complete.

By the time we had left Bepoaka behind I was already regretting those midday THBs. I could feel a cushion of blisters on the balls and heels of my feet, aggravated by the grit of all the riverbanks where I'd had to remove my boots. There was also the constant irritation of plucking needle-like grass seeds from my socks.

The plain climbed slowly into the west, immensely wide and wild, beyond a single dome-shaped mound known as *Ny Trafo* – the Zebu's Hump. The hills rolled away from us and actually seemed to be rippling as the wind brushed the grass. The stark red wounds of lavaka were clearly visible here and there, where the hills tucked themselves too tightly into the creases of darkly wooded valleys.

The view inspired a few scattered lines of such Country greats as 'Country Road' and 'El Paso'. Eloi, who, I was impressed to discover, was familiar with both of these songs, even agreed to dedicate a duet of 'Rhinestone Cowboy' to my little sister. When we eventually ran out of lyrics, Eloi changed tack somewhat and began tuning up for 'Silent Night, Holy Night'. I had to quieten him by explaining that, in my country, at least, carols were unlucky – 'fady' I said – except at Christmas.

'You have fadys too?' he asked in surprise.

'Yes, I s'pose some people do.'

'What's your fady?'

'My fady ...' I thought for a moment. 'My fady is that I can only eat rice three times a day. Four times is too many!'

All around us in the undergrowth were strange, cube-shaped rocks like huge dice which – if we'd been mpanandro – might have foretold the chances of our reaching Soa Tana village, on the Manambolo River, by nightfall.

The scale of the country was so vast that the view hardly seemed to change for the next hour as we climbed steadily towards a row of bare hills. The tall grass whispered in a light breeze but we were walking directly into the glare of the sun and I was grateful for the wide brim of my hat.

'You know what's *kleebatata*?' asked Eloi, with the air of elaborate carelessness he reserved only for the most bizarre facts about his country or beliefs.

'No. What's kleebatata?'

'Not klee-ba-ta-ta,' he mimicked. '*Keli* – as in small, and *betratra* – meaning big chest. *Kelibetratra* is a small animal with a big chest. I saw one in Tana in December, 1997,' he added, displaying his usual attention to detail. 'It's like a dog, but longer with a long tail ...'

'Ah-hah! Fosa!' I guessed, wondering simultaneously what Madagascar's largest carnivore would be doing in Tana.

'No, not *foosh!* Fosa is like a panther, kelibetratra is more like a dog. Its eyes shine at night and it attacks people – or dogs – as soon as it sees them. It doesn't eat them, but just attacks.'

I had to save my breath now to climb the pass around the first hill and directly up the face of the second, higher one. Even so, little of it had been saved by the time we slogged our way over the crest to find a soaring rock face ahead of us, twice as high as the last. Worse than this, we had to descend first, squandering some of our hard-earned altitude in a darkly forested canyon.

We climbed down into the shade of a dry wood and walked through a gap in the high canyon walls. At the foot of the mountain, the gully opened out unexpectedly into a dusty, bowl-shaped depression. A large, well-built kraal, big enough to hold several hundred zebu, had been built here using the canyon wall and the foot of the mountain as natural boundary fences on two sides. We were out in the open before we realised that there were four men working on the fence!

They were equally surprised to see us and only smiled silently at our salutes as they watched us cross to the foot of the mountain. Their looks were somehow cold and threatening, far from what I had come to expect in the villages, and we carried on moving – not stopping to talk, not wanting them to realise how much the odds were in their favour.

One of them shouted at our backs as we started up the escarpment: 'Be careful, if you go up there the Dahalo will know where you are. They will follow you!'

We laughed and waved back, but didn't stop.

'They'll rob you! Maybe kill you!'

We could still hear their laughter as we leaned into the hill, finding new energy in our anxiety to get away – or at least gain a height advantage in case they decided to pursue us. The herd of zebu for which that hidden kraal had been built would need a veritable army to protect it and I knew that there was only one army of any size in the Zone Rouge: the Dahalo themselves. I was certain that we had stumbled upon the Aladdin's Cave of a big Dahalo gang but I was unable to expend any breath on confirming this with Eloi until we finally stopped to rest against the sun-heated rocks near the crest of the mountain. The kraal was again hidden from view but I panned my telescope around the slope below us and was immensely relieved to see that nothing moved there.

'Were they Dahalo?' I asked.

'Could be … Maybe not real Dahalo. Just bandits.'

'What do you call *real* Dahalo?'

'Real Dahalo are more than just bandit thugs. They have their own magic … For example, they carry charms. If you try to shoot a Dahalo, all he has to say is *"rano"* – water – and your bullets will turn to rain. They're not allowed to eat tenrec or sheep or any other cowardly animal,' Eloi continued, as he picked up his pack to move on. 'And, above all, they must never, ever wash their shirts.' He was warming to his subject: 'You can recognise a real Dahalo because his eyes are bright red and his shirt is yellow with dirt ... For this they're sometimes called *Mavo* – The Yellows.'

We hurried onwards and cast a last backward glance over the ridge as we stepped onto an immense, grassy-humped plateau. It was known as *Bezavona* (Place of Many Mists) and in the hour before sunset a hazy blueish light hung dreamily over the whole plateau. It was certainly the eeriest landscape that I had ever seen. Rolling hummocks swept ahead of us, rippling with tall grass so that they looked like the backs of a pod of travelling whales. Between these hummocks ancient lavaka gullies had blossomed, leaving petrified stone forests of tsingy. These spreading amphitheatres had somehow been recolonised by tangled vegetation, giving an impression that great, bulbous trees had been painted on the canvas of the hills – dark green on light green. And the whole picture was washed in that strange blue light.

Wildflowers of every colour had fixed their roots among the grasses to take advantage of the permanent mists. Termite mounds jutted up here and there like snow-capped volcanoes above a green sea. There are over seventy endemic termites in Madagascar and this particular species had a strange habit of 'roofing' their castles with a heavy, white quartz rock. Perhaps the termites had begun to build their mounds under the rocks for protection from rain. Eventually the combined labours of thousands of tiny workers, reinforcing the red cement of their fortress, had, in the termite equivalent of moving mountains, raised the rock up to ninety centimetres off the ground! The Bezavona plateau was a place of fairytale beauty but the thought of the bandits rushed us across it, racing the setting sun westwards to the village of Soa Tana.

CHAPTER 3

'SWEETSVILLE'

> Beyond an unpeopled region of hills … there lies a
> mighty valley. And we peered into it from the brink
> of that long eastern wall, wondering if any great sea-
> flood had ever poured between there and the
> answering heights, far-drawn in rock-breasted cliff,
> thirty miles nearer sunset across the void.
>
> – Rev. William Clayton Pickersgill

'Can't we use the torch?' I whispered, as we stumbled over loose
stones and hummocks of grass amongst the impenetrable shadows of the gully.

'Yes, we can't,' Eloi replied, in the manner that still threw me
mentally off-balance every time he used it. He pulled me down
into a crouch and whispered: 'The village will have a guard out
and if we flash a light he might shoot at us'.

'But if we creep around like this they'll never believe we're
not up to no good.' I felt like standing up and shouting ('Yoo-hoo,
it's only me!'), but I knew who was the greenhorn in this outfit
and was ready to trust Eloi's experience. 'Can't we at least light a
signal fire?'

'Yes, we can't … and shssssh! – If we light a fire the Dahalo
might find us before the guard. We'll just sit here and wait. The
village is just across there and the guard will probably patrol
around this way.'

I stared into the darkness beyond Eloi's pointing finger, but
there was nothing to see. As we waited I prayed that the guard
wasn't feeling as jumpy as I was.

'On y va!' – Suddenly Eloi stood up and moved confidently forward.

As I rose doubtfully to follow him, a shadow broke away from the creek-side trees and climbed towards us. The moon glinted on the barrel of a rifle and I wondered who had been watching whom.

'Bonsoir, m'sieur.' The guard, who was no more than a boy, held out his free hand. It was no surprise to find out that this phrase was the full extent of his French 'repertoire'. Eloi and he chatted animatedly in Malagasy as I shuffled after them into the darkened village. Soa Tana (Sweet Town) would be revealed by daylight to be no more than a collection of eight small but well-built huts, with mud and dung walls forming sharp, meticulous right angles, and thatch roofs spanning out into wide eaves. The headman's hut was twice as long as the others were and, although the sound of laughter came from the left-hand side of this 'presidential palace', the guard led us directly to the silent right-hand door. Eloi was sure that the headman would offer us a 'safe house' for the next few days but the old man was away buying supplies and it fell to his wife to welcome us.

Mme Laza was a delightfully bright-eyed lady in her late forties (knocking at the gnarly portals of old age for a rural Malagasy). Even the wispy goatee that curled in a few long hairs from the tip of her chin seemed to sprout forth as a testament to her easygoing attitude. Chattering and laughing all the while she fixed us a meal of rice, cold shredded beef (with congealed lumps of something that I took to be stomach) and bitter cassava leaves. The beef tasted dubiously high and I was pleased when Eloi told me that this was the usual flavour of wild cattle meat. There were apparently a lot of wild cattle around Soa Tana and, as the sound of Malagasy pop music blared at us from the next room, Eloi described some of the stranger bovine inhabitants of the Zone Rouge.

'Songaomby runs like the wind and lives on the blood of men! It's bigger than a zebu bull but it's fat and has no horns. *Tokantongotra* –'single-foot' – is smaller, more like a shaggy goat … but it has one foot on its front and one on its back.'

Mme Laza – intelligent enough to stay with the conversation even though it was in a language she had never heard – gestured with her hands to describe the songaomby's speed and the tokantongotra's feet.

'Even with its feet like this, tokantongotra can run almost as fast as songaomby,' Eloi continued. 'It feeds on men too, but it really hates dogs – I don' know why but it steals the eyes of dogs. A man from my hometown once tried to hide in a tree when he saw a songaomby. This was very silly because everybody knows that it plays a wicked trick to get you down. It stood underneath the tree and it … how you say?' – he paused, searching for *le mot juste* – '… it peed. And it swished its tail. The pee burns like acid and the man fell out of the tree when he got splashed. The songaomby ate him.'

I was relieved to see that Mme Laza refrained from acting out this scene, and instead rose to lead us into the next room, where it seemed that the whole community was gathered. Radio Bungolava was doing its utmost to pipe the sounds of the twenty-first century into the Zone Rouge.

'Soa Tana disco!' Eloi laughed as – with an eruption of giggles – three girls froze in mid-dance. Shining darkly with sweat in the lamplight, they managed to mask their amazement and like the rest of the village came forward to greet us with double-handed handshakes. Apart from that fleeting moment's surprise there was nothing in the faces of these people to betray the fact that our arrival had not been expected.

I had been a 'victim' of these same good manners before, in Indonesia. It had been distinctly unnerving to realise that my arrival had been so obviously anticipated in communities that were isolated by almost unexplored rainforest. I assumed that the bush telegraph had travelled ahead, as it almost always does but, as we moved onto remoter, more untrodden trails, I realised that this was impossible. Even in the most far-flung village it was regarded as simple good manners that we should be treated exactly like old friends who were paying their weekly visit.

But now the door grated open behind us and Mme Laza came

in carrying what I later realised was the only chair in Soa Tana. It was simply a beaten metal frame with wooden slats but here it was a treasure: the fact that someone had once had to carry it for three days to get it to the village was proof enough of this! Now it was being offered as the seat of honour for the first vazaha ever to visit Soa Tana. I set it against the wall and bowed my head: *'Misaotra.'*

I appreciated Mme Laza's thoughtfulness but felt uncomfortable to be propped so high above the heads of the others in the room. I didn't want to be treated like the vazaha I was and, as Eloi finished relating the story of our day's adventures, I slipped off the chair and sat cross-legged on the mud floor.

'Tsy misy vazaha,' I said in clumsy Malagasy, smiling at Mme Laza – 'I'm not a vazaha … I'm Malagasy!'

The circle of brown faces broke into ivory-toothed laughter. The girls started dancing again and I leaned back to watch, content just to have made it safely to Soa Tana – and to be amongst friends.

It was strange that there were no children here and, as we slouched against the wall, I asked Eloi where they were.

'At this season they are away with some of the adults at the far paddy fields, in the next valley. They must guard against locusts.'

We must have looked more deeply relaxed than we felt because very soon Mme Laza called a halt to the evening's entertainment and signalled for the music to be switched off. But, although nobody showed their disappointment, it was obvious that the vazaha's arrival had thrown a wet blanket over the Soa Tana disco.

'Can you ask them to turn the music back on?' I asked Eloi. 'Then we'll dance too.'

The packed mud floor was smooth and cool under the water-filled balloons of my blisters. Mick helped the party along, from his Tsiroanomandidy studio, with the jumping, tribal beat of Jaojoby's *salegy* dance music. The whole village was up and dancing and Mme Laza was in the thick of it, roaring with laughter as she did a very passable twist.

As Eloi and I lay out our sleeping-mats in the empty 'dance hall' later that night, Mme Laza knocked on the door. Like a considerate hostess bringing her guests late-night cocoa she handed us each a spear: 'Don't worry too much if you hear footsteps in the night,' she explained, 'my son will stay out with the rifle … Just leave the assegai close to your mat where you can reach it in the night if you need it.'

With this frightening possibility on my mind it was a full ten minutes before I fell asleep.

When the nightly battle against darkness must be fought more vigorously than through the prod of a light switch (or with remote control TV from the comfort of an armchair) people must live their lives in the daylight hours. Even so I found it difficult to chew salted beef and wet rice at 7 am! And Eloi's breakfast-table conversation was equally hard to digest: 'Like I started to say las' night,' he began, suppressing a yawn. 'Like songaomby and tokantongotra – I forgot to tell you 'bout Sagittaire.'

My drowsy brain tried to tell me that this was a creature I had heard about somewhere already. Then I realised that he was talking about Sagittarius: 'You don't mean the man-horse?' I gasped.

'You have him too? We call him like that: *bibyolona* – animal-man. I've seen him twice … For example, once when I was 'bout twelve I was waiting for my father to come home and I was leaning in the window. I thought I saw my father coming down the street but it was the bibyolona and I was so scared I was frozen. He had a horse's bottom half and a man's top and, like always, he was with a man. Bibyolona only comes when it is a half-moon and he is always accompanied by a man – a mpanandro or a politician or something, I'm not sure. But if he had seen me he would have killed me.'

After a sobering cup of coffee, Eloi and I decided to take a slow walk through the rice terraces to check the condition of the river. The rice plants grew in tall regular bunches out of the black water and we had to perform a balancing act along the dykes between the flooded paddies. I went barefoot so that I could use my toes for extra grip. The water cooled my blisters and soothed the grass-seed splinters in my ankles. I tried not to think about the likelihood of it being infected with bilharzia.

The Manambolo River swept in a wide *café-au-lait* curve between the neon-green paddies and a shadowy wall of liana-tangled forest. Although it was running fast, the level was considerably lower than Eloi had feared. As if to demonstrate, three young men in ragged shorts stepped out of the trees on the far bank and walked down the sandy beach to the river. They held their assegais to their chests as the current reached up to tug powerfully around their ribs. Their unusually muscular hunting dogs were intelligent enough to run further upriver before beginning their swim. They reminded me immediately of the Dayak dogs of Kalimantan. Like the boar-hunting Dayaks, these young warriors would also be fearless in dispatching dangerous wild cattle with their spears – once the dogs had cornered them.

In 1971 Nigel Heseltine wrote that 'the Merina kings hunted wild cattle *(baria)* 150 years ago, and some are said to survive between Belobaka and Ankavandra on the western edge of the Hauts-Plateaux'. Their dark skin goosepimpled from the chilly river, these young men confirmed that there is no shortage of baria in the Zone Rouge today: that very morning a young bull had hurt one of their dogs before making good its escape. They would pick up its trail later, they said. The dogs ran up, wagging their tails to shake water over us, and I saw that one of them was dragging a paw.

The smiling men wore ody charms of coloured beads around their necks and each was tattooed with three small marks between his eyebrows. Tattoos are rare in Madagascar but I remembered hearing about these facial marks. James Sibree (missionary and editor of the *Antananarivo Annual*) wrote in 1870 that marks on the forehead were frequently seen amongst 'the lowest caste of slaves'. Eloi said that the tattoos were just a recent fashion and had no cultural importance. But these hunters didn't look like fashion victims: perhaps their forefathers were the slaves who guarded the herds of Merina kings.

It suddenly dawned on one of the golden-haired dogs happily sniffing around my ankles, that there was something unusual about me. It leapt away with a yelp, its hackles bristling. Only then did the other dogs – never having seen (or smelt) a vazaha before – notice my 'offensive odour' and back away snarling. I look on dogs as infallible judges of character and have always been pleased that they invariably trust me. It was a blow to my very soul therefore, that during the time I stayed in Soa Tana, these hunting dogs demonstrated such instinctive hatred for me.

Not so long ago, the inhabitants of these same isolated villages might have met me with the same fear and loathing that their dogs now showed. In some parts of Madagascar, even today, there remains a suspicion that vazaha are *mpakafo* – zombies who come to the island to steal the healthy internal organs of the Malagasy! Perhaps this belief was rooted in the 'political propaganda' of the xenophobic Ranavalona the Cruel. Or maybe it was a relic of the Arab slave trade. A hundred years ago Sibree's missionary friend, E. O. McMahon, wrote:

> One African who is now free told us how, when the dhow they were on was becalmed near the Madagascar coast and a man-of-war boat was in chase, the Arabs called up the strongest of the slaves to row the dhow, and to make them work harder told them that those in pursuit were cannibals, and were only chasing them to catch them for food.

Late that afternoon a mysterious old man battled across the wide current of the Manambolo. For unexplained reasons he was walking eastwards with a battered old double-barreled shotgun as his sole companion. Nobody knew from whence he came or where he was bound ... and with typical Malagasy manners nobody thought of asking. He wore a dark-blue lamba held tight, Sakalava-style, with a thick belt from which hung a leather pouch. He was tattooed with the three marks between his eyes, his head was shaven but his chin sprouted a wispy grey goatee – only slightly more substantial than that of Mme Laza.

'About fifteen Dahalo,' he nodded, 'hiding down the valley ... waiting for someone'. He shrugged his wiry shoulders with the air of a man who had seen more than his share of bandits.

We strained our eyes across the emerald patchwork of paddies, across the muddy sweep of the Manambolo and into the shadows of the trees. Nothing stirred in the last of the day's heat. It was unusual for anyone to travel alone here and paradoxically the dangers were enhanced for a man with a rifle: there were many in the Zone Rouge who would happily kill for a shotgun like this one. We wondered how he was unafraid to travel alone.

'How's he know they're waiting for someone?' I asked.

'He heard them preparing magic,' Eloi translated, his forehead furrowed with what I took to be healthy concern.

I weighed up the options. We could retreat back to Fierenana, through the Place of Many Mists and back along the numerous twists of Kalashnikov River – but that would mean trying to slip back past the big Dahalo kraal. In front of us lay a vast expanse of uninhabited savannah and forested valleys before the craggy Bungolava peaks. We would have to cross what is probably the wildest territory in all Madagascar before we reached 'civilisation' of a sort at Ankavandra – an island in the wilderness, boasting three or four satellite hamlets linked by a few miles of dirt track.

Back in Mme Laza's hut Eloi voiced his suspicion over the old man's information. Was this a set up? Was the old man a Dahalo? Or even a mpanandro? If the Dahalo wanted to trap a vazaha they would certainly use a mpanandro – was the old man trying to make us change our route and lead us into a trap? The peaceful inhabitants of Zone Rouge hamlets have learnt to keep their guard up against strangers. In many cases it had been obvious that the bandits were acting on information that could only have come from within the village. As Eloi said: 'Nobody really knows who's Dahalo and who isn't'.

The old man was a guest in the village and, like ourselves, he would be sleeping in the 'dance hall', but both Eloi and Mme

Laza expressed concern over which way his precious shotgun would be pointed in the event that there was a raid on the village. It crossed my mind for the first time that I might be placing the people of Soa Tana in serious danger. As their guest, I was certain that they would fight in my defence and it was a lonely moment when I realised that the best thing that I could do would be to move on and take that responsibility with me.

Amongst his other talents Eloi was 'trained' in karate (although possibly only by a prodigious diet of Van Damme movies). With this educational background – clashing somewhat with his religious aspirations – he considered it absolutely natural to ask how many Dahalo I thought I could 'take out' if it came to a fight. I didn't want to disappoint him with my extreme reluctance to take *anyone* out with a stabbing spear so I paused for a moment – as if planning my moves – and hedged at a confident: 'Two ... Maybe three on a good day'.

We felt nightmarishly vulnerable as we lowered ourselves into the swirling current of the Manambolo at first light the next morning. The sun was just climbing over the hill at our backs and it was still cold under the shadowy trees. I had bundled my cameras and films into a thick PVC kitbag that had proved its worth through many dunkings in rougher rivers than this. I held my pack above my head and entrusted the kitbag to the surefootedness of our diminutive new guide, Legali, who somehow managed to keep his feet even when the current came halfway up his chest.

Pickersgill wrote on 23 June 1875:

> Yesterday we safely passed the spot around which all the terrors of this lonesome way are forever flitting like ghostly shadows. It is a few yards of path between two dark glens, where the woods have hidden murderous men, and convenient boughs served as rests for their levelled guns. Several travellers have lost their lives there.

We sat still for a few minutes, listening for the crack of twigs underfoot. But all was peaceful and I strapped the kitbag onto my pack. Legali led us, scrambling through a wall of giant bamboo, up the steep slopes of the valley. He was a tough, pigeon-chested little guy who in my imagination lived up to his name wonderfully; I could only think of him translated into Spanish as *El Gallo* – the Cockerel.

Legali was dressed in long, threadbare shorts that had long ago given up their last trace of colour and a bright yellow T-shirt that was invariably hitched up over the top of his chubby belly. His only luggage was an assegai and a plastic shopping bag, containing a comb and a spare shirt. Wrapped around his head was a yellow, green and red 'turban', made from a lurid floral lamba. Despite Mme Laza's trust in him, I couldn't help but think that if the Dahalo wanted a beacon to show them where we were, they could only improve on Legali by making him a foot taller.

As we peered carefully over the lip of the hill towards the Bungolava Mountains, from where the Cockerel's turban probably already appeared as a blot on the landscape, I could still imagine a hoard of whooping Dahalo, tearing towards us on the backs of thundering stallions. But the swaying grassland ahead of us appeared to be as lifeless as ever and we set off almost at a jog, striking directly towards the Bungolavas. This was Eloi's plan, known only to Mme Laza and the three of us, and since it would mean going directly across the worst of the bandit country, it would be the last thing that anyone would expect.

We had only been travelling like this for about ten minutes when Eloi saw a movement on the hilltop opposite and we ducked into the grass. I fumbled for my telescope but before I had focussed I heard the Cockerel exclaim: 'Baria!'

It was a herd of eight wild cattle including, as far as I could see, an old bull and two calves. They were altogether stockier than the local domestic zebu, had almost no hump and all were a rich brown colour. Pickersgill had also seen wild cattle in this region.

He wrote:

> Travellers west become owners of all the cattle which
> they can pick up on the road. At least so I was told, and
> on the strength of the information, shot one of two young
> bulls which were grazing on a hillside.

We kept up a brisk trot all morning over a seemingly endless
chain of hills that were covered with what I came to think of as
'man-eating grass'. Swaying over a metre above our heads, *vero*
grass not only sliced like razor blades but I realised that it was
also seriously reducing our (already slim) chances of successful
'pygmy-spotting'. Even so, these vero patches were no more than
islands in a Sargasso Sea of a far more vicious nature.

Danga grass, as Eloi called it, was crowned at knee-height with
a row of black spines sprinkled with tiny silver hairs. It was deceptively beautiful when the sun shimmered across it but the sharp
seeds, which jabbed painfully into our flesh, had already made both
my ankles swollen and sore. The Cockerel was barefoot – and therefore had no socks that could be transformed into pincushions – but,
being close to a pygmy himself, he was tormented by seeds that got
trapped in the hem of his baggy shorts. Furthermore, the grass seeds
that had been a mere irritation on the hills further east had matured
into a veritable torment west of Soa Tana. On these hills, the heads
of this devilish grass seeped resin so that a whole sea of danga was
able to mass together in a single prickly 'hessian mat' that hovered
at knee level. The only way to get through this mat was to drag
your feet, thus collecting more and more of the painful spines.

There has long been a myth of people-eating vegetation in
Madagascar – but the story was of something more gruesome even
than the slow, creeping insanity that is caused by danga seeds. In
1878 one Carle Liche wrote a letter to a Dr Omelius Fredlowski
describing the terrifying spectacle of a human sacrifice to what he
called the great tree devil. The horrified reporter wrote:

> … The atrocious cannibal tree that had been so inert and
> dead came to sudden savage life. The slender delicate

palpi, with the fury of starved serpents, quivered a moment over her head, then as if by instinct with demoniac intelligence fastened upon her in sudden coils round and round her neck and arms; then while her awful screams and yet more awful laughter rose wildly to be instantly strangled down again into a gurgling moan, the tendrils one after another, like great green serpents, with brutal energy and infernal rapidity, rose, retracted themselves, and wrapped her about in fold after fold, ever tightening with cruel swiftness and savage tenacity of anacondas fastening upon their prey ... And now the great leaves slowly rose and stiffly, like the arms of a derrick, erected themselves in the air, approached one another and closed about the dead and hampered victim with the silent force of a hydraulic press and the ruthless purpose of a thumbscrew. A moment more, and while I could see the bases of these great levers pressing more tightly towards each other, from their interstices there trickled down the stalk of the tree great streams of the viscid honey-like fluid mingled horribly with the blood and oozing viscera of the victim ... May I never see such a sight again.

The retracted leaves of the great tree kept their upright position during ten days, then when I came one morning they were prone again ... and nothing but a white skull at the foot of the tree to remind me of the sacrifice that had taken place there.

The letter (despite the Poe-esque richness of gurgling moans, savage tenacity, viscid fluid, oozing viscera – and the doubtful existence of a Dr Omelius Fredlowski) was published in scientific journals across the world. Almost fifty years later it inspired the classic *Madagascar: Land of the Man-Eating Tree* by Chase Salmon Osborn, who commended Liche on the detail and character of his report. Yet nobody but Liche ever saw the people-eating tree, or even the Mkodo tribe – 'one of the smallest races, the men seldom exceeding fifty-six inches in height' – among whom he travelled.

For now I was busy being 'hampered and strangled' in my own nest of 'great green serpents'. I had followed Eloi and the Cockerel down into a depression that was metres deep in vero grass. No breeze penetrated this plantation and the heat was suffocating. I kept my arms out ahead of me to form a battering ram and ran to keep up with my guides. There was no time to look where I was putting my feet and when I stumbled, the wall of greenery closed neatly around me. It was impossible to see in which direction Eloi's bulletproof back had disappeared. For all I could see of the horizon I might as well have been in a sea of grass and I could do nothing other than squawk until somebody came back for me!

Pickersgill dealt with vero in a rather more cavalier fashion. He wrote: 'At every stage we left miles of it rolling in fire. The next traveller would be grateful for the clearance.'

We sat on the hillside above the 'vero plantation' chewing on some wild beef jerky that Mme Laza had given us. 'In Bungolava,' said Eloi, 'The cattle bird – the white one – is fady.'

I guessed that he meant the long-legged snowy egret that is found all over Africa, picking the parasites from grazing animals.

'That's right, the white one. It's fady – you cannot eat it – because when the cowboys come to collect their animals the only way they can find them is with the help of this bird which rides on the zebus' backs.'

In his characteristic, ultra-informative style Jørgen Ruud described another bird fady connected with vero grass (from Iavomalaza, Mandritsara canton, Betafo district, if you must know). It seems that the Iavomalaza villagers hid themselves in the vero grass when they were being chased by bandits. Immediately a flock of sparrows landed on the grass. The bandits reasoned that, if people were hidden in the grass, the birds would not have alighted. This fady shows clear parallels with the Betsileo tenrec fady and in both cases the escapees would have expressed their gratitude in similar terms: anyone killing or eating sparrows/tenrecs should be cursed. Let them become lepers, may they be cut to pieces, or sold as slaves, may they be childless and may their families die out.

We moved onwards in single file, sweating under the midday sun, across hills that were silver-plated by the hateful danga spines. Suddenly the Cockerel dropped to the ground and signalled us to do the same. There was a herd of zebu on the opposite side of the valley. As I scanned the hillside I picked out a white lamba. I handed the telescope to The Cockerel, who was already inordinately proud of his new-found ability to use this piece of technology, and lay back in the grass, closing my eyes against the searing sun. After five minutes, during which only one unarmed man had been seen, the Cockerel stood up. We had only moved a few metres when the white lamba jumped to its feet and took off at a run. We stopped and watched as he sprinted over the back of the hill … abandoning his charges to their fate!

We were still a long way distant and the sun was at our backs so the cowboy could not have distinguished our appearance. The question was: did he think we were bandits? Or was he running to collect the rest of his Dahalo gang? We deliberated for a while but, in the end, it was just too hot and the sound of running water at the bottom of the valley was too tempting. We decided to rely on what Joseph Conrad called 'do nothing heroics'. As I sat in the cool water listening to Eloi and the Cockerel singing a Malagasy ballad while a billy can of rice bubbled on the pebble beach, it seemed to be well worth the risk.

Neither the cowboy nor his friends reappeared as we trekked onwards. As the afternoon progressed the rocky saw-tooths of Bungolava (Long Mountain) spread out before us. The naked peak of Vatosira (Rock-and-Salt) Mountain rose high above the jagged skyline. Somewhere beyond Bungolava, down in the great Manambolo rift valley, lay the little town of Ankavandra.

A barely discernible trail (I'd have thought it was an animal track if I could have imagined any reason why an animal would wish to climb there) zigzagged its way tortuously up the escarpment. As Pickersgill noted: 'Our progress measured in direct line would not amount to very much, seeing that once or twice the road has doubled upon itself like – "a sheep's bowels," said our unfastidious followers'.

I didn't have to ask why Vatosira was so-called as we worked our way carefully across treacherous landslides made up only of loose black stones like volcanic rock, 'salted' liberally with gleaming white specks of quartz. Near the top of Vatosira we stopped to gaze back across the rolling hills that we'd spent the last week crossing. We were faced with the most immense panorama that I had ever seen. The savannah seemed to billow out from the foot of the salt and pepper mountain face, apparently into infinity. In the 160 square kilometres that lay before us, there was not a single lonely hut, charet track or even the smudge of a campfire. My shoulders ached and my ankles throbbed where they had been stabbed by the malignant spines, but I had to admit that this enthralling view was almost worth the pain of the trek.

Below the western slope of Vatosira peak we came out in a wide basin where a beautiful tarn, surrounded by reeds, reflected a single fluffy cloud in its deep blue mirror.

'This is very important – it's a sacred lake,' said Eloi. 'There are crocodiles here.'

I thought of pointing out that it was improbable that crocodiles would ever have climbed up Rock-and-Salt Mountain, but it would make no difference: no matter how enticing the tarn looked we could not swim in a sacred lake. As we stood looking at the gleaming circle of water I noticed something about the size of a ping-pong ball, swaying near the top of a vero 'blade'.

'What's this?' I asked, pulling the three-metre stalk down to face level.

'Aah, this is an egg – from an insect … you know the one that makes like this.' Eloi put his hands together under his chin.

'Praying mantis?'

'Tha's 'im. We give it to babies for strength. It makes energy!' With that Eloi plucked the egg and broke it in two. It was creamy white, with the texture and appearance of a meringue. The white foam had hardened as protection around the dozens of yellow specks that were the 'yolks'.

'Eat one,' he said.

I'd had more attractive gastronomic invitations but it was an experience that was unlikely to be repeated. Besides, any supplementary energy would certainly be greatly appreciated. The praying mantis egg tasted like a cold chip – one of the disgusting green ones that you leave on the side of your plate. And, worse, I didn't notice any bursts of incredible energy.

In fact I was still feeling slightly queasy an hour later when we reached the cliff face on the western edge of Long Mountain, where we stared down into the 'mighty valley' that Pickersgill had been so struck by a century before. The giant silver snake of the Manambolo River crawled southwards, and way beyond its western bank the 'rock-breasted cliff' of the Bemaraha Plateau was hazy, 'thirty miles nearer sunset across the void'. From this distance the regular line of the cliffs looked as featureless as a railway embankment.

Very probably Pickersgill's caravan of seventy, bristling with guns and spears, were called to a halt while Mr S. 'foraged for hilltops'. For our part, we chewed some more jerky and Eloi made the brave decision to take off his bulletproof vest, complaining that the stiff leather straps had become considerably more painful than the bullets would have been!

Ankavandra lay somewhere to our north, tucked under the western edge of the Bungolava chain that plummeted vertically almost a kilometre to the valley floor. We should make it to the town the next day, but for now I wanted nothing more than to make camp for the night. Still the Cockerel hurried us onwards along a track that showed promising signs of human passage in a constant chain of cairns, called *katao*, where wayfarers had given thanks to whatever guiding spirit had led them thus far. Since my own 'guiding angels' – Eloi and the Cockerel – went out of their way to respect the tradition, I too had to stoop painfully under the weight of my pack to collect an errant rock and place it ceremoniously atop each of the growing heaps.

An hour before sunset we spotted a lean-to shelter on a hilltop to our right and went cautiously to investigate. Eloi explained that settlers here were especially wary and, in the hours around darkness, had a habit of shooting strangers on sight. But nobody was in residence and the abandoned hut – with a door that you could only enter by crawling – looked to be a perfect place to spend the night. We'd covered almost fifty kilometres since dawn, over rough mountainous country. I was prepared to take a chance on sleeping anywhere but the Cockerel seemed to be strangely shaken by this palm-thatched 'Wendy house'.

Just as the light faded altogether we crawled on hands and knees into a dense, festering thicket in the bottom of a gully. It was an awful camp site; its sole benefit being that nobody would be able to clamber in here without us knowing about it. I slashed around with the Cockerel's coup-coup until I had cleared the minimum of space for my little mozzy-net cocoon, and checked around by torchlight for unwanted arachnid bed partners. Then I sat down, unlaced my boots carefully and used my Swiss army knife to cut out some danga splinters that I could see had actually penetrated halfway under my skin. Both ankles were sensitive and swollen and several of the splinters had already turned a poisonous yellow. I had given my last tins of milk and sardines to Mme Laza and all we had to eat was rice and dried jerky. The hypnotising flicker of a subdued 'fugitive's campfire', as small and smokeless as possible, revived my strength more profoundly than could a second helping of wet rice!

Eloi and I crawled into the mozzy-net and I gave the Cockerel the fly-sheet to wrap himself in. Several times during the surprising chill of the night I was woken by the croak of hundreds of frogs in the creek. It was a fine clear morning when I awoke once and for all to the clatter of a billy can being dragged through the undergrowth. A smoky fire – with which the Cockerel had obviously tried to defend himself from the aerial barrage of mosquitoes – sent wisps of blue cloud up into the tangled canopy.

Our little guide estimated we had a gentle three-hour stroll down the winding cliff-side track to the river, then along the flat valley bottom to the town. I decided that, since I would hardly have time to break into a sweat, I might as well put on a fresh change of clothes for this final stint. I was already celebrating our successful crossing of the Zone Rouge and was looking forward to arriving in Ankavandra where I could feast on cold Three Horses beer and whatever solace I could find to ease my tormented sweet tooth. I was also congratulating myself that I had resisted the temptation to hire the Cockerel as a porter and so deprive myself of some of the sweetness of the achievement. Nevertheless, I did wish that he had at some time had cause to lift my pack, so that he could imagine what those twenty-five kilos felt like over such a trek.

At either end of the day the light in Madagascar is incredibly clear and bright. Colours leap out to hit you. Back on the hillside the tall stands of vero were shimmering with the vibrant green that you usually associate only with young rice plants and the sky covered us in a neon-blue dome.

We kept up a steady progress northwards for two hours, expecting Ankavandra to come into view at any moment. The occasional cigarette butt and sweet wrapper by the trail were signs that 'civilisation' was just around the corner. After four hours these were *still* the only signs that we were approaching the town. Then we came to an army patrol post of two mud huts and a concrete guardroom. Here a solitary soldier laboriously copied my passport details into a tattered exercise book. Other vazaha had been through within the last year, he said, but they had all come from the south. He had never heard of a vazaha crossing the Zone Rouge from the east. The old Merina garrison who had once guarded this outermost portion of Ranavalona's kingdom – 'too weak to fight, and too confirmed in their squatting to run away' – might have had greater cause to remember the Reverend and Mr S. riding along this trail on their palanquins with 'the two-and-thirty', their bearers.

The trail swept onwards over the Bungolava ridges and, if it weren't for the cigarette butts, it would have been easy to imagine that there was not a town within a hundred kilometres. By the six-hour mark my blisters had swollen and burst and swollen again so that I was trying to walk on the sides of my feet. My morale was at an all-time low and I was cursing the Cockerel under my breath: 'If you hadn't told me *three* hours – "jus' *three* hours" – "easy, all downhill"'.

Every danga-matted hill that rose up in front of us promised to be the last. Yet beyond it was another, and another and still another. Seven and a half hours into that bitter three-hour stroll we sat for a rest under a solitary sun-bleached tree. Nothing moved on the blistering hillside but a fifteen-centimetre collared lizard that flickered over a pilgrim's cairn.

I made a grumbling and slightly hysterical note in my diary:

> You can psych yourself up for a three-hour march – No problem! A six-hour march? – Well, that's okay too. Another full day? – Okay, if you have to, you have to. It's just a little more pain at the end of what was already a long trek. But when your easy three-hour downhill stroll runs to six, seven, eight – each of those hills, beyond that three-hour mark, becomes an increasing torment.
>
> Sometimes I think I travel through reasonable difficulties – not incredible difficulties, but certainly reasonable ones – just to remind myself how to appreciate simple everyday pleasures like a nice cold coke and something to eat at the end of the trail ... Something different from rice ... or even rice with plenty of sauce ... or something.

After a while it began to seem literally impossible that there could be another ridge behind the one we were hauling ourselves up, but there always was. Eloi spotted a plane that he said was taking off from the dirt track runway at Ankavandra, but it was a long way off. I prayed fervently that he was wrong.

Looking ahead I swore that this steep slope must the last ... Wrong!

But surely only Ankavandra itself could lie over this crest ... Wrong again!

And so it continued, until ten hours after leaving the camp in the thicket we saw the tin roofs of the town! The climb down the Bungolava cliffs was slow; it was steep, dangerous and the rocks were baked so hot that they were untouchable. By now I knew that I was seriously run-down: the soles of my feet were a mass of white bubbles, both ankles were poisoned and I was almost entirely deaf in my left ear (a common symptom of exhaustion). I didn't realise that, on top of all this, I was carrying a dose of Amber Mountain malaria. It would take a few days rest before I could get going again.

Lalisy Louisette ran her kitchen and three rented rooms, under the name of Hôtely Fihaonana (Hôtel Rendezvous), with the generosity of a mother caring for her vast and transient family. She was a voluptuous and delightful *métisse* who – despite the contradictory evidence of her gargantuan proportions – claimed to be descended from the Vazimba.

'But some people say that the Vazimba are very small and hairy with sharp nails,' I said one day, leering meaningfully at Lalisy's monumental curves.

She roared with laughter and slapped me on the back with enough power to knock the wind from my lungs:

'Aah ha ha! You too funny vazaha. Befo', one hundred years befo' they were like that. They changed!'

'How changed?' I croaked, still reeling from the blow.

'They mix. Mix with other people. You can look for tiny ol'-time tombs down the river but Vazimba's not so small today. Eh?' She winked and began to roar with infectious laughter again.

Eloi and I rented a twin room in a compound at the back of the hôtely and the Cockerel bedded down on a sleeping-mat in a storeroom behind the kitchen. I punctured the awful pads of my blistered feet and strung them through with little lengths of cotton thread that would help them to drain and dry, and dug the danga spines out of poisonous ankle chains strung with yellow sores.

At a long timber table Lalisy served her guests (and whoever else happened to be around) with vast platefuls of fried chicken, beef, rice, green papaya with garlic, rice, custard apples, rice-cakes, yoghurt, rice, hot zebu milk, little smoky bamboo grubs known as *sokondro* … and rice. As she served she roared with a laughter that made mealtimes a delight and her big bosoms rolled around on the table as she watched the vazaha try his first plate of sokondro.

At this time of year Ankavandra was still totally inaccessible to any form of transport other than the weekly bush-hopper and any imported goods were prohibitively expensive. Main Street consisted only of two bars and three Indian-owned general stores, one of which doubled as the Air Mad office. The coke that I had craved so deeply was in short supply and on our arrival Eloi, the Cockerel and I had drunk six of the small warm bottles between us. It was the Cockerel's first taste of coke. There now remained one single bottle of coke in the whole town. One small, lonely bottle sat on a shelf in one of the two Main Street bars and the barman absolutely refused to sell it to me.

'There is no coke,' he shrugged. 'We have no more coke.'

We stood together and looked at that single, forlorn little bottle on the otherwise empty shelf. I came to the conclusion that this last bottle of coke had become a status symbol. This was now the only bar in Ankavandra that could honestly boast 'we stock Coca Cola', even if there was only one bottle and it wasn't for sale!

I asked Eloi if he wanted to take a flight home to Tsiro but he decided that he would prefer to complete the trek with me, right across to Antsalova on the other side of the Bemaraha Plateau, and catch a plane from there. I was delighted because although he was educated and westernised he had proved that he was totally unabashed about sharing his beliefs and 'superstitions' with me. I could make my way in French but I was aware that if I were to collect all my material from people who were also speaking the language as badly as I was there was a *double-chance* that I might often get hold of the wrong end of the bâton.

I paid rent and food for the Cockerel for three days and then loaded him with coffee, rice, sugar and condensed milk for Mme Laza and our friends in Soa Tana. I had paid Eloi up to date and he bought our little friend a present of a pair of plastic shoes for the return journey. The Cockerel was so delighted with these shoes that, when he shyly shook hands at the hôtely and wandered away to tackle that awesome vertical climb back onto the ridge, I noticed that he had them securely wrapped up in his plastic bag.

CHAPTER 4

LAND OF THE FIGHTING SAKALAVA

> He is limbed like a young Hercules, and dressed like
> a noble savage ... Gun and spear are almost as much
> part of himself as teeth and nails.
>
> – Rev. William Clayton Pickersgill

A small-town wide boy – *un petit coq du village* – had been try-ing to convince me that I'd need a local guide *('Moi, par exem-ple')* to lead us up the pass onto the Bemaraha plateau. Apart from the dollar signs flickering across his eyes I saw little indication of any genuine interest in the trek or even real confidence in his own abilities. I decided instead to place all my faith in my GPS and a 1967 Operational Navigation Chart, revised (but to what extent?) in 1989. In many remote parts of the world these are still the best maps available; but I had set off before to trek through remote country to villages that no longer existed or to a mountain that was 100 kilometres deeper into the jungle than the chart showed.

Fortified by Lalisy's rice-cakes and black coffee, Eloi and I hauled on our packs once more. We strode down to the Manambolo River just as the first hints of dawn were showing above the Bungolava ridge at our backs. Eloi had arranged for some kids to ferry us across the hundred-metre stretch of rushing water, although I was doubtful that anyone would actually be around at this ungodly hour. But when we arrived on the muddy bank a zebu charet, fitted with a huge water butt, was already being backed into a current that threatened to carry the whole rig downstream, animals and all. The water vendor would try to make as many trips as possible between the river and the town before the sun became too fierce.

Our two young ferrymen were already sitting patiently in a huge dugout that had been hewn from a single ancient tree. They fought valiantly as the canoe slewed sideways against the powerful tug of the river, to paddle us across and hold the boat against the bank while we clambered out. We turned our backs on the mighty Manambolo and started towards the cliffs that were still just a paling blue line in the distance. We had eaten and rested well at Lalisy's; my feet were comfortable, our clothes were clean and we were happy to be moving again.

We covered a lot of ground that morning through scrubby desert, but when we stopped for lunch the western ridge still did not appear to be any closer. We would be crossing the forty-five kilometre breadth of the Manambolo valley until we arrived at the Bemaraha cliff-face the next afternoon.

For a while we followed a strange old man who was dressed in blue nylon football shorts, a neat linen shirt, pink plastic sandals, *two* hats (one propped on top of the other) and carried an umbrella. He seemed to know the quickest way across a section of patchy swamp that we were struggling through and we hustled to keep up with him. I left my boots hung around my neck and hobbled across the short spaces of dry land between the waterlogged sections. The old man posed for a photograph, doffed his hats, then shot off into the wilderness like a Malagasy version of Carlos Castaneda's Don Juan.

When I put my boots back on I suppose it should not have surprised me to see that the sun-heated rocks had so quickly raised the blisters on both my feet again! The country here was networked with animal trails leading between watering holes, but we didn't spot another human footprint for the rest of the day to reassure us that we were on course. My GPS was limited to pointing a straight line directly towards the village of Tsiandro, but in the darkening shadows of the still distant cliffs there was no sign of the steep pass that would give us access to the Bemaraha Plateau.

Tsiandro has, with a certain poetic licence, been dubbed 'The Village Where Time Stands Still', though the name translates more literally as 'There is No Time'. Locally this name is attributed to a

Sakalava king who had arranged to meet an enemy there to do battle. The enemy, perhaps wisely, was otherwise engaged and the disappointed king named the area Tsiandro: 'This is Not the Day'.

In Ankavandra we had been told that it was possible to get to Tsiandro in a single day but, for us too, it was clear that this was not the day. We contented ourselves with pitching camp in a beautiful creek-side clearing. We found a pool that was deep enough for swimming and let the campfire smoke waft over us as protection from mosquitoes while we ate our noodles and paté.

We climbed a hill the next morning to get our bearings and saw a lone cowboy. He was driving six zebu across our path but he ran away, leaving us alone again in the vastness of the valley. We kept following the arrow of my GPS westwards and after a couple of hours saw two hunters on a low hillside to our left. We watched for a while to check that there were no more and then went cautiously towards them.

After hauling away their loathsome curs (my respect for hunting-dogs as judges of character had diminished by now) the men accepted some lukewarm coffee from my metal water-bottle. A village that according to my map should be only a few miles further on had apparently been abandoned more than fifteen years ago! The hunters directed us instead to follow the edge of a deep ravine until we saw the mango trees that surrounded another village, called Manitsy, about four hours distant. From there we could climb onto the plateau and make Tsiandro in half a day; thus the hunters gave lie to the oft-reported belief that it was possible to walk from Ankavandra to Tsiandro in a single day.

The danga here was more mature and almost gushed with sticky resin, so that our hands were constantly covered with 'glue' from plucking off bunches of sharp spines. If we tried to grit our teeth and ignore the stabbing pain in our ankles, the seeds would work their way into our skin with such speed that it was hard to imagine they didn't possess a diabolical intent of their own. The malicious splinters must have contained some sort of poison because, within minutes, an ignored seed could become a swollen, yellow pustule.

There were occasional flat 'sandy' areas that looked like they should provide easy footing. But this, we had already discovered, was sinking sand. I had walked confidently onto this deceptively dry, dusty surface and was already several strides onto it before it cracked. My right leg sank, halfway up my thigh, into sticky mud and still I had the horrifying impression that there was nothing of substance under my boot! It was easy to imagine that a person could disappear in a moment into that sandy paste. We skirted it warily from there on.

The countryside levelled out as we approached the region called Beramabom – 'Above the Swamps' – and we began to see the square stone blocks of Sakalava tombs on distant hillsides. Although there was no village within miles we didn't risk causing offence by going close to the tombs and I noticed that when Eloi pointed at them he invariably did so with his whole hand, his fingers directed at the ground.

These tombs were built in a way, divined by the mpanandro, that would maintain mutually respectful relationships between the communities of the living and the temperamental and all-powerful communities of the dead. The Malagasy say that 'a house is for a lifetime but a tomb is forever', and in some areas eighty per cent of income is still spent on the dead. These tombs had clearly been built with eternity in mind, whereas the ramshackle wattle-and-daub dwellings of the villages, built for this fleeting mortal sojourn, had long ago crumbled and disappeared.

The Sakalava, perhaps with the outlook of a warrior tribe who had no shortage of enemies, were always on guard for signs of evil destiny. A child who was born on an inauspicious day might nevertheless grow to be ten or twelve before the mpanandro had decided his fate. If they then decided that he was a danger and a curse to the village then the most awful of death sentences might be pronounced. He would be buried alive with only his head sticking out of the ground and left to die, at the mercy of the sun and wild animals. In the area through which we were walking it was said that, even a century ago, cowboys and hunters would sometimes hear the cries of these wretched children for two days before weakness and then death silenced them.

About midday we spotted a clump of bottle-green mango trees and the bleached-grey of a few palm roofs. Manitsy was almost deserted; the mangoes were not in season and there was little reason to stop. Almost everybody was out in the paddies, but a young man in an indigo lamba and a huge straw hat offered to guide us to the next village. Benôit, as he was called, offered us some strange fruits that looked outwardly like a dusty kiwifruit. Eloi had never seen them before and Benôit showed us how to slice them into thin biscuit-like discs. They tasted exactly like digestive biscuits (to someone who had been in Madagascar for the last two months) but all thought of 'a biscuit tree harvest' was promptly quashed by Benôit's complicated description of the three-day drying process.

In his enthusiasm to prove himself a competent guide Benôit rushed us out of Manitsy and across the wilderness at breakneck speed. We crashed headlong through walls of blinding vero grass, hopped cursing across hills of danga, and tore our boots off periodically for splashing stream crossings, until three hours later we stumbled knee-deep into a muddy paddy field.

The headman of Bekignana greeted us with typical, cheerful composure and asked us for 'the news' as we munched our way through a whole heap of sweet bananas. We sat in the shade of a hut, while five handsome young Sakalava ladies, with lambas tucked around them like towels, wove hats from palm leaves for their menfolk in the paddies.

After returning from a hunting trip to find the righteous Mr S. enjoying just such 'picturesque' company, Pickersgill wrote:

> The spreading waves of crinoline have not yet come upon the squaws of the roving Sakalava. Let me be careful on this occasion to guard my hale old friend from all suspicion of being a participator in these wanton pleasures

[speaking of the hunting] He was otherwise occupied. And now I'll be revenged on him for not taking more interest in the sport. This is where and how I found him: He was comfortably seated beneath a shady tree near a Sakalava village, eating his dinner in the focus of an admiring semicircle of highly-ornamented women-folk, who seemed quite fascinated by the cheerful spectacle, for when I happened to sit down so as to shut out their view, they immediately shifted to another post of observation, from which they could gaze as before. The object of their undisguised admiration now responded by giving them each a biscuit ... Of course I was naturally led to be similarly gallant and added a little jam; and our servants said: 'Eat ladies.' Such is the force of example.

We asked the headman and the ladies about the Vazimba but they only remembered some vague and disjointed story about a Vazimba king who had travelled across the valley from the east with his sister. Eloi translated that there had been an argument about 'something or other' and their paths had split to 'different places'. More than this, nobody could say.

Unfortunately the smallest banknote that I now had in my possession was 25,000 FMg (almost US$6); there was nothing in Bekignana for sale for such a large sum and no change to be had anywhere. Thus one note covered Benôit's pay (he would collect later when change was finally made), twenty bananas, seven cups of rice and a hen. The latter was summarily boiled by the headman's wife and brought to us with the good news that the corpse had contained six half-formed eggs – apparently this was a good omen in Bekignana. According to local tradition we ate some of the chicken and rice and then returned the drumsticks – the choice pieces – as a token of gratitude to the headman. But strangely, despite the bird being cooked in his house, the old man had to refuse: chicken was fady for him!

The guest hut was newly built and appeared to be very clean, yet it was more heavily infested with cockroaches than any of the much dirtier huts in which I'd stayed. I considered that this might be because the zebu dung walls had not yet fully hardened and the whole structure was still no more than a monstrous, but carefully moulded, cowpat. Since visitors were rare the hut was used for storage: baskets of rice were stacked in the corners and corncobs hung from the ceiling in thick rustling bunches.

A constant parade of rats trotted up and down the rafters to feast on the corn. I remembered reading a report that claimed that the proximity in which rural Malagasy live with rats could, even today, lead to a full-blown epidemic of bubonic plague in western Madagascar. 'Black Death', the disease that wiped out a quarter of the population of Europe in the Middle Ages, is still a very real danger in the mid-west. It arrived as a parasite in the fleas of black rats at the end of the 1800s but didn't penetrate into the interior and the capital until the Diego-Tana-Tamatave railway began running in 1920. Now it seems that the Black Death is on the increase. Numbers of fatalities have doubled in recent years and in 1996 L'Institut Pasteur de Madagascar reported 1,629 suspected cases of this highly infectious disease. When the Zone Rouge villagers bring their rice supplies inside for security the rats come with them; and when they burn the land, as they do every year, more rats take refuge in the village in growing numbers.

Black rats can give birth to 400 offspring a year and the only way to fight the plague is a simultaneous campaign against the rats *and* the fleas. If you kill the rats the parasite immediately deserts the body to go in search of a new host … and if there are insufficient rodents they will happily move onto a human. Luckily there was no shortage of rodent hosts in our giant cowpat and our greatest problem was trying to sleep in the hailstorm of corn kernels that rained down from the rafters all night.

I had dug the danga thorns out of my ankles with the point of a penknife and covered the wounds with antiseptic cream. But by the next morning, my right foot in particular was swollen to the point where I had difficulty forcing it into my boot. The skin was peeling where the circulating blood had been poisoned and I could feel the infected nerve all the way up to my groin.

'It looks like a dead man's foot,' I said to Eloi, laughing. Little did I realise that long after I left Madagascar I would still be carrying around a calcified lump on the front of my leg as a permanent reminder of the danga poisoning. Eloi – who suffered from the first stab as the thorns entered the skin but was never infected – suggested staying in Bekignana for another day. But I decided that it would be better to press onward up onto the plateau and take the 'rest period' in Tsiandro.

Realising that it was going to be a difficult day I swallowed my pride (along with some antibiotics and a couple of codeine painkillers) and hired a happy-go-lucky kid called Eugene to carry my pack up the cliff. Thus I waded with Eugene and Eloi back into the paddy fields, encumbered only with a photographer's waistcoat, cameras, boots hung around my neck and one bulbous right foot, so tender that even the touch of a rice plant root could be excruciatingly painful.

After two creeks I pulled my boots on, fearful that if I didn't confine the swelling now it would soon be impossible to do so. Eugene and Eloi chatted happily in Malagasy and I luxuriated in the freedom to stop and take photographs whenever I chose before hobbling back to catch up with 'the caravan'. After two hours we climbed down to the densely forested banks of a rocky river. Our trail led us towards the highlands in a stone-hopping obstacle course, occasionally leading us in and out of thickets and over and under rotting logs. Big trees obviously collapsed regularly on the steep slopes, so that this valley, though never cleared by humans, was to all intents and purposes a tangle of secondary jungle.

There were many snakes here and I caught a whip-like grass snake by the tail as it slithered into the undergrowth. Taking shameful advantage of my (reasonable) confidence that a venomous Malagasy snake should have made itself known to science by now, if any existed, I picked this individual up for a closer look. When, at the insistence of my gentle tugging, its head finally appeared, at the end of a metre-long body, I was surprised to see the hind legs of a frog kicking feebly from between its jaws. Now I was struck by a dilemma: should I play God and liberate the frog or should I allow the snake at least to keep its dinner? I liberated the frog, which hopped unsteadily away without even a grateful glance, and left the snake to follow it if it so desired.

On a pebble beach Eugene stopped and pointed to the tops of the highest trees soaring above the valley walls. There, lounging comfortably in the forked branches, was a group of magnificent, fleecy-white lemurs. They were Decken's sifaka and looked strangely human staring haughtily down at us, with their black faces and snowy fur coats. One of them was a young animal displaying a magnificently thick tail, longer than his body, and I estimated that of the three adults none could have weighed less than four kilograms. These animals are rarely seen and very little is known about them other than their habit of insulting ground dwelling predators with cries of: 'Shi-fahk! Shi-fahk!'

Apparently they did not consider us a threat worthy of such abuse. We stayed to watch them sunbathe until Eloi translated Eugene's wistful comment: 'Good meat'.

I decided to remove them from his hungry stare. Obviously sifaka were not fady for Eugene.

In his twenty years of study and travel Jørgen Ruud reported as many stories of wanton cruelty to lemurs as he did of protection through fadys. Being skinned, sprinkled with cayenne pepper and roasted alive seems, strangely, to have been an all too common occurrence. Malagasy people find a sadistic pleasure in torturing animals, Ruud concluded, they have no feeling of remorse until some curse befalls them as a result of their cruelty: 'Then they become frightened, and a new taboo is made'.

The indri, a huge black-and-white teddy bear of a lemur that bears a single young every three years, is happily protected by a fady that its now extinct larger cousins were never blessed with. Long, long ago, so the legend goes, a man called Koto and his son left their village to collect honey in the forest. They were gone for so long that their fellow villagers went to look for them. After they had been searching for a long time the rescue party became aware that two big indri were watching them from the treetops. Naturally they concluded that this was in fact Koto and his son who had been transformed into indri by some magic spell. From that day on the indri became a fady animal known locally as *Babakoto* – Papa Koto.

The vegetation thinned and the river got narrower and steeper with every curve. Soon we had stepped out of the tree cover altogether and were back in the eye of that fiery African furnace. Two rosy clumps of rock about six hundred metres above us guarded the gateway onto the plateau ... and it was now that Eugene decided to rebel. Having carried my pack up the relatively flat lower valley he now baulked at making an attempt on that cliff-face with a twenty-kilogram pack (without photographic gear).

I could fully relate to the 'deed of violence' to which William Clayton Pickersgill confessed on Saturday, 19 June 1875, after being similarly abused by just such a tyke as Eugene:

> And now let me come to confession, by way of preparing for the Sabbath. I had a great row this morning with one of Mr S.'s bearers who happened to come into the house whilst some of my own were asking whether we intended going on to-day or staying over tomorrow. On hearing me answer that possibly we might choose to start after dinner, and that all had better be prepared, he squatted himself down uninvited, and impudently replied to the effect that Mr S. and I could go on if we pleased, but that all the men would stay behind. Whereupon he was bidden at once to take himself and his impertinence out of the place, which he refused to do. In two seconds more he was tumbled out, head-first; and that's my humble confession. Certainly it was either a deed of violence, or a healthy exercise of muscular Christianity that I indulged in.

Looking up that treacherously winding trail, I couldn't pretend that Eugene's reluctance was wholly without reason and resisted the temptation to tumble him headfirst back down the river. But, somehow, both my pack *and* myself had to get up there. With

Eugene sticking unshakeably to his mutiny (even in the face of a reluctant wage increase) it fell upon me to shoulder *his* responsibilities … and *my* pack.

Cursing under my breath I followed the now fleet-footed Eugene and the trudging Eloi towards the craggy rock face. The path wound upwards in such steep, narrow switchbacks that our fingers were soon blistered from hauling on the sun-scorched rocks, but we quickly raised a stunning horizon back across the Manambolo Valley. The Bungolavas – more viciously jagged than the massive Bemaraha tabletop – now appeared as a blue smudge through the vapour that rose from the river.

Often we had to edge fearfully around tree trunks that encroached on the narrow trail, seemingly suspended over a vertical drop of fifty metres. In the end, it took less than an hour to reach the cliff-top, where Eugene offered to take the pack again! I didn't have Pickersgill's experience in handling 'bearers' (nor his flair for discipline) so I rebuffed 'the tyke' grimly and limped onwards with what I imagined was stubborn bulldog tenacity. We stopped briefly at a spring where someone had left half a coconut as a cup and Eloi tried to reconcile our 'bearer' problems – but I staggered onwards with mulish stubbornness.

Not far from the edge of the cliff we passed through an enchanting collection of smooth rock formations. Bizarre moulded shapes were arranged singly or in picturesque still-life groups across the grass. The illusion that these 'sculptures', some four metres high, had been 'arranged' by some divine hand was all the more powerful because of their vivid gunmetal colour. I thought they could never have been thrust from the dusty red earth on which they lay. We left the 'gallery' as suddenly as we had entered it and thereafter not a single blue sculpture was to be seen amongst the windswept danga.

Here and there we cut around an oasis with a shallow pool and a thick clump of palm trees. For a full half-hour we walked through a burgeoning locust swarm that would have disastrous implications if it left this savannah for the Tsiandro rice paddies. The vero grass seemed not to be any different on this patch than it had been elsewhere and it was easy to believe that the three-centimetre-long black grasshoppers were merely congregating – ten to a stem – for company.

Quicker than expected we emerged onto a rock shelf and the village of Tsiandro lay spread out before us, nestling neatly in its patchwork of paddies. The tiny, almost Lilliputian, huts lay clustered in little groups near the shade of ballooning mango trees. Eugene shrugged off my pack (okay, so my 'bulldog mulishness' had finally cracked). I paid him what we had agreed in Bekignana and resisted the temptation to slip him a bonus. It's always a humbling experience to hire a guide for what I consider to be a full day's trek only to see him turn around at the end of it to walk back home.

With his western education and outlook, Monsieur Gaston knew that it was not considered bad form to show his surprise as two hot, sweaty backpackers limped towards him surrounded by a growing army of kids:

'*Nom d'un chien!* Where the devil did you come from?'

Gaston was in his mid-twenties, fresh-faced but capable looking. He was trained as a *technicien forestier* and spoke excellent French. He was also officially the head of the Project Bemaraha office in Tsiandro and, by proxy, the district délégué.

It was fitting, considering the island's wealth of unique flora and fauna, that Madagascar was one of the first countries in the world to establish a national system of nature reserves, in 1927. There are now over fifty reserves (only a few of which are accessible to tourists) covering twelve per cent of the island's uninhabited land. But in many cases their inaccessibility and a shortage of staff means that there is little to back these figures up. Réserve des Tsingy de Bemaraha, stretching north to south over 150,000 hectares of largely inaccessible wilderness, is the largest tract of 'protected' land in Madagascar.

The Tsingy reserve is listed as home to six species of lemur (including the rare Decken's sifaka, which had already blessed us with a sighting) and over fifty-five species of birds. Nobody knows what wonders might still exist in the largely unexplored rainforests and the impenetrable regions of towering limestone needles.

The towering tsingy rock formations make a monstrous pincushion out of much of the southern half of the reserve. Some claim the name comes from the ringing sound that the narrow bacon-slicer formations make when struck. But Eloi explained that it really derives from *tsingy-tsingy*, the Malagasy word for tiptoe: the needles often lie so close together that there is not space at their base to lay your foot flat.

The few vazaha who come to the park enter with the help of tour companies through the village of Bekopaka, far down the Manambolo River. Scientists occasionally visit the more isolated north-western section near the town of Antsalova but rough trekking or, season permitting, even rougher travel by zebu charet keeps numbers to a minimum.

Gaston summed it up nicely: 'You'd better have a drink!'

He led us into a concrete shed which a rickety trestle table and collection of well-thumbed wall maps identified as a Project Bemaraha 'boardroom'.

'*Everything* that arrives in Tsiandro from the outside world has to be carried here on a man's back for at least two days,' he said. No wonder the Three Horses *grand modèles* that had just been rustled up were among the most expensive that I'd yet bought in Madagascar. Not for the last time did the high price of 'imported goods' conjure up a picturesque image to accompany the Malagasy word *mandoa*, which can mean both 'to pay' and 'to vomit'.

'This tin roof,' said Gaston, drawing my attention to the sheets of corrugated steel, ' was carried here by fourteen men. Anybody who has a reason to go "back to the world" will always return with the things that people are running short of here.

'The two stores in Tsiandro operate on a barter system and rarely handle money. The recognised currency here is a kapoka measure of rice – a Lucky Cow milk tin-full. For instance' – and he rattled some words of Malagasy at the crowd of children blocking the doorway – 'at current exchange rate, one kapoka of sugar equals five of rice, and a *grand modèle* THB equals ten kapoka of rice!'

Thus the exchange rate was loosely based upon the equation that a man could carry one hundred kapoka of rice or ten litre-bottles of beer over a two-day trek. But prices could fluctuate almost weekly, depending upon supply and demand.

'Last year, after the locusts came, the price of rice almost doubled and the people were forced to live on cassava leaves. In the early morning the children went out to collect the locusts. In a couple of hours – before the dew had dried off their wings so that they could fly – it was possible to collect six five-gallon cans of the insects … but nobody could afford the oil to fry them.'

An economical alternative to THB turned out to be Tsiandro's sugarcane rum. Until recently the villagers used to make sugar but now they trade their rice for sugar and devote their own sugarcane harvest to the production of rum. So, as Gaston expounded on the difficulties of policing such a huge tract of wilderness, we transferred our allegiance to the local firewater.

'It's very difficult to stop either the farmers or the Dahalo from driving their zebu across the reserve,' he said. 'The Dahalo are very powerful here. If a cattleman wants to sell some animals he needs to hire men to drive them to Tsiroanomandidy – over two weeks away. The cowboys try to avoid the Dahalo but they might have to fight so they're expensive to hire. They are paid from the profit but when they return home it's expected that the cattleman will set aside a certain amount for *le dépenser ceremonial* – to celebrate the happy termination of the expedition.' Gaston raised his glass with a smile.

'So the Dahalo are still a problem here?' I asked.

'*Mais oui! Un grand problème!* Some of the surrounding villages refuse to send their children to school because of the danger of walking through the countryside.' He rose abruptly: 'Follow me'. The children scattered as he led us around to the side of the boardroom.

A slab of rock, like an oversized tombstone, had been painted in yellow with the words:

MAHERY
Fun I
BEMARAHA
– RAZAFIMAHATRATRA ALFRED
– RASOLOARIMANANA ETIENNE
Maty tamin 'ny
03–01–95

Eloi translated: 'Heroes of Bemaraha, Alfred Razafimahatratra and Etienne Rasoloarimanana, died on third of January 1995'.

'The Dahalo blew their whistles at dawn,' Gaston began. 'There were twenty-one of them. My predecessor, Severin Rasabotsy, ran out of his hut and a Dahalo spear shot past his thigh. Severin killed the Dahalo with the Dahalo's own spear. Luckily these bandits only had two guns between them, but they shot Alfred Razafimahatratra before they were driven back out of Tsiandro and into the forest. The villagers sent a runner to another village to get them to attack the Dahalo from the rear. Then they chased the Dahalo into the forest where Etienne was shot.'

'What did they want from Tsiandro?' I asked.

'It seems that they had inside information. A young cattleman, who is now a prominent politician, was staying here. The Dahalo went straight to the house where he was, to rob and kill him, or to take him as a slave, nobody knows, but they didn't get him. In 1997 this monument was erected to honour the two villagers who died defending Tsiandro. In the same year Alfred Razafimahatratra's Betsileo family arrived to carry his bones home to the family tomb.'

Although the Betsileo are the most widely travelled of Madagascar's tribes, they maintain a deep-rooted horror of dying away from home. If a relative who has been buried in a distant land appears in a dream, it is taken as an unmistakable sign that his spirit is restless and feels abandoned. Speedy arrangements must be made to bring him back to the ancestral tomb as soon as possible, and at any cost. There are endless sagas of loyal Betsileo trekking for weeks on end carrying suitcases containing the remains of wayward loved ones.

Gaston was a Tsimihety from the north – 'a vazaha' like myself, he said – but most of Tsiandro was Sakalava. There was also a large minority of Betsileo and a few Bara but 'nobody had claimed to be a Vazimba for a great many years'.

We settled into a simple room among the flame trees in the Project Bemaraha compound and stayed for several peaceful days in Tsiandro, while I picked Gaston's brains shamelessly for whatever he could tell me about the region.

'I think that the Vazimba in this area have long ago been integrated into the Sakalava peoples,' he said one evening as we tucked into a hearty meal of rice, fried duck (*duk-duk* in Sakalava!) and shredded papaya at the boardroom table. 'But there are many kalanoro in the countryside here. I myself, have seen one.'

'You *saw* a kalanoro?' I asked, choking on a piece of duk-duk. 'What did he look like?'

'He was like a little man, less than a metre tall, with long hair all over his body and long fingernails.'

In 1924, Chase Salmon Osborn reported on the kalanoro:

> ... a kind of wild men of the woods, who are represented as very short, covered with hair, men with flowing beard and both sexes almost fire worshippers ... I was told of an eye-witness to an occurrence that is in common report. When spending a night in the heart of a deep forest he was awake, watching the fire that had burned to a bed of glowing coals, when suddenly one of the wild men appeared without a stitch of clothing, sat down by the fire, rubbed his hands together in a manner of enjoyment and seemed perfectly happy. The brave but inhospitable Betsimisáraka [an east coast tribe] grasped a stick, dug into the coals and sent the hot embers in a shower over the naked visitor, who ran precipitately, uttering frightful shrieks. Another tale has it that in the middle of a black night campers were disturbed by the appearance of a naked man who looked around and, finding some rice left

in a cooking pot, went away and presently returned with
a nude woman. It must have been a honeymoon couple,
the natives say, because they caressed, made love and fed
each other with their hands, and appeared to communicate by grimaces. When they were interrupted they ran
away into the jungle.

I remembered Mlle Josephine's father's meeting on Montagne
d'Ambre with what she described as a small, hairy Vazimba 'with
long, dirty fingernails'.

'In the north,' I began, 'they said that Vazimba were little hairy
men who like to eat the burnt crust around the edge of rice pots ...'

'Everybody likes to eat the burnt crust,' said Eloi, helping himself to a second plateful. 'But you're talking about kalanoro, not
Vazimba. Kalanoro is animal, Vazimba is human. You can never
catch a kalanoro because they know what you're thinking ...'

'They're telepathic then, like Vazimba?'

'Yes, and also it's said that their feet point backwards so
hunters always track them in the wrong direction!' Gaston
laughed. 'But if you fry pistachio nuts they find the smell irresistible and you can see them easily.'

But according to a report by L. H. Ransome in the 1889
Proceedings of the Royal Geographical Society, a kalanoro *was*
caught ten years earlier in the forests of the northeast. An eyewit-
ness described the 'wild man' as:

> ... a powerfully built man of about five feet nine inches
> in height, his face and body being thickly covered with
> long black hair; his mode of walking was peculiar, as he
> travelled very fast, with his head down, occasionally
> going on all-fours, his eyes (which resembled in expres-
> sion those of an animal rather than of a human being)
> invariably being fixed on the ground.

The kalanoro was apparently caught:

> ... while asleep on the branch of a tree, and when taken
> resisted violently, biting his captors severely; after a few

days confinement, however, he ceased to be aggressive ...
When caught he was perfectly nude, but wore clothes
when provided with them. He could never be induced to
eat flesh or any kind of cooked food, subsisting entirely on
manioc and other roots; nor would he sleep in a recumbent
position, but when resting preferred to squat on hands and
feet on a stool in a corner of the house. After some weeks
he commenced to learn a few words, and by means of
these and signs it was understood that he had a father and
two brothers in the forest where he was taken. These were
found and surrounded by a search party one night, but
being disturbed, easily eluded their pursuers, jumping
from tree to tree like monkeys and running on all-fours.
The captured man died five months after being taken.

'For example ... I saw one of these animals in Analavory, near
Tana,' Eloi said. 'The people there, they're scared of kalanoro
and they wear charms to protect themselves!'

These two educated, westernised Malagasy chuckled at the
naivety of the simple country people, displaying a disarming confidence in their own knowledge of the characteristics of this hairy,
pistachio-craving dwarf with backward-pointing feet!

'Kalanoro isn't dangerous,' Gaston confirmed. 'In fact sometimes they help people who look after them.'

Later, in Tana, another Malagasy friend explained: 'Kalanoro
can help you. If you capture one or find one and treat it well, it
can get you anything you want – cars, motorbikes, money, girls
...' His speech faded with a wistfulness that I feared had put an
end to the story before it began. 'Near the house of my parents,
here in Tana, there lived a powerful man. He was a politician and
a close friend of President Ratsiraka. Everybody in the neigh-
bourhood knew he had a kalanoro. We knew this because one day
he had the big security wall and gates outside his house all painted
black. Inside, the house was green but he painted black all around
the walls, in every room, up to a height of one metre.

'Black is the favourite colour of the kalanoro and, when it went
out to get him money or power or girls, the politician wanted to
be sure that the animal would always be happy to come home.

This is why he painted his house black up to kalanoro-height and left it green above for himself!'

Despite these magical powers I found it strange that a kalanoro was still invariably referred to 'merely as an animal' (never promoted to the ranks of a spirit, a mpanandro or even a human), until it dawned on me how many weird and wonderful creatures are already known to exist in Madagascar. The aye-aye – with a beaver's teeth that never stop growing, a fox's tail, huge ultra-mobile bat's ears and a long, almost skeletal, third finger – was so strange that for a long time zoologists considered it to be one of the more imaginative (and less believable) Malagasy myths. It took them a hundred years just to come to the conclusion that the aye-aye is a lemur. Its evolution has finetuned it to fill the niche that woodpeckers occupy in other places, but in many Malagasy villages it is still killed on sight as a harbinger of death. Fosa, snakes, crocodiles, chameleons and lemurs have been attributed powers far beyond the already impressive ones that are acknowledged by science – yet nobody ever disputed that they were 'merely animals'.

Since the aye-aye is not found in western Madagascar neither Eloi nor Gaston felt qualified to explain its nature. This again seemed to emphasise the honesty with which they had spoken about the more 'familiar' kalanoro. Although I was amazed by their claims to have seen these creatures first-hand, I struggled to show only the same objective interest that I would have used in listening to reports of a sighting of the 'rare' Decken's sifaka or the 'fabled' wild cattle of Bungolava.

The songaomby, which Eloi had described as being like a fat bull with no horns that swishes its tail from side to side when peeing, has been interpreted by some experts as proof of the continuing existence of a pygmy hippo which is otherwise believed to have become extinct since human arrival on the island. Although hippos have never been known to 'eat people', they do kill more humans than any other African animal, often with an errant swipe of their long teeth. Nobody denies that there is undiscovered fauna in the remote rainforests and deserts of the world's fourth largest island. If we have time to discover it, who can say for sure that there will not be creatures equally as strange as the aye-aye, the pygmy hippo … or the kalanoro?

Gaston was a mine of information on everything to do with the area and I was sorry when it was time for us to move on. Antsalova, he told us, would be completely cut off from the outside world except by air at this time of year – it might take another six weeks before the Project Bemaraha jeep could battle its way south to Bekopaka.

The Tsingy Reserve is run by the National Association for the Management of Protected Areas (shortened, in French, to ANGAP), who are careful to protect its natural resources. Eloi and I would need permits and an ANGAP guide before we could enter the Reserve, and our passage would be limited to three days.

Via Gaston's radio, Tsiandro's only link with 'the world', Eloi booked a seat on the plane back to Tsiro from Antsalova in five days time. I decided to wait and see what options would be open for travel onwards to the west coast.

'I've been asking around about your white, telepathic pygmies,' Gaston smiled on the evening before our departure. 'Your guide, Georges, can take you to a village where people say the headman is Vazimba. He might be able to tell you what you want to know.'

Georges appeared early the next morning, wearing a miniskirt made from bright orange plastic!

'To keep out danga,' he grinned sheepishly.

Georges was a short, wiry man, deceptively strong, with a trim moustache, bright eyes and a head of springy Sakalava curls. He was a master of bushcraft and could survive indefinitely in the Tsingy, but was hoping to be back with his family in Antsalova in two days time for the Labour Day celebrations.

We stocked up – on rice, coffee and one of the two remaining tins of tomato purée that Tsiandro could boast – and tramped out westwards with Georges swinging a live hen for fresh meat.

'In five kilometres cross river. After, no more danga,' he promised. '... Almost.'

We prayed he was right as we strode across a wide open plain that was blanketed thickly with the stuff. In the early light the countryside created a powerful illusion: the burnt yellow expanses of danga looked like wheat and a few grand old mango trees were like royal oaks. If I soft-focused my eyes, the open spaces of the Bemaraha Plateau at first light became an English midsummer's day, complete with wisps of cumulus cloud over distant woodland.

There even appeared to be sections of dry-stone walling, like ruined shepherds' cottages, on the low western hills. These were the block-like Sakalava ancestral tombs and they had been built here according to the instructions of local mpanandro. A tomb that was built east of Tsiandro might form a barrier of death between the village and the life-giving powers of the rising sun. I had been surprised nevertheless to see a group of tombs to the east of Tsiandro and asked Gaston about it.

'Those belonged to another village that was here before – so they are not fady for us,' he explained, once again illustrating the extent to which 'one man's meat is another man's poison' in Madagascar.

Like Gaston, Georges was an authority on the wildlife of the Tsingy, both fabled and familiar. It wasn't long before Eloi had drawn him into conversation about a creature that seemed to span both these worlds.

'Fandrefiala snake lives on other side of forest,' he said. 'Very, very dangerous. Has spear point for a head and kills anybody who walks underneath.'

Eloi could not resist elaborating: 'It's very clever. For example ... if you stop under his tree he will drop three leaves, one at a time, onto your head. He does this to check the wind and the angle of his drop. After the third leaf he drops out of the tree and springs his body straight like a spear and kills you ... and him also.'

Georges was not to be outdone: 'Near here a fandrefiala dropped on a metal rice pot and broke it! It too died.'

The Malagasy fandrefiala is a snake that is known to modern science as *Ithycyphus perineti*. It has a blood-red tail and a V-mark on its head that, though actually little more than a shadow, does suggest a spearhead. Perhaps this reptile has, on an island where all its kind are harmless, been accredited with such wilfully violent (and suicidal) behaviour simply to satisfy a natural human impulse to fear snakes.

Georges and Eloi were still discussing Madagascar's weird and wonderful creatures as they led me limping onto the packed red earth between some collapsing ochre huts. Two men came forward: one tall and lanky, the other short and bandy-legged. Both were dressed in the shorts and T-shirts that are now the dress of choice across most of the country.

A teenager appeared, firing off a volley of cheerful French: *'Bienvenue, m'sieurs. Comment allez-vous?'*

With his lamba worn toga-like over one shoulder and a large plastic comb stuck in his hair, he appeared to be the traditionalist in this motley group. An old man came out of one of the huts, screwing his eyes up against the sun. I wondered if we had interrupted his siesta. Mahatoky could have been seventy, but was probably not much older than fifty. He was the headman of this modest collection of seven huts that was bestowed with the impressive name – even by Malagasy standards – of Ankazomandiladongo. He was dark-skinned, with finely chiselled features that clearly betrayed more Asian blood than African and wore a ragged denim jacket onto the back of which somebody had – in another lifetime – painstakingly embroidered: 'HARLEY DAVIDSON'.

At just under 1.5 metres, Mahatoky might have qualified for the textbook definition of a pygmy if it weren't for the fact, as he explained later, that all Vazimba were not created equal. He had a disconcerting way of smilingly redirecting my questions – 'Are all vazaha the same height as you?' – so that I had the impression that he preferred to guide me into answering them for myself.

After Eloi had given 'the news' of our journey I asked him to find out what Mahatoky could tell us about the Vazimba. The old man led us to some low stools in the shade by his hut.

'This is not my own lie,' he began – using the traditional disclaimer with which any self-respecting old-time Malagasy sage
started his tale – 'this is a lie that the ancestors told me.'

He massaged his salt-and-pepper beard while his grandson filled
some enamel cups with syrupy sugarcane wine, then he leaned forward to tell me the story of the Vazimba's arrival in the west.

'At the time when the Merina tribe defeated the Vazimba and
drove us from our highland capital, near where Antananarivo
stands today, we had a great king called Andrianavaovao. He led
his people westwards from the Central Highlands, across the
Bungolava Mountains to the Manambolo River. Another king,
who was with him was called Rangoromana but he travelled only
as far as Bungolava where he eventually died. He had said that
after his death his vast zebu herds should be allowed to go wild
and they were the ancestors of the baria cattle that are to be seen
in Bungolava today.'

He paused and cast a peaceful eye over the village, with the air
of a man who could no longer see any reason to hurry.

'The great king's sister, Ampelamana, was also a great leader,
but she had a son who was bad. Betandra, the son, was in love
with one of his uncle's wives. He wanted to kill the king but
Andrianavaovao got to hear of the treachery. He got Betandra
drunk, reached into his nephew's lamba and killed the young man
with the knife that was meant for himself.'

Mahatoky leaned back against the wall of the hut and this time
held his silence for so long that I began to wonder if he was going
to continue. Only when our cups had been refilled with the delicious wine did he break his silence.

'Words are like rice plants,' he said, 'they must be carefully
arranged … and watered.

'Ampelamana, heartbroken by the death of her only son and
tired of the journey, decided to settle her followers by the
Manambolo River. They became Vazimba Andrano – Vazimba of
the Waters. Their blood was soon lost among the people of the
long valleys but their tombs can still be seen near the riverbank.
Our king continued the trek with his wives and subjects along the

trail by which you came here and finally they stopped to plant their rice and raise their zebu here. They became the Vazimba Antety – Vazimba of the Plateau. I'm the last Vazimba Antety,' Mahatoky sighed. 'My children are Sakalava-Vazimba.'

'When did all this happen?' I asked. 'How many generations ago?'

'It's impossible to say,' came Eloi's translated answer, 'Monsieur Mahatoky says that the story's always been this way.'

Until the French colonisation, rural Malagasy did not recognise any time structure beyond agricultural cycles and specific obligations relating to ancestral loyalty. But there was something else that I wanted to ask, going back even further in time. Would the old man be able to tell me how the Vazimba first arrived in Madagascar?

'Ask him where his people first came from. In other words, what's his belief of the beginning of life?'

Mahatoky waited patiently while the question was interpreted and then turned slowly to fix a crooked smile upon me. I'm not saying it was telepathy but I didn't need a translator to tell me what he was thinking: 'Nobody knows that. Did this vazaha come all this way to ask me?'

If only Mahatoky could have known just how far I had travelled to meet him. But how could I explain all this?

Alfred Grandidier, probably Madagascar's greatest explorer (clocking up twenty journeys) and certainly the most prodigious writer on the country (with thirty-eight illustrated volumes), believed that the Vazimba had arrived from Africa. He based this theory on the existence of an African group called the Wazimba.

Nigel Heseltine, a later expert on the country, added his support to the popular theory that the Vazimba arrived with an earlier, less successful, wave of Indonesian pioneers. He explained:

> The word *simba* in modern Malagasy means 'broken' or 'spoiled'. Thus the word can take on the sense of abandoned or degraded, and can be applied to a relic or something that has been displaced as primitive by a new wave of immigration.

Despite unanimous scientific claims to the contrary (backed principally by the total lack of evidence of human occupation before two millennia ago), thousands of islanders still revere the Vazimba as the most ancient of all ancestors and the indigenous Malagasy.

'They've always been here,' they say.

I would have liked to stay in Ankazomandiladongo longer, but it wasn't to be. We only had a couple of days to get through the reserve, Georges wanted to get home and Eloi was anxious to get back to Poussy in Tsiro – and I was desperately in need of some home comforts myself. So I shook hands with Mahatoky and followed Georges out through the slippery mud of the rice paddies towards the west. Within minutes we were tagging along, in blind faith, through acres of three-metre vero grass.

An hour later we skirted a swampy basin at the boundary of the reserve, where Georges said that the Andafiabe River was born, and stumbled – in my case, literally – upon the first of the tsingy. These rocks were not as dramatic as the spectacular forests of thirty-metre limestone needles that lay far to the south but they were equally as mysterious. These gunmetal grey slabs were exhibited artistically on their grassy cushions in a way that again made me think of the careful arrangement in a sculpture gallery.

In parallel lines over the upper surface of each of these slabs ran razor-sharp ridges, some fifteen centimetres high. Sometimes there were eight rows of ridges – each sharp enough to slice your thumb if you tested their edges – rising and falling uniformly so that they looked like the marks on a crocodile's back. They were as viciously jagged as the rocks in the gallery above the cliff had been smooth and serene but there was still no clue to explain how this gunmetal rock came to be on the rusty laterite of the plateau.

The danga grew only in occasional patches now, as Georges had said it would, but as I followed him through the undergrowth towards a well-trodden path I felt a tingling sensation on my knee. In an instant it was burning painfully and I realised that something had stung me. I bent to rub my leg and the pain stepped up another notch – now it was a fiery stabbing, as if the hairs on my knee were being pulled out half a dozen at a time! As I clutched at my leg and hobbled around, clawing and feeling sure that the searing sensation must subside in a moment, Georges turned and saw me.

'Scratch NOT!' he shouted. 'You are stung by *agy* tree. You must scratch NOT!'

In 1879 a missionary traveller called W. Montgomery reported an attack by the agy tree:

> My hands were on fire and my face and head burned as if they were being held against a red-hot stove. The burning increased and was accompanied by severe pain and dizziness. I thought I would die and strove to get back to my wife and children. My men started when they saw me coming, so great was the agony as indicated by my face. One of them cried out 'he is smitten by an agy'.

The agy's sting has been described as like that of a nettle but ten times more virulent. It was clear from Eloi and Georges's expressions that – to borrow another of Montgomery's choice turns of phrase – agony was 'writ plain enough over every line of my face'.

At least Pickersgill was able to see the humour in what he, with a certain undeniable justice, called the very mother of all nettles. 'It was a laughable sight to see our guide scrubbing his bare back against a rough tree to relieve the torment,' chuckled the fun-loving missionary.

I clenched and unclenched my hands, trying to overcome the almost irresistible urge to scratch, just to do *something* about the terrible burning sensation.

'Is there ... I can do ... nothing?' I stammered to Georges, my French grammar deserting me.

'You can scrape with wet mud but not really work. Wait is the best – wait and scratch not.'

Sure enough after a minute more the scorching did begin to cool and Georges showed me the agy pods that I'd brushed up against. They were innocuous-looking seed cases, about eight centimetres long, covered with fine dart-like hairs that were designed to work their way quickly into the flesh. The agy tree is really a type of vine and when the pain had finally loosened its hold I went back to the tree to take some close-up shots of those unforgettable seed cases.

Even in this thoughtless activity I didn't realise the risk I was taking. The silver hairs that are the vine's defence – although it seemed perilously close to a blatant attack – are so fine and light that, as you pass innocently underneath, as the unfortunate Montgomery discovered, they can be wafted down to you even in the gentlest of breezes. With both ankles already poisoned and my left knee burning ferociously I entered the Bemaraha forest feeling that the idea of a people-eating tree in Madagascar was not so far-fetched after all.

The Tsingy Reserve now protects virtually all that remains of the vast tropical forest that once covered Madagascar's 'wild west' and I realised that this was the first real forest that I had seen since leaving the waterlogged slopes of Montagne d'Ambre.

'Tsy misy ala, tsy misy rano, tsy misy vary!' Georges quoted a phrase that had been used at village level, as a rallying cry for Madagascar's conservation efforts: 'If there is no more forest, there will be no more water; if there is no more water, there will be no more rice!' It was a maxim that was designed to get to the heart of the matter – to hit the Malagasy where it hurt.

Within minutes under the canopy we were sweating profusely. The trail bucked its way around rotting logs and across mossy rocks, so that very soon we were speckled with the slime of the jungle. Chameleons froze as we passed, pinpoint volcano-eyes swivelling around – placing, as far as I could see, all too much faith in their reputation as masters of camouflage. Tiny emerald lizards flickered away from us and soldier ants marched in orderly single file across our path. In a patch of sunlight, where a forest giant had brought down one or more of its brothers, a flash of crimson alerted me to the flight of a red fody (bringing back more memories of Montagne d'Ambre). But the forest here was essentially of a drier nature – thank God!

Once we had to step aside to let a convoy of four Tsiandro-bound traders pass. The boxes that were strapped to their backs and foreheads rattled and clanked in time with their step, betraying a cargo of beer bottles and milk tins. The last one carried a plastic five-gallon drum of fuel for Gaston's generator. This supply would have to last a long time, but telltale rainbow swirls decorating the puddles along the trail told us that the drum was leaking slowly.

In mid-afternoon we heard the sound of rushing water and walked out into the sunlight of a canyon that was flanked on both sides by towering green curtains of hardwood forest and sliced through by a churning rush of silvery water. The river tumbled over a wall of boulders to fall swirling into a deep blue sump that was almost glacially clear, sparkling as only water that is very near its spring can.

The Andafiabe River was undoubtedly one of the most beautiful rivers I have ever seen. Eloi translated the name as 'Place of Big Fat Rocks' and, although it was well-named for the huge slabs that channeled it into a dozen separate rushes of water, I could have wished for something more picturesque.

Further on, at a spot where the river slowed and deepened, we stripped off and dived in before setting up camp on a big fat rock shelf that the benevolent *zanahary* (god) of this place had thoughtfully covered with fine silver sand.

When the afternoon began to cool I took my camera and set off to explore the forest around the campsite. I found a large Colubrid snake – about one and a half metres long and thick as a man's wrist – that was busy excavating a hole in which some unfortunate creature was cowering. It was so unconcerned by my presence that it allowed me to set up my tripod and photograph it from a distance of half a metre. Even when I tugged its tail it only looked back at me for long enough to allow me to snap off a couple of frames, then stuck its head back down the hole. Perhaps, having only had 2000 years to get used to the presence of the world's most dangerous predator, the creatures of Madagascar have simply never developed a fear of humans. The *Aepyornis*, the giant lemurs and the pygmy hippo never had time to learn the all-important lesson and a few other creatures were only spared by the timely creation of a protecting fady.

I hoped that this particular colubrid was a local fady animal. Had I been so inclined, before I pulled it out of the hole to kill it I would have had ample time to light a fire, get a pot of water boiling *and* shoot another roll of film. Luckily I didn't have to mar the spiritual ambience of Andafiabe with slaughter; I could leave that to Georges, who had dispatched our luckless hen and set the rice cooking by the time I got back to the camp. As we ate chicken smeared with tomato purée, Eloi and I talked about everything that we'd seen in our weeks in the mid-west. Then we watched in silence as a violet sun deepened to a bleeding scarlet and sank, with incredible speed, right into the point where the river disappeared in the converging darkness of the trees. The Andafiabe River appeared to be running with fiery lava.

There's an old Malagasy proverb that says: 'It is the destiny of the hen to die at the moments of humans' greatest happiness'.

Eloi had shared Georges's tent and I had already been for a chilly early morning dip by the time they stepped bleary-eyed out into the sunlight. Now that we were nearing our objective I was getting less anxious that our journey should come to an end. I sipped my coffee slowly, watching the river shimmer in the early light, and took my time in packing up my tent. But it was Labour Day (1 May); there was a big celebration starting in Antsalova and both my companions were in a hurry to get to the party.

I doped myself with co-codamol to alleviate the throbbing of my poisoned ankles and passed the first part of the morning in blissful contemplation of the delights of nature. There were fewer of the tantalising blue pools but the Andafiabe seem to run with cut diamonds as it hustled its way westwards to the Mozambique Channel. Some of the treetops were occupied by squabbling flocks of grey vasa parrots that crashed around the branches with all the finesse of flying squids. A wild boar – one of the few animals that Madagascar shares with mainland Africa – crashed away in fearful desperation as we stepped onto the sunny beach where he was snuffling.

For over an hour we walked through a shadowy gully that was bound on one side by dark trees and on the other by a raggedly eroded rock face that Georges, rather freely I thought, referred to as 'tsingy'. We found a hollow that was sprinkled with belemnite fossils, finger-like casts of marine animals, that showed that the Tsingy had once been the bed of a prehistoric sea. Georges told me that the Sakalava had used belemnites as bullets as recently as the French invasion, when warring hardware had been in short supply.

The forest ended in an abrupt – and, one suspected, steadily retreating – line on the grazing lands of the immense zebu herds of this region. The lyre-horned cattle trotted out of our way as a rutted charet track enticed us onwards through their rolling pastures. To our left lay the hamlet of Berano (Where there is Water). According to Georges, the headman of that collection of a dozen well-dunged huts owned more than a thousand zebu … and a bigger house in Antsalova.

Our first sight of the town, as always, was a riverbank blanketed with paddy fields. A woman in a colourful lamba and a conical 'coolie' hat waded tenderly through the knee-high plants and I could have imagined that we'd walked straight back to Indonesia. We'd trekked more than two hundred kilometres, since leaving Tsiroanomandidy almost three weeks ago, to arrive barely forty kilometres from the west coast. Still, scant attention was paid to us as we walked past the concrete buildings of the Red Cross clinic and the larger blocks of a French-built primary school.

It seemed that the whole community was gathered in the central marketplace and as we eased our way into the crowd and craned to look over shoulders the reason was all too clear. Our arrival had coincided with the first rounds of the annual Sakalava street-fighting festivals! In the dusty clearing that had become an improvised boxing ring four young warriors prowled like caged tigers. Although they glowered aggressively, the ferocity they were doing their best to exude was – at least to the eyes of a vazaha – somewhat diminshed by floral lambas and little Homburg hats that were perched upon stacked Sakalava curls.

One, clearly the leader, carried a short baton that he rapped constantly against his thigh and chewed a toothpick as he scanned the faces of the crowd with snake eyes. Another, taller with a yellow lamba wrapped tightly over his shoulders, slouched along behind him and cast slightly mournful glances at the audience from underneath a wide straw hat.

Some subtle and unseen signal answered the challenge and a man from a rival group stepped into the 'ring'. Three of the 'warriors' walked off to crouch, with airs of soldierly anticipation, on the edge of the shuffling crowd. Yellow Lamba shrugged the covers off his muscular brown shoulders and tightened his belt as two apparently sadistic 'marshals' drove the crowd back with whip-like branches that swung in whistling arcs.

The two fighters circled each other. The challenger crouched low, weaving his left hand, outstretched, towards his opponent's stomach. Yellow Lamba still gave the impression of slouching even as he circled with his right fist poised near his cheek and his left reaching out as a block. Above the murmurs and hoots of the crowd I could hear the challenger mumbling as his hand waved across the taller man's body.

I don't know what I had expected from the fight but the speed and sudden burst of violence shocked me. The challenger charged in, swinging wildly and seemingly out of control, landing three or four thudding blows to the ribs of Yellow Lamba, who threw his cocked right fist downwards with all the force he could put behind it. But the crouching man came in closer swinging treacherous right hooks and managed to clinch with his left arm around Yellow Lamba's body.

They shuffled around the ring, kicking up dust as the crowd whooped and a marshal pulled them apart. When they closed in again, in the same style, Yellow Lamba's searching right managed to catch his opponent above the left ear with his third power-driver jab. The challenger's knees gave way and he fell into the dust. Yellow Lamba lazily raised one arm and slouched mournfully out of the ring as his gang rushed up, cheering and slapping, to congratulate him. The fallen warrior was helped to his feet by his own friends and as they led him off the battlefield I saw him aim a befuddled smile at the crowd.

Morengy is a ritualised form of street-fighting and it has been described as the national sport of the Sakalava. The Labour Day bouts in Antsalova were the first, and most important, bouts of a season that would take place every Saturday afternoon throughout the winter months. Anybody who wants to fight is free to walk around the ring until he finds a challenger, but honour demands that the two be of roughly equal stature.

Another group, six warriors this time, prowled the ring and I began to see in their body language that each would-be pugilist had his own way of attracting opponents. Some slouched lazily, almost sleepily, trying to give the impression that they were utterly unprepared for a challenge. Others looked tough, wore their hats at a rakish angle, chewed toothpicks and tried to bully watchers into a challenge with piercing eye contact. One even pretended drunkenness, with an exhibition of unconvincing staggering and eye-rolling that he hoped would make him look like 'easy meat'.

With their flowery lambas and the tiny shocking-pink or electric-blue shirts that were the height of Sakalava fashion some did, in fact, look deceptively like easy meat, even to me. But when they circled in the dust – often uttering strange screams designed to intimidate the enemy – and then went crashing fearlessly into battle the viciousness of the attack was invariably frightening.

Queensberry Rules don't apply in morengy and windmilling fists (making up in quantity what they lack in accuracy) is the usual strategy. But some fighters had their own style of combat. Several took up karate stances, gleaned from the careful study of cheap kung fu comics (although kicking is illegal). Others fancied themselves as boxers but invariably found that it was impossible to float like a butterfly through the hail of scrabbling blows that the bouts usually degenerated into. Some hoped to weaken their adversaries with magical strength-sapping movements or unnerve them with muttered curses.

None of this worked on Yellow Lamba and always that smashing right fist found its target. His gang whooped their low, swooping victory song all afternoon. Each group had its own deep song that never more than underpinned the clamour of the crowd, yet seemed to echo from all around the marketplace at once.

This eerie Sakalava whoop, certainly used effectively many times in Madagascar's history to unnerve an enemy, had met its match when it was used to intimidate our favourite missionary-explorer and the unshakeable Mr S.:

> … a special performance of whoop and stamp and clanging of weapons, extemporised at once for our edification. 'Yes, that's pretty good,' we said, accosting our visitors, the moment there was a slight lull in the row, 'but wait a little and you shall have a specimen of *our* singing.' We then called out the two-and-thirty, and led them off in a favourite hymn …

What could the guns and spears do in the face of that but go home to bed?

After an hour of adult fights the children were allowed into the ring for their own chance to beat somebody to a bloody pulp. In imitation of their heroes they swaggered around until, amidst playful jostling and shouting, a small boy jumped out of the crowd. These children were no more than seven years old but they faced each other fiercely and fought brutally until a lucky head-lock gave one the advantage and he managed to give his opponent a severe pummelling in the face before he was pulled away. Two gangs dashed in to collect their 'warrior' friends and to my surprise and admiration, even the bloody-nosed loser rushed away in joyful laughter!

The bouts were usually mercifully short and a marshal would

try to stop the fight as soon as the first effective punch was landed – but if a victor managed to land a few more before he was pulled away, well, so much the better. I suggested to Georges that there must often be serious bad feeling between two fighters for long after the twenty or so seconds that their bout lasted. But he explained that a loser was not allowed to fight his vanquisher twice in one session; if he wanted to try again he would have to wait until the following Saturday, giving him time to reconsider. Even if he took the punch but was ready to keep fighting, the marshals would haul him away to ponder the wisdom of his determination for a week.

Appearance was important here. The heaped coiffures, sometimes in three separate piles of curls, bright clothes and manly bravado were clearly for the benefit of the groups of girls who watched the fights hungrily. Sakalava girls dig street-fighters and just in case any further temptation was needed, Georges explained that the town hall offers a 10,000 FMg (about US$2.50) bounty for each clean knockout!

As Georges answered my questions I came to realise that what had at first sight appeared to be brutal, bare knuckle, blood or glory slugfests were, in fact, something much more meaningful. They were brutal, bare knuckle, blood or glory slugfests founded in sorcery and ancestor worship. According to Georges, many of these fighters carried charms made by their mpanandro. It might be the mohara zebu horn of the Dahalo or it a talisman of glass beads and sacred wood. The charm could not be worn in the fight otherwise the warrior's adversary might recognise the type of ody and could be able to use his own to overcome it. A fighter could also make an incision in his knuckles or forehead and rub mysterious oils into it to give him power.

'For example ...' – you could always trust Eloi to be good for an example – 'if they have powerful ody and hit you in the eye, maybe you don't bleed in the eye. But afterwards, slowly you begin to bleed somewhere else. If a fighter hits me and I don't have ody I can go to you and you can pass your ody in front of my face and it'll stop me bleeding!'

Another way in which a morengy fighter might hope to make himself invincible is by having his body temporarily occupied by the spirit of an ancestor: a famous warrior or a fearless bandit leader. In a practice called *tromba* the young man might enlist the help of a mpanandro and could spend several hours before the tournament working himself into a trance, until he believed that he was occupied by a powerful spirit.

In *The Possessed and the Dispossessed*, the anthropologist Lesley A. Sharp went so far as to claim that tromba possession is 'the quintessence of Sakalava religious experience'. Among the Sakalava, there are even frequent cases of involuntary tromba where a living person's body is forcibly taken over by the ghost of an ancestor, traditionally warriors or queens who died in violent ways. But tromba has moved with the times. As Sharp reported from her extensive studies in the Sakalava town of Ambanja:

> The spirits active in town are not the staid and powerful royalty of the past, instead they are cowboys, boxers, soccer players and prostitutes ... They have been in automobile accidents, they like to drink and dance, they frequent boxing (morengy) matches and several have died at the hands of their lovers or rivals.

The tournaments were once the breeding grounds for the Sakalava warriors who became masters of most of western Madagascar, but today they are reputedly used as the recruiting grounds of the Dahalo. Although we did not realise it, as we crossed the Zone Rouge, gangs of Dahalo bandits (or just 'fighting Sakalava' who hoped to become Dahalo) had also been trekking westwards towards this biggest of all morengy festivals. If the Zone Rouge, with its prairie hamlets, cowboys and bandits, was like the old-time Wild West then the dusty, brawling streets of Antsalova were Dodge City.

Antsalova during the Labour Day celebrations was so full of strangers that the authorities could have no reason to question the appearance of gangs of young warriors of dubious origins and

213

intents. There were certainly no dirty shirts in the crowd (everybody was in their best, most luminous colours) and there was nobody who I could identify as likely Dahalo. On the other hand, as I looked around I had to admit that any of the prowling pugilists, swaggering, loping or stumbling around the ring, could have been bandit warriors come to make a reputation or connections for themselves.

'See that tall one in the yellow lamba?' I whispered to Eloi. 'He's won all his fights and he thinks he's "The Daddy". Go and teach him.'

'Not for me – I'm Betsileo ... but I think it's okay for a vazaha!'

In fact certain Sakalava citizens, with typical Malagasy hospitality, appeared to be somewhat concerned that here was a guest in their country who might be waiting politely for a formal invitation to join in their little Labour Day 'celebrations'. But the vazaha – never one to wilfully inflict his presence upon the local populace – retreated shamelessly into the journalistic ethics that demanded his presence only as a reporter and not, God forbid, as an active participator. Diligently fumbling a fresh film into his battered camera he was, to all intents and purposes, deaf to the burgeoning shouts of a crowd that appeared to be disproportionately enthusiastic to see a little bit of British blood spilt on the hallowed dust of Antsalova's marketplace.

CHAPTER 5

FIHAVANANA

> ... I thought of my friends in far-off social Old
> England. God bless them every one, and incline
> their hearts to write me more letters and expect but
> a few to be answered.
>
> – Rev. William Clayton Pickersgill

Two days later an Air Madagascar Twin Otter went bouncing away over the grass runway, carrying Eloi back to Tsiroanomandidy. He was delighted to be going home loaded with stories (and 'examples') and I asked him specifically to 'give the news' to my friends at Best Western.

Having travelled so far westwards I now wanted to reach the sea before turning back. The nearest coastal airstrip was Maintirano – Black Water – but that was 160 kilometres further on. To reach it at this time of year I would have to trek through the extensive mangrove swamps that gave the town its name.

I had pitched my tent in the Project Bemaraha compound in Antsalova. When I wandered down to bathe in the nearby river, the tranquil current lured me into investigating the possibility of buying a dugout and drifting lazily down to Soahanina. This was apparently nothing but a tiny fishing village of the Vezo tribe (some of who are supposedly descended from shipwrecked Portuguese sailors) but there was a chance that if I waited long enough, a dhow might call in on its southbound trading voyage. But money was running short and if nothing arrived soon I might end up 'shipwrecked' myself – just a danga-riddled piece of flotsam on the beach.

Finally I hopped a Twin Otter myself and skittered gratefully above the shimmering hills of vero with their gigantic red 'tree-drawings' of lavaka bulging from the banks of rivers that bled the heart out of the island. As the plane circled above Maintirano I saw the red wash of muddy water stretching well over a kilometre towards Mozambique.

I spent eight days in Maintirano walking on perfect white beaches amongst the outrigger boats of the Vezo and waiting for some dhow or tramp steamer to cruise into the harbour behind the sheltering mangroves. An Englishman who had thrown up his job as an accountant in London to buy a twin-masted clipper and pursue a Conradian life, trading coconuts and hardwood down the Mozambique Channel, offered me a lift northwards to Mahajanga. Then his crew mutinied and his captain (and brother-in-law) stole the clipper and left us both marooned! I now only had three weeks left on my already-extended *recherche* visa so I opted for the first plane back to Tsiroanomandidy and the 'predictability' of overland travel.

Another Air Mad bush-hopper banked out over the mangroves, before swooping across the pale savannah. Very quickly we saw the dense greenery of Réserve des Tsingy de Bemaraha. We bucked and bounced wildly in the thermals above the Bemaraha cliffs and in a few minutes we'd crossed the dusty Manambolo rift valley that had taken two difficult days to cross on foot.

We were buffeted again as we shot over the Bungolava Ridge. Then I was looking down on mountains that were entirely flattened by this new perspective but had almost succeeded in making me lame and deaf the last time I tried to cross them. There were only three other passengers, businessmen in white button-down shirts, reading the business pages of the *Midi Madagasikara*. They never gave a thought to Zone Rouge: to the Dahalo bandits or to the peaceful, fun-loving villagers over whose heads we sailed.

Mick and Tiana promised to pray for me and Maman Suzanne shed another ladylike tear as I hitched away from Tsiro after failing to find a bush-taxi heading for the highlands, or anywhere else. A ride on the back of a motorbike carried me several kilometres towards Tana up the RN1 and a pick-up truck carried me several more before it broke down at dusk in a back country hamlet, somewhere near where Eloi had seen his kalanoro.

Just as I was beginning to look for a place to sleep I found a ride in the back of a truck full of watermelons and at 2 am I woke up in Tana. I looked around, drowsily doubtful, and it was a minute before I recognised Lac Anosy with the darkened shapes of jacaranda trees leaning out over its lily-covered waters. I hauled my pack onto my back and hiked up over the hill and up the steps of Analakely to hammer once again on the familiar doors of Hôtel Lambert.

And here, as the tireless Reverend Pickersgill would say, the light goose-quill must be restrained and compelled to summarise the last of my frantic skirmishes into the Malagasy wilderness.

Somehow, the weeks of slow travel on foot had left me with a heightened wanderlust and I had a desperate urge now to cover ground. So I took a bush-taxi southwards – for twenty-seven sleep-deprived hours – to Morondava where dawn was greeted, as we rattled past the awesome 'avenue of the baobabs', by the gentle chanting of the Bara migrant workers who were my travelling companions.

In Morondava I was again frustrated by this record-breaking rainy season; flooded roads had cut off the southern 'deserts' and adverse winds had affected waterborne traffic. I turned back after only two days to retrace my steps to Tana – this time taking only twenty-two hours.

Now I wanted to make a pilgrimage down to the eastern forests to pay homage to the legendary indri, the mightiest – and most vocal – of all lemurs. I spent more sleepless nights on the edge of the Périnet Reserve while troops of red-fronted lemurs leapt through the branches over my tent, grunting inquisitively.

I saw a family of babakoto, and heard their awesome dawn cry, carrying like an air-raid siren over three kilometres; and I stood rooted to a jungle track one day as a troop of golden bamboo lemurs, seemingly unaware of my presence, leapt across the trail. This cuddly little snub-nosed teddy bear has evolved to fill a niche that is almost entirely free from competition; it lives on giant bamboo, every day eating twelve times enough cyanide to kill another animal of its size. Even in a reserve as accessible as Périnet, the golden bamboo lemur was not discovered until 1986 and I counted twenty-three of them in this procession!

Flushed with this success I hitched back up the steep canyon road that leads out of the eastern rainforests, towards Tana and home. In Moramanga (where the 1947 insurrection had been answered by the slaughter of so many villagers at the hands of Senegalese troopers) I found a bush-taxi that would take me on my last Malagasy journey. There was the usual three-hour delay while everybody sat around, waiting for the minibus to fill with passengers and then an American tourist arrived, toting cameras, guidebooks ... and the wherewithal to save us all.

To the surprise of the other passengers he paid for all of the remaining five seats, explaining to me that they were so cheap that it wasn't worth waiting. I was naturally embarrassed to see a vazaha so deliberately flaunting his wealth in front of these poor farmers but, other than that, I was neither relieved nor disappointed that we were finally leaving. I had been infected by a severe case of *mora-mora* – Malagasy take-it-easy fever. (It would take city life – and my future wife – several months to knock it out of me.)

I've always been a firm believer that with enough patience there is always a way to travel forward, but on the Isle of the Moon my faith in this theory was constantly shaken. Overland travel in Madagascar can be excruciatingly uncomfortable. It is often hot, usually dusty and always noisy. It is invariably slow but it is never, ever boring.

Fihavanana is a Malagasy word that literally means blood-kin but has been extended in common use to mean friendship towards all men. In Madagascar fihavanana is more than just a word and it is this concept that prevents travel through the island from ever becoming a trial.

The Malagasy say 'It is better to lose money than friendship' but ask them why fihavanana is such an important part of their culture and they'll simply shrug and say: 'It's always been this way'.

FURTHER READING

Brown, Mervyn. *Madagascar Rediscovered: A History from Early Times to Independence*. London: Damien Tunnacliffe, 1978.

Dodwell, Christina. *Madagascar Travels*. London: Hodder & Stoughton, 1995.

Durrell, Gerald. *The Aye-aye and I: A Rescue Expedition in Madagascar*. London: HarperCollins, 1992.

Heseltine, Nigel. *Madagascar*. London: Pall Mall Press, 1971.

Jolly, Alison. *A World Like Our Own: Man and Nature in Madagascar*. New Haven, Connecticut: Yale University Press, 1980.

Madagacar and Comoros. Melbourne: Lonely Planet, 1997.

Madagascar Wildlife: A Visitor's Guide. Chalfont St Peter, UK: Bradt Publications, 1996.

Murphy, Dervla. *Muddling Through in Madagascar*. London: John Murray Ltd, 1985.

Osborn, Chase Salmon, LLD. *Madagascar: Land of the Man-eating Trees*. New York: Republic Publishing Co., 1924.

Ruud, Jørgen. *Taboo: A Study of Malagasy Customs and Beliefs*. Trans. Jon Egil Ofstad. Oslo: Oslo University Press, 1960.

Sibree, James. *Fifty Years in Madagascar: Personal Experiences of Mission Life and Work*. London: George Allen & Unwin Ltd, 1924.

Stratton, Arthur. *The Great Red Island: A Biography of Madagascar*. London: Macmillan, 1965.

Tyson, Peter. *The Eighth Continent: Life, Death, and Discovery in the Lost World of Madagascar*. New York: William Morrow, 2000.

Wilson, Jane. *Lemurs of the Lost World: Exploring the Forests and Crocodile Caves of Madagascar*. London: Impact Books, 1990.

LONELY PLANET JOURNEYS

JOURNEYS is a unique collection of travel writing – published by the company that understands travel better than anyone else.

It is a series for anyone who has ever experienced – or dreamed of – the magical moment when they encountered a strange culture or saw a place for the first time. They are tales to read while you're planning a trip, while you're on the road or while you're in an armchair, in front of a fire.

These outstanding titles explore our planet through the eyes of a diverse group of international writers. JOURNEYS books catch the spirit of a place, illuminate a culture, recount an adventure, or introduce a fascinating way of life. They always entertain, and always enrich the experience of travel.

'Lively, intelligent and varied . . . an important contribution to travel literature' – *Age (Melbourne)*

AFTER YUGOSLAVIA
Zoë Brân

Sarajevo, Mostar, Dubrovnik . . . the names are carved into the psyche of any-one who watched a news broadcast between 1991 and 1996. Zoë Brân visited these places long before the crises of the 1990s, and returned to what are now the countries of Slovenia, Croatia and Bosnia-Hercegovina to try to make sense of what had happened in the intervening years.

'Lucid, informed, and entertaining, this is a smooth, accomplished treatment of a complex topic' – *Library Journal (USA)*